ARGUMENTS FOR
LIBERTY

ARGUMENTS FOR
LIBERTY

edited by
Aaron Ross Powell & Grant Babcock

eBook ISBN: 978-1-944424-13-8
Print ISBN: 978-1-944424-12-1

Library of Congress Cataloging-in-Publication Data available.

Cover design: Faceout.
Printed in the United States of America.

Cato Institute
1000 Massachusetts Avenue, N.W.
Washington, D.C. 20001
www.cato.org

CONTENTS

Introduction

Aaron Ross Powell and Grant Babcock

If you value political liberty—or reject it in favor of, say, material equality—you have reasons for doing so. Your reasons might be unexamined or thought through, compelling or flimsy. When we think rigorously about the reasons we believe what we believe about morality and politics, we're practicing philosophy. "Practical men who believe themselves to be quite exempt from any intellectual influence, are usually the slaves of some defunct economist," wrote John Maynard Keynes.

Similarly, many people, even most people, are the slaves of some defunct philosopher. If you think your political beliefs are simply based on "common sense" or "practicality," you're probably not digging deep enough. What seems like common sense today often turns out to be a once-controversial idea from the cutting edge of philosophy decades or centuries ago. Thus, chances are that your politics either originate with or have been thoroughly examined and articulated by some philosopher.

In this book, nine philosophers give their reasons for believing that political liberty is the most moral and just system. But they do so from within nine different schools of moral thought. Although a single best moral and political philosophy might exist, philosophers have been offering theories for at least 2,500 years and have yet to reach consensus. That doesn't mean progress hasn't been made. As libertarian philosopher Robert Nozick reassuringly said, "There is room for words on subjects other than last words."

We assembled this book for two reasons. First, because freedom matters. We are convinced that the only just political order is one that enshrines liberty to the highest good. Second, because philosophy matters. Libertarianism without philosophy is libertarianism without foundation. Without principle. It's not enough to *have* reasons for one's political views. We need to understand those reasons, to examine them, to critically evaluate them. We need to appreciate not only why people might reject political liberty, but also why those who embrace it do so—especially when they disagree on reasons and foundations. Libertarians often argue about philosophy. Recognizing and understanding the source of libertarians' differences helps us to better appreciate what it is they hold in common, and reveals weaknesses that might otherwise lie undiscovered and unaddressed. Having a more robust understanding of the philosophical foundations of liberty will better enable those of us who seek to promote it to engage with our critics. And for liberty's critics, better understanding the moral foundations of liberty will help you argue more fruitfully and avoid straw men.

Arguments for Liberty is not an easy book, but neither is it a book only for scholars and experts. The chapters don't assume the reader has a strong philosophy background, though some are necessarily more complex than others, given the theories they're articulating. The chapters are written to stand on their own, and they can be read in any order.

Each chapter begins by explaining its featured moral theory. Then, it traces out the implications of that theory, arguing that it is best understood to have *libertarian* conclusions in the realm of politics. In some cases, that conclusion isn't very controversial among academic philosophers. For example, almost everyone agrees that the moral theory espoused by Ayn Rand implies libertarianism, or at least something very close. In other cases, the opposite is true. John Rawls's moral theory, considered in Chapter 5, is usually thought to justify social democracy, not libertarianism.

The book begins with the simplest theory, though its simplicity is deceptive. Utilitarianism holds that the right thing to do is whatever produces the most happiness, and in Chapter 1, Christopher Freiman argues that, among competing political systems, libertarianism best fits the bill.

In Chapter 2, Eric Mack takes up natural rights. If it is true that humans, by our very nature, have certain rights that restrain how we may treat one another, then governments, just like ordinary people, must respect those rights.

In Chapter 3, Jason Kuznicki looks at arguably the most important philosopher since the ancient era, Immanuel Kant. Kant offered a moral theory grounded in reason and respect for the separateness and dignity of each of us. Kuznicki shows how this moral system points toward a government that does the same, namely, a libertarian one.

If we gave everyone a say in which rules should govern society, but they all had to agree on a single set, what would those rules look like? In Chapter 4 on social contract theory, Jan Narveson shows how the rules most likely to meet that standard would be those supporting political liberty.

John Rawls's *A Theory of Justice*, which advanced a form of social contract theory, revitalized political philosophy in the late 20th century. Kevin Vallier shows in Chapter 5 how Rawls's work, both in that book and in his later *Political Liberalism*—although often considered antithetical to libertarianism—can actually provide a compelling case for a robust system of political and economic liberty.

Virtue ethics, explored by Mark LeBar in Chapter 6, is at once the oldest and youngest theory in the book. First discussed by the ancient Greeks, it largely disappeared from academic moral philosophy until its revival in the mid-20th century. Virtue ethics puts a person's character at the center of moral theory. It asks what traits enable a person to make good choices and live a good life. In the realm of politics, it asks what institutions are most conducive to this task.

Neera Badhwar discusses Ayn Rand's theory of Objectivism in Chapter 7. Rand's Objectivist philosophy holds that political liberty is the only system compatible with an appropriate understanding of the value of human life and the importance of human reason.

When facing moral questions in our everyday lives, most of us don't apply carefully constructed theories; instead, we go with what our intuition tells us. In Chapter 8, Michael Huemer develops this approach into a full theory of morality, known as intuitionism, and shows how our moral intuitions expose the immorality of most, if not all, of what governments do.

The book ends with Jason Brennan discussing pluralism, which can be roughly seen as a theory that says all the other theories go wrong in thinking that morality has an underlying framework. The various theories get at important truths, but morality doesn't reduce to a unitary good, value, or set of rules. Brennan argues that this imprecise but arguably more realistic account of morality gives plenty of support for liberty.

Is it a problem that the authors disagree with each other about fundamental moral questions? Are we stuck with ad hoc reasoning toward a desired conclusion—in this case, libertarianism?

We can talk about right and wrong on several levels. The contributors to this volume agree, for the most part, at the level of applied ethics—if you asked them some concrete questions about specific situations or behaviors, they would answer in similar ways. They would likely agree, for example, that the state cannot legitimately ban recreational drugs, or censor a newspaper critical of the president, or conscript people into the armed forces. Yet they have disagreements. If you asked *why* the state cannot legitimately ban recreational drugs, you would get very different answers. The explanatory frameworks philosophers use to give reasons for their moral judgments are called "moral theories." The chapter titles in *Arguments for Liberty* are all the names of moral theories or of their inventors. Now, if you start asking questions about moral theories—questions like, "What do terms in moral theories, like *good* or *justice*, really mean?" or "How do we come to have knowledge about moral theories?"—you're asking questions of a different kind. The subfield of philosophy dedicated to such questions is called "metaethics." The contributors to this volume have diverging opinions about metaethics, just as they do about moral theories. In some chapters, disagreements about metaethics won't matter much. In others—especially the chapter on intuitionism—these disagreements matter a lot.

Each chapter presents a different argument for liberty, not because the authors are making things up to justify a predetermined conclusion but rather because of good-faith disagreement among them about issues in ethical theory and metaethics. Even then, we shouldn't count such disagreements against libertarianism. There are similar disagreements about how to justify libertarianism's competitors, too.

You might find some or even all the moral theories presented here unpersuasive. Does that mean that reading the chapters about those theories was a waste of your time? We don't think so. Even if, for example, you don't believe that maximizing human happiness is the right way to think about morality, it would still be useful to learn that libertarianism maximizes human happiness. Likewise, it would still be useful to learn that libertarianism is conducive to developing personal virtue, even if you think that's the wrong foundation for ethics.

Indeed, you may finish *Arguments for Liberty* thinking that libertarianism satisfies *multiple* theories of morality, even though you think only one of the theories is correct. If that's the case, then it simply means that liberty is overdetermined: the fact that libertarianism meets someone else's standard of morality, a standard you don't necessarily hold, doesn't mean it can't *also* meet your standard.

If you find none of the arguments persuasive, that's okay. We hope you'll at least have a better sense of the kinds of arguments one can mount for liberty, and so be better able to engage with such arguments.

Regardless of how many—if any—of the book's chapters you find compelling, our goal is to inspire you to continue your study of ethics and libertarianism. At the end of the book, we've included a bibliography with suggestions for further reading, including introductory texts and primary sources, many of which are available for free online.

Utilitarianism

Christopher Freiman

Suppose there's been a shipwreck and you're on the rescue mission. Your boat has only enough fuel to save the people on one of two life rafts. The first raft has four survivors; the second has three. Which do you save?

You should, it seems, rescue the first raft. Why? Because rescuing the first saves more people. It does the most good. This idea—that you should do as much good as you can—powers the moral theory known as *utilitarianism.*

What Utilitarianism Is

Put simply, utilitarianism says that the right thing to do is the thing that produces the best results.[1] An action, rule, or institution is morally right just in case no available alternative does more good.

---

[1] For a classic work on utilitarianism, see John Stuart Mill, *Utilitarianism*, ed. George Sher (Indianapolis: Hackett Publishing Company, 2001 [1861]). For an accessible introduction, see Russ Shafer-Landau, *The Fundamentals of Ethics* (New York: Oxford University Press, 2014), chaps. 9 and 10.

More specifically, utilitarianism tells us to maximize *utility*. I'll focus on the version that identifies utility with happiness, understood as the satisfaction of our preferences.[2] On this sort of view, we should not equate happiness with something specific, such as physical pleasure or wealth. Rather, happiness is—by definition—whatever you want to get out of life. In this respect, utilitarianism defers to our own opinions about what sorts of things are valuable rather than dictating to us what we should care about. Give people what they want.

Utilitarianism doesn't tell us simply to promote our own happiness, however. Morality requires impartiality—that we regard equal amounts of happiness equally. So we're obligated to maximize *social* happiness rather than our own individual happiness. If you see a child with a broken leg by the side of the road, you should stop and drive her to the hospital even if it makes you late for your party. The happiness that the child's healthy leg brings her is far greater than the happiness that your party brings you, so it would be morally wrong to neglect the child for the sake of the party.

Lastly, utilitarianism tells us not simply to promote social happiness, but to *maximize* it. If you are faced with two choices and one produces more good than the other, you should take the one that produces *more* good. On a personal level, if you need money and if you can have a $5 bill or a $10 bill, it's hard to see why you

---

[2] Utilitarians disagree here—some think that there are a variety of intrinsically good things that we should promote (e.g., knowledge, beauty, etc.). Others focus on pleasure in particular. In the interest of space, I'll have to leave these alternatives unexplored.

would take the $5 bill. On a societal level, if you have a choice between doubling people's happiness and tripling people's happiness, a utilitarian would insist that you would not be justified in choosing *less* happiness.

To make the idea of maximizing social happiness more concrete, think of it like this: when you face a range of options, look at how much happiness each one is going to produce for those affected, and how much suffering each one is going to produce for those affected, and then pick the one that has the greatest *net* happiness. Utilitarianism is about the bottom line. For any action, add up the benefits, subtract the costs, and then look at the bottom line of the calculation: Does it maximize the benefits once you've subtracted the costs? In summary, utilitarianism tells us that we should select those actions, rules, and institutions that produce as much happiness as possible for those affected.

So why think that utilitarianism is correct? For one, it seems plausible at the abstract level. The idea that happiness is the ultimate point of morality is compelling, as is the thought that we aren't justified in doing less good than we can. At a concrete level, utilitarianism makes sense of much of commonsense morality. It provides a reasonable account of *which* actions are right and wrong and *why* they are right or wrong. For instance, actions like lying, theft, and assault are generally wrong because they generally decrease social happiness. Lying is wrong because, if we can't trust one another, then we can't have promises or contracts. This result would be bad for our relationships and for business. Victims of assault endure serious suffering. Regarding virtuous actions, generosity is good because it relieves poverty and suffering—it makes people happier. And so on. Morality is important because it helps us prosper, not because it is good in itself.

Now, according to utilitarianism, moral rules will not be *absolute*. We can justifiably break them in certain conditions—namely, when breaking them does the most good. But this conclusion seems right, too. To use a famous example, if you're hiding an innocent person in your home to protect him from a murderer, you would be right to lie when the murderer asks whether you're hiding the person.[3]

Lastly, utilitarianism gives us a perspective from which we can criticize and jettison the indefensible parts of commonsense morality. It helps us make moral progress. Moral rules that don't relieve suffering or promote happiness don't merit our allegiance, no matter how rooted in tradition or convention.

To be clear upfront, this chapter is a preview of utilitarianism, not the whole feature. So here's a confession: things aren't always sunny for utilitarianism. Consider that utilitarianism has no problem asking us to take unpalatable means to the end of maximizing social happiness. Here's a famous case:

TRANSPLANT: Five patients are dying because they lack suitable organ donors. A delivery person enters the hospital. The chief of surgery knows he is a match for all five

---

[3] This case is most famously discussed by Immanuel Kant (who argues, counterintuitively, that it is *not* right to lie under these circumstances). See Immanuel Kant, "On a Supposed Right to Lie from Altruistic Motives," in *Immanuel Kant: Critique of Practical Reason and Other Writings in Moral Philosophy*, ed. Lewis White Beck (Chicago: University of Chicago Press, 1949 [1976]).

dying patients. If the surgeon kidnaps him and harvests his organs, she will save five and kill one. (Assume word of the killing never gets out.)[4]

Killing the delivery person maximizes social happiness but, intuitively, is the wrong thing to do. *Transplant* is just one illustration of a broader worry about utilitarianism: any action, no matter how reprehensible, can be morally justified so long as the results are good enough.

Undoubtedly, this is a problem for utilitarians. But it's less of a problem for the kind of utilitarianism I'll be talking about here. An *act utilitarian*—someone who thinks that the morally right action is the one that produces more social happiness than any available alternative action—might need to accept the rightness of killing one to save five. But I'm going to focus on institutional questions. So I'll be discussing what has been called *institutional utilitarianism*—the view that our social, economic, and political institutions should maximize social happiness.[5] The relevant question from the perspective of institutions is whether we should have a *law* permitting the surgeon to kill one to save five. And the answer to that question seems to be no. The reason is straightforward. A society that legalized organ harvesting would have a hard time running functional hospitals, as patients and delivery

[4] See Judith Jarvis Thomson, "The Trolley Problem," *Yale Law Journal* 94 (1985): 1395–415.

[5] See Russell Hardin, *Morality within the Limits of Reason* (Chicago: University of Chicago Press, 1988); and Robert Goodin, *Utilitarianism as a Public Philosophy* (Cambridge, MA: Cambridge University Press, 1995).

personnel could never be sure of getting out alive. Thus, all those in need of medical treatment would not receive it. The benefits made possible by the hospital would be lost.[6]

Now, we might worry that utilitarianism would have no objection to violating rights as long as it was done secretly. We could imagine a hospital administrator who has the policy of authorizing organ expropriation only in cases where she is sure it will go undetected. In this way, she could save lives on net *and* maintain the hospital's reputation as a safe place. This worry generalizes: Why wouldn't a utilitarian endorse a *government* that secretly violates rights for the greater good?

The answer, in brief, is that such secret powers would create huge opportunities for abuse—with no oversight to keep abuses in check. In a related discussion of whether utilitarianism would recommend that the government commit acts of injustice so long as they were hidden from the public view, utilitarian philosopher and psychologist Joshua Greene writes: "For such policies to fulfill their utilitarian aims, government officials would have to maintain, indefinitely, an enormous conspiracy of Orwellian proportions while forgoing daily opportunities to abuse their power. This cannot be expected to lead to a happier world."[7]

---

[6] See David Schmidtz, "Separateness, Suffering, and Moral Theory," in *Peter Singer under Fire: The Moral Iconoclast Faces His Critics*, ed. Jeffrey Schaler (Chicago: Open Court, 2009), pp. 429–54, 435.

[7] Joshua Greene, *Moral Tribes* (New York: Penguin, 2013), p. 269. Here, Greene is specifically discussing the possibility of a government's faking punishments, but I think his point applies generally.

A happiness-maximizing society, then, will recognize a person's rights, such as the right to her body. This means that others must not expropriate her organs even if they can put the organs to a better use in a particular case. The justification for this restriction is simple, although it comes with a hint of paradox: institutions will produce the best results if they stop people from relentlessly pursuing what they take to be the best results.

To illustrate further, imagine a law that says, "Generally speaking, don't burglarize your neighbor's house—but you have some wiggle room to make an exception when you think you need your neighbor's stuff more than she does. Use your best judgment." That's a bad law on utilitarian grounds, despite its nod to good consequences. There's a lot of value in living in a world in which we can count on being safe in our home, make long-term plans about how to use our possessions, and so on. As David Schmidtz writes, "There is enormous utility in being able to treat certain parameters as settled, as not even permitting case by case utilitarian reasoning."[8] If we thought that other people were ready to steal from us, assault us, or kill us whenever they thought it was *just* beneficial enough, the consequences would be disastrous. People would be too scared to go to school, work, or the hospital. This result would make everyone unhappy. A utilitarian will say that institutions should protect our lives and property because property rights create an environment in which we can flourish.

---

[8] David Schmidtz, *Elements of Justice* (Cambridge, MA: Cambridge University Press, 2006), p. 171.

On a utilitarian account, then, rights aren't morally important in themselves—only as a means to producing good results. Rights are justified because they are useful. Now, plenty of philosophers think that rights are important in themselves. That's a plausible position, but I believe the view that rights are a means has merit too. To say that rights aren't valuable in themselves doesn't *de*value them. After all, oxygen isn't valuable in itself, but it's still pretty valuable.

Utilitarian Libertarianism

So much for the broad strokes of utilitarianism. Which specific institutions and rights will it endorse?

In what follows, I argue that it will tend to favor libertarian institutions. By "libertarianism," I mean, roughly, the family of views united by certain institutional commitments, such as the legal recognition of civil liberties, robust private property rights, freedom of exchange, and freedom of contract; the central place of markets in the production and distribution of goods; and the minimization of forcible interference in people's private choices. More specifically, libertarians tend to support something along the lines of a "minimal state" that supplies only a military, police, and courts. There are some intramural disputes among libertarians about the particulars of the state's role (perhaps it should do more than the minimal state; perhaps it should do less), but I'll concern myself mainly with the minimal state for the sake of discussion.

Here's the one sentence argument for utilitarian libertarianism: compared with other institutions, markets do the best job of promoting social happiness without depending on people *trying* to promote social happiness. Markets solve two major problems for utilitarianism. First, most people don't *desire* to maximize social happiness as opposed to their own happiness and the happiness of a relatively small circle of family and friends. Second, even if people desire to maximize social happiness, they generally don't know how. As individuals, we know very little about the distribution of the world's resources and particular people's desires for those resources. Consequently, we lack the information we need to produce an optimal match between resources and people. But markets provide both the incentives and the information that people need to advance the happiness of strangers. Markets generally make our moral and cognitive limitations work for us rather than against us. They channel self-interest toward the public interest.

Private Property Rights

Let's start with private property. Private property rights are one of the characteristic features of a free-market system. We claim private ownership of such things as houses, gardens, land, cars, paper, and computers. Others are thus obligated not to hop our fence and trespass on our lawn, or break into our car, or use our computer without our permission. To privately own something means that you possess the right to *exclude* others from using it.[9]

---

[9] For a more detailed discussion of this idea, see David Schmidtz, "The Institution of Property," *Social Philosophy and Policy* 11 (1994): 42–62.

To begin to see why the right to exclude is socially useful, let's think about the alternative—a world in which no one has the right to exclude anyone else from the use of his or her property. At first blush, that world might seem ideal. All resources are held in common and everything is shared. Thus, everyone has an equal right to drink from the stream or to swim in the lake. They can all sit under whichever tree they like whenever they like and enjoy its shade and fruit. They can hunt the deer and rabbits that run across the communal land to their heart's content.

But problems arise. Suppose Stan is thinking of starting a garden so that he can grow some tomatoes and make ketchup for his family to enjoy. However, as things stand, he has little incentive to endure the labor involved in growing tomatoes, because he has no assurance that he will reap what he sows. Because there is no private property, he has no right to exclude anyone from his garden. If Stan can't exclude others, he might ask why he should expend the time and resources needed to grow tomatoes when Morty can simply take as many as he likes without offering Stan anything in return. So Stan decides that cultivating the land isn't worth the trouble. Consequently, Stan's desire to feed his family some homemade ketchup doesn't suffice to motivate him to plant the tomatoes, because the tomatoes are unlikely to end up on his family's table.

Stan's problem generalizes: no one has much of an incentive to invest his time and effort into producing food, shelter, clothing, and so on because he has no assurance that he will enjoy the benefits of those productive efforts. This is an example of what is known as the *tragedy of the commons*: people will tend not to use resources efficiently when they are held in common, leading to suboptimal results.[10] When resources are held in common, there is little incentive to use them efficiently because efficiency doesn't pay.

A standard solution to the tragedy of the commons is to introduce private property rights. By granting Stan the right to exclude others from plucking his tomatoes, we give him an incentive to produce those tomatoes in the first place. Property rights encourage people to be productive because they enable people to capture the benefits of their productive efforts. Classical liberal philosopher John Locke writes:

> [H]e who appropriates land to himself by his labour, does not lessen, but increase the common stock of mankind: for the provisions serving to the support of human life, produced by one acre of inclosed and cultivated land, are (to speak much within compass) ten times more than those which are yielded by an acre of land of an equal richness lying waste in common. And therefore he that incloses land, and has a greater plenty of the conveniencies of life from ten acres, than he could have from an hundred left to nature, may truly be said to give ninety acres to mankind: for his labour now supplies him with provisions out of ten acres, which were but the product of an hundred lying in common. I have here rated the

[10] See Garrett Hardin, "The Tragedy of the Commons," *Science* 162 (1968): 1243–48. Also see Schmidtz, "Institution of Property."

improved land very low, in making its product but as ten to one, when it is much nearer an hundred to one.[11]

To be clear: private property is useful even for well-meaning people. Stan isn't mean or selfish—he just wants to feed his family. Still, without private property, he has little incentive to realize that aim by improving the productivity of the land and thereby increasing the total amount of goods available—as opposed to, say, consuming existing resources via hunting and gathering. He won't waste his time growing a fresh bounty of tomatoes; he'll scavenge for berries instead. However, this is a recipe for stagnating at the status quo rather than working toward greater prosperity for all.

Voluntary Exchange

Suppose Stan is now secure in his possessions thanks to his newfound property rights, and so he goes about growing tomatoes and making homemade ketchup. Morty likes ketchup, but because Stan has the right to restrict access to his property, Morty cannot simply take it from Stan's table. If he wants some ketchup, he has to make it worth Stan's while. Morty plants some mustard seeds, makes mustard, and trades some to Stan for a bottle of ketchup. Both Stan and Morty are happier than before. It's win-win.

In a market economy characterized by voluntary exchange, if I want something you have, I have to give you something you want, and vice versa. Thus, I have a strong incentive to serve

[11] John Locke, *Two Treatises of Government*, ed. Peter Laslett (Cambridge, MA: Cambridge University Press, 1988), p. 37.

your interests. As the philosopher and economist Adam Smith says:

> Man has almost constant occasion for the help of his brethren, and it is in vain for him to expect it from their benevolence only. He will be more likely to prevail if he can interest their self-love in his favour, and show them that it is for their own advantage to do for him what he requires of them. Whoever offers to another a bargain of any kind, proposes to do this. Give me that which I want, and you shall have this which you want, is the meaning of every such offer; and it is in this manner that we obtain from one another the far greater part of those good offices which we stand in need of. It is not from the benevolence of the butcher, the brewer, or the baker that we expect our dinner, but from their regard to their own interest.[12]

When I walk into a store and buy a Mountain Dew for 99 cents, I do it because I want the Mountain Dew more than the 99 cents. The shopkeeper does it because she wants the 99 cents more than the Mountain Dew. The exchange leaves us both happier than we were before—otherwise, we wouldn't agree to the deal.

Here's one of Smith's vital insights: when I give the shopkeeper my 99 cents, I do it because I expect the Mountain Dew to make *me* happier, not because the 99 cents will make the shopkeeper happier. Still, my action has the *good consequence* of making the

---

[12] Adam Smith, *An Inquiry into the Nature and Causes of the Wealth of Nations* (New York: Bantam, 2003 [1776]), 1.2.2.

shopkeeper happier. So one crucial feature of markets is that they lead people to promote the happiness of others even when they intend only to promote their own happiness. As Smith puts it, in a market, "By pursuing his own interest, [a person] frequently promotes that of society more effectually than when he really intends to promote it."[13]

Prices

Suppose that I've done such a powerful job of elucidating utilitarianism that you're already convinced it's the correct moral theory. Motivation isn't a problem; you don't need any financial incentives, and so perhaps it's unclear what, if anything, the market can do for you. You're ready to go out and maximize the world's happiness. OK—how? More specifically, what's the happiness-maximizing distribution of the world's resources?

The short answer is that I don't know. No one knows. That said, we can be confident that markets will tend to place goods in the hands of those who derive the most satisfaction or happiness from them. Imagine that a scientist in Arizona is frantically buying up coffee beans. Coffee bean extract is a key ingredient in the new arthritis drug she is developing, a drug she expects to sell to thousands of people. In short, she *really* wants coffee beans. In buying up lots of coffee, the scientist brings about an increase in its price.

In contrast to the scientist, an ultramarathoner in North Dakota has a slight preference for coffee over tea as his morning beverage.

[13] Ibid., 4.2.9.

When he sees that his morning cup of joe has gotten more expensive, he switches to tea. He isn't cutting back on coffee to help society; he's doing it to fatten his wallet. Nevertheless, in cutting back, he *does* help society. His switching from coffee to tea means that the coffee is going to a more highly valued use—it's better for society for the coffee beans to go into the arthritis drug than the ultramarathoner's travel mug. Critically, the ultramarathoner has no idea what the researcher is doing or what she needs (or even that she exists). Still, he frees up the coffee for a more highly valued use simply by responding to the increase in its price. Economist F. A. Hayek argues that market prices supply us with information about the scarcity or abundance of goods, information that in turn motivates us to use those goods in efficient ways.[14]

Now, a minute ago I had you assume that you didn't need any financial incentive to promote the happiness of strangers. That assumption is probably optimistic. Not to worry, though: as the coffee example suggests, prices provide not only socially useful information but also socially useful incentives. The ultramarathoner is led to conserve coffee not out of concern for the public interest but out of self-interest—he just wants to spend less on his daily caffeine fix.

The same point applies to labor. If a lot of people want to watch animated sitcoms and demand for such shows increases, then the wages paid to those who make these shows will increase. Here again, the high wage supplies both useful information and useful incentives. Critics of capitalism might lament that *Family Guy*

---

[14] F. A. Hayek, "The Use of Knowledge in Society," *American Economic Review* 35 (1945): 519–30.

rakes in hundreds of millions, whereas Fellini, well, doesn't. But a utilitarian couldn't find fault with this (full disclosure: I prefer *Family Guy*). *Family Guy* does a better job than Fellini of giving people want they want. The wealth of Seth MacFarlane, the creator of *Family Guy*, represents a feature of the market, not a bug. The high wages of in-demand jobs create a powerful incentive to do work that makes people happy. (And in a free market, no one will stop you from going to the independent movie house to watch Fellini if you really want to.)

Intentions or Outcomes?

Is the market's ability to mobilize self-interest for the common good really a *virtue*? According to one objection, the market motivates you to do the right thing—helping others—but for the wrong reason. Even if you give your customers what they want, you might be doing it only because you want to make money for yourself. Sometimes, critics of capitalism argue that we should oppose markets on moral grounds because they work by recruiting our baser motives, such as self-interest.[15]

It's worth clarifying that evidence suggests that markets do not draw upon or cultivate the worst of human psychology.[16] But let's grant the objection for argument's sake. It still won't faze the utilitarian.

---

[15] G. A. Cohen, a prominent philosophical opponent of libertarianism, acknowledges capitalism's productiveness but still finds it worthy of moral criticism on these sorts of grounds. See G. A. Cohen, *Why Not Socialism?* (Princeton, NJ: Princeton University Press, 2009).

[16] For a review of some of the relevant social science, see Herbert Gintis, "Giving Economists Their Due," *Boston Review*, May–June 2012, http://new.bostonreview.net /BR37.3/ndf_herbert_gintis_markets_morals.php.

For a utilitarian, results are what matter. The famous utilitarian John Stuart Mill writes, "He who saves a fellow creature from drowning does what is morally right, whether his motive be duty, or the hope of being paid for his trouble."[17] There's no shame in paying lifeguards to save lives. Think about it from the perspective of the drowning man saved by the lifeguard: *he* doesn't care what motivates the lifeguard as long as he gets saved. Similarly, the shopkeeper doesn't care *why* I'm giving her 99 cents; she just cares about the 99 cents.

A utilitarian would tell us not to wring our hands over the nobility of the lifesaver's motives—the important thing is saving the life. Imagine a kind-hearted surgeon with uncorrected astigmatism who regularly kills her (pro bono) patients. We'd want her to stop. Conversely, imagine a narcissistic virtuoso surgeon who operates only to gain fame and fortune. We'd want her to continue. The question that matters most is this: Which surgeon do we want? The one that produces the best results. Which institutional arrangement do we want? The one that produces the best results.

So a utilitarian would object to the idea that efficiency arguments for free markets are not enough—that we also need *moral* arguments that are somehow distinct from the economic ones I've been giving so far.[18] According to utilitarianism, the economic arguments *are* the

---

[17] Mill, *Utilitarianism*, p. 18.

[18] See, for instance, Walter Williams, "The Argument for Free Markets: Morality vs. Efficiency," *Cato Journal* 15 (1995/6): 179–89. Williams writes: "Economic efficiency and greater wealth should be promoted as simply a side-benefit of free markets. The intellectual defense of free-market capitalism should focus on its moral superiority" (p. 182). Williams argues that the moral superiority of markets rests on their voluntary nature and respect for individual rights.

moral arguments. Free markets are moral *because* they are beneficial. Think of it like this: no one would say that it is true, but morally insufficient, to argue that hospitals make us better off. The fact that hospitals bring us more health, enjoyment, and life seems like all the justification they need. Similarly, the fact that a political or economic institution brings us more health, enjoyment, and life seems like a good moral justification for it, just as the fact that an institution causes poverty and suffering is a good reason to think it's bad.

What about Market Failure?

The utilitarian case for markets is simple: they're efficient. But open any introductory economics textbook, and you'll read about plenty of ways in which markets are *inefficient*—that is, cases of "market failure." So shouldn't market failure curb a utilitarian's enthusiasm for the market?

To start to answer this question, let's consider a specific case of market failure: public goods. Public goods are *nonexcludable*, meaning that you cannot be excluded from enjoying them even if you didn't contribute to them. Public goods are also *nonrivalous*, meaning that my enjoyment of the good doesn't subtract from yours.

Here's an example. A storm threatens to flood the river, an event that would destroy your town. If the townspeople join together to build a levee with sandbags, the town will be spared. However, your individual contribution won't make or break the effort. The levee is a public good. If it prevents the flood, my house will be saved whether or not I helped stack the sandbags. And the levee will protect the entire town, so protecting my house doesn't detract from the protection afforded to other houses.

It's typically assumed that people won't voluntarily contribute to public goods like the levee. Your individual contribution won't make or break the existence of the levee, and if the levee does somehow get provided, you enjoy its protection whether or not you helped. You get the benefit without paying the costs. So the self-interested choice is to watch TV while your neighbors get sore backs from lugging sandbags around. The problem is, your neighbors have the exact same incentive to stay home—if enough others contribute to the levee, they'll enjoy the benefits whether or not they contributed themselves. Consequently, no one has an incentive to contribute to the levee. As a result of this *free-rider problem*, the town will flood even though the flood is bad for everyone. The public interest and individuals' self-interest break apart.

Here's the moral of the market-failure story: markets aren't as efficient as they could be. Sometimes, they leave welfare gains on the table. But that doesn't spell doom for the utilitarian case for markets.

To see why, consider that a utilitarian doesn't regard the right institutional arrangement as the best *imaginable* arrangement but rather the best *available* arrangement. Think back to the shipwreck case. You could rescue either the raft with four passengers or the one with three passengers. Obviously, you'd produce more happiness by saving all seven passengers—but that option wasn't available. You had only enough fuel to save one raft. In a perfect world, we could save all seven (or rather, no one would need saving in the first place). But we don't live in a perfect world. We can choose only the least imperfect alternative from a menu of nothing but imperfect alternatives. So simply showing that markets are imperfect does not show that they are the wrong institutional structure. To draw that conclusion, we'd need an *available* alternative that does better—an alternative that realizes the welfare gains that markets do not.

By way of analogy, let me tell you about my theory of "LeBron James failure." That theory alleges that the Cleveland Cavaliers should cut LeBron James because he misses roughly 50 percent of his shots. Because James fails roughly 50 percent of the time, he should be replaced.

The "LeBron James failure" theory is not compelling, and it's easy to see why. Perfection isn't the standard we should use to judge basketball players. Rather, the standard is the best player available to replace them. If LeBron James's backup is better than James, then, by all means, let's replace James. But James's backup *isn't* better—he misses even more of his shots—so James's roster spot should be secure.

The same analysis applies to institutions. Markets sometimes leave welfare gains on the table just as LeBron James sometimes leaves points on the table. But the standard we should use to judge the market is not perfection; rather, it's the best available institutional alternative. Markets are the wrong choice only if there is a feasible alternative that will do a better job. As the utilitarian Henry Sidgwick writes, "It does not follow that whenever laissez faire falls short, government interference is expedient; since the inevitable drawbacks of the latter may, in any particular case, be worse than the shortcomings of private enterprise."[19]

---

[19] Henry Sidgwick, *Principles of Political Economy* (London: MacMillan, 1887), quoted in Charles Wolf, *Markets or Governments: Choosing between Imperfect Alternatives* (Cambridge, MA: MIT Press, 1993), p. 17.

Of course, governments might sometimes outperform markets. Indeed, that is often how the system is drawn up on the chalkboard. Take the levee case. To solve the public goods problem, the town could authorize a 1 percent sales tax to fund a levee-building public works project. That way, citizens are *forced* to contribute to the levee. They have no grounds for complaint, though, because the tax works to their advantage: better to pay 1 percent more for bubble gum than to lose your home to a flood. So it looks as if we have a formidable utilitarian reason to depart from a free market.

However, it's not enough to stipulate *that* the government will somehow efficiently provide public goods—we need to know *how*. After all, a libertarian could just stipulate that the market will *somehow* efficiently provide public goods, but that clearly won't do. As we've seen, people won't contribute to the levee because they have nothing to lose by not contributing. But here's the rub: the exact same analysis applies to the government intervention meant to fix this problem and efficiently provide the levee. People won't contribute to good government because they have nothing to lose by not contributing.

Let me spell out this argument more thoroughly. Suppose that in the upcoming election, the mayoral candidates field their policy proposals for flood prevention. To determine which candidate actually has a good proposal, you will need to inspect each proposal for its economic cost, feasibility, and environmental impact. To form an educated opinion on those matters, you'll need to brush up on your economics, engineering, and ecology. You'll also want to research how closely candidates' promises align with their legislative history. For instance, you'll want to read the fine print of the incumbent's legislation to see how often tax revenue actually goes toward its intended purpose rather than pork-barrel projects designed to gain the support of special-interest groups; you'll want to learn that the firms hired for public works projects are the best ones for the job rather than the ones that donated the most to her reelection campaign; and so on.

This sounds like a lot of hassle. But citizens need to do it if they are going to hold the government accountable and ensure that it efficiently provides the public good. So will you roll up your sleeves and get to work? Probably not. Indeed, you won't do so for exactly the same reason you won't work on the levee in the first place: your incentive is to free-ride. In all likelihood, your individual vote won't tip the scales in favor of the best candidate, and if the best candidate does somehow get elected, you enjoy the benefits whether or not you voted for her.[20] You get the benefit without paying the costs. So the self-interested choice is to watch *Family Guy* while your neighbors spend their weekends scrutinizing the fine print of the Efficient Levee Act. The problem is that your neighbors have the exact same incentive—if enough others vote for the best candidate, they'll enjoy the benefits whether or not they cast a good vote themselves. So no one has an incentive to cast a good vote. As a result of the free-rider problem, the town won't get good government even though this outcome is bad for everyone. The free-rider problem that generates the call for government intervention in the first place undercuts the intervention itself.

---

[20] For an overview of democracy and "rational ignorance," see Ilya Somin, *Democracy and Political Ignorance* (Stanford, CA: Stanford University Press, 2013).

Think of it this way. Suppose Stan is feeling too sluggish to walk to the coffee shop. Morty suggests that Stan can perk himself up for the walk by drinking an espresso—an espresso that happens to be sold at the coffee shop. Needless to say, Morty's suggested solution isn't very helpful. It's unraveled by the very problem it intends to solve. Stan isn't energetic enough to walk to the coffee shop, so Morty shouldn't suggest caffeinating strategies that hinge on Stan's being energetic enough to walk to the coffee shop. The same analysis applies to the public goods argument for state intervention. If the cause of the market failure is that people are assumed to be free riders, we shouldn't suggest government solutions that hinge on people *not* being free riders.

Historically, an important feature of libertarian institutional analysis has been the insistence that we use the same assumptions about human behavior when thinking about economics and politics, instead of modeling people as greedy in the marketplace and saintly in the voting booth.[21] The economist George Stigler writes:

For some, market failures serve as a rationale for public intervention. However, the fact that self-interested market

---

[21] Indeed, this insistence is at the core of *public choice* economics, which is, roughly, the economic analysis of politics. For more on the general idea that our analysis should apply its behavioral assumptions across institutional contexts, see James Buchanan and Gordon Tullock, *The Calculus of Consent* (Indianapolis, IN: Liberty Fund, 1999 [1962]); Geoffrey Brennan and James Buchanan, *The Reason of Rules* (Indianapolis, IN: Liberty Fund, 2000 [1985]); Harold Demsetz, "Information and Efficiency: Another Viewpoint," *Journal of Law and Economics* 12 (1969): 1–21; Milton Friedman, *Capitalism and Freedom* (Chicago: University of Chicago Press, 2002 [1962]), conclusion; and Jason Brennan, *Why Not Capitalism?* (New York: Routledge, 2014).

behavior does not always produce felicitous social consequences is not sufficient reason to draw this conclusion.
It is necessary to assess public performance under comparable conditions, and hence to analyze self-interested
political behavior in the institutional structures of the
public sector. Our approach emphasizes this institutional
structure—warts and all—and thereby provides specific
cautionary warnings about optimistic reliance on political
institutions to improve upon market performance.[22]

It's no surprise that fictitious, idealized governments look better than realistic, imperfect markets. But that's not an apples-to-
apples comparison.

The broader point here is that we must compare like to like.
Markets fail and governments fail. Our goal should be to favor
institutions that fail less frequently and less severely when their
participants are operating within the same limitations of incentives and information. Economist Tyler Cowen suggests that a
like-to-like comparison will generally favor private solutions to
public goods problems:

> The imperfections of market solutions to public-goods
> problems must be weighed against the imperfections
> of government solutions. Governments rely on bureau-
> cracy, respond to poorly informed voters, and have weak

---

[22] George Stigler, "The Economists' Traditional Theory of the Economic Functions
of the State," in *The Citizen and the State: Essays on Regulation* (Chicago: University of
Chicago Press, 1975), p. 103.

incentives to serve consumers. Therefore they produce inefficiently. Furthermore, politicians may supply public "goods" in a manner to serve their own interests rather than the interests of the public; examples of wasteful government spending and pork barrel projects are legion. Government often creates a problem of "forced riders" by compelling persons to support projects they do not desire. Private means of avoiding or transforming public-goods problems, when available, are usually more efficient than governmental solutions.[23]

As Cowen indicates, there are private means of solving public goods problems. The levee, for instance, could be built via "crowd-funding," whereby individuals pledge x dollars toward some large-scale project on the condition that enough others pledge as well. If not enough others contribute to make the project work, then you aren't charged anything. This structure ensures that you won't make a contribution in vain. It doesn't *eliminate* the free-rider problem (perhaps nothing can), but it does lessen the problem.

Granted, private solutions probably work better for public goods like the levee than for large-scale public goods like national defense. Sometimes, the best solution might be a mix of market mechanisms and government regulation, such as in the case of clean air. According to the market-failure argument, you won't voluntarily contribute to clean air because your individual purchase of a hybrid car (for example) won't make or break whether

[23] Tyler Cowen, "Public Goods." *The Concise Encyclopedia of Economics*, Library of Economics and Liberty, 2008, http://www.econlib.org/library/Enc/PublicGoods.html.

our air is clean, and if enough others buy hybrids, you'll breathe clean air whether you bought one or not.

Before examining how we might best provide clean air, it's worth noting that our inability to provide the public good in this case is plausibly due to the absence of any sort of private property rights. What we have here is a tragedy of the commons: air is a resource that is held in common, and so no individual has an incentive to manage it wisely. I have no way to capture the benefits of my individual contribution to cleaner air. My decision to buy a hybrid (or not) makes virtually no difference to the overall quality of the air I breathe. For this reason, libertarians tend to recommend that we expand property rights into the realm of natural resources insofar as possible to supply people with an incentive to treat them well. (You are far less likely to absentmindedly toss your crumpled gum wrapper on your front yard—and to let others do so—than on a public sidewalk.)

Of course, establishing private property rights in air isn't feasible. Here, the best available solution might be a system of emissions trading, which takes advantage of some of the virtues of private property and market mechanisms to produce clean air. Under this system, the government caps the total amount of pollutants, and companies are allotted pollution permits that can be bought and sold on a market. Companies have an incentive to reduce their pollution because they can sell unused permits and, conversely, must pay more if they want to pollute beyond their initial allotment. Moreover, the system will tend to channel pollution permits to those who value them most and are thus willing to pay the most for them, thereby ensuring that when pollutants are emitted, they go toward a highly valued use. As with any sort of institutional arrangement, though, we must make a sober assessment of its likely real-world efficacy. No form of regulation is immune to inefficiencies or special-interest pressure. We can only choose the least flawed alternative.

To sum up: at the level of moral philosophy, we cannot say how governments should intervene in the economy in specific cases (if at all), just as we cannot say how a particular hospital should allocate its particular supply of medicine to treat its particular patients. However, we can determine the moral standard for evaluating those decisions—namely, we should favor the arrangement that does better than all of its *feasible* competitors.

Utilitarian Redistribution

I'd wager that most utilitarian philosophers aren't libertarians. One major reason concerns the economic inequalities that tend to result from market processes. A free market in labor provides both the information and incentive we need to give people what they want. If you're really good at giving people what they want, you'll get rich. But there are plenty of people who have more than enough money to meet all of their needs and wants alongside others who don't have enough to meet even their basic needs. We could, it seems, maximize happiness by redistributing resources from rich to poor.

This argument relies on the phenomenon of the *diminishing marginal utility of wealth* (DMU). The idea is something like this: each additional dollar that you get brings less happiness than the dollar before it. We tend to allocate our resources to their most highly valued uses, and so we satisfy our most urgent needs first. Someone with no money whatsoever will benefit enormously from $100—he can spend that money on goods like food and water. By contrast, a billionaire will barely notice an extra $100 because all of her urgent needs were met long ago. Maybe she'll spend it on something trivial, like extra fireworks for her extravagant birthday celebration. Although $100 worth of fireworks might be nice, they surely don't create as much happiness for the billionaire as $100 worth of food creates for someone dying of starvation. So transferring wealth from someone with more to someone with less will increase overall happiness.

The DMU forms the basis of a number of utilitarians' criticisms of libertarianism. In a review of libertarian philosopher Robert Nozick's *Anarchy, State, and Utopia*, Peter Singer writes:

> Utilitarianism has no problem in justifying a substantial amount of compulsory redistribution from the rich to the poor. We all recognize that $1,000 means far less to people earning $100,000 than it does to people trying to support a family on $6,000. Therefore in normal circumstances we increase the total happiness when we take from those with a lot and give to those with little. Therefore that is what we ought to do. For the utilitarian it is as simple as that. The result will not be absolute equality of wealth. There may be some who need relatively little to be happy, and others whose expensive tastes require more to achieve the same level of happiness. If resources

are adequate the utilitarian will give each enough to make him happy, and that will mean giving some more than others.[24]

More recently, Joshua Greene expresses his sympathy with a number of libertarian policies but stops short of fully endorsing the view.[25] One of his reasons is the DMU argument: "Taking a bit of money from the haves hurts them very little, whereas providing resources and opportunities to the have-nots, when done wisely, goes a long way."[26] Before I offer a philosophical rejoinder to the DMU argument against the free market, let me first make some preliminary remarks.

Libertarian Redistribution

To start, plenty of libertarians and classical liberals endorse some wealth and income redistribution. F. A. Hayek, for example, supported "the assurance of a certain minimum income for everyone."[27] Milton Friedman proposed a negative income tax, whereby people who earn less than some specified amount receive income from the government rather than pay it in taxes.[28]

---

[24] Peter Singer, "The Right to Be Rich or Poor," *New York Review of Books*, March 6, 1975, http://www.nybooks.com/articles/archives/1975/mar/06/the-right-to-be-rich-or-poor/.

[25] Greene writes, "I believe that libertarians are probably right—righter than many liberals—in some cases." Greene, *Moral Tribes*, p. 367. He discusses school choice, organ markets, prostitution, and sweatshops as possible cases (with some reservations).

[26] Ibid., p. 368.

[27] F. A. Hayek, *Law, Legislation, and Liberty*, vol. 3 (Chicago: University of Chicago Press, 1979), p. 55.

[28] Friedman, *Capitalism and Freedom*, chap. 12.

It's crucial to note that support for something like a guaranteed minimum income does not amount to support for what we think of as a "welfare state" that puts the government in the business of directly providing goods like education or health care. Rather, extra income is distributed directly to the poor, who can use it as they please. One major advantage of this policy is that it doesn't face the same information problems as the "in-kind" provision of goods and services by the government. Given the diversity of citizens' preferences, it's hard for governments to determine the happiness-maximizing allocation of the goods it provides. What if I prefer half as much health care but twice as much education as you? It's more efficient to simply let us buy the basket of goods that best satisfies our preferences.

Poverty and Priorities

Next, the emphasis on domestic redistribution is gravely misplaced from a utilitarian perspective. Utilitarianism counsels us to care equally about equal amounts of happiness, regardless of whom we are making happy. Thus, utilitarianism doesn't provide any basis for prioritizing the happiness of our fellow citizens above the happiness of those on the other side of our national border. And because the global poor are far poorer than the domestic poor in the United States, the DMU argument should lead us to make the alleviation of global poverty a more urgent priority than the alleviation of domestic poverty.[29]

---

[29] For a discussion of why the "difficulties [of the poor in the United States] are of a different order than those of the world's poorest people," see Peter Singer, *The Life You Can Save* (New York: Random House, 2010), p. 8.

One incredibly powerful and underrated tool for fighting global poverty is a free market in labor, that is, opening the border to immigrants. Studies suggest that we could potentially *double* world gross domestic product by eliminating all immigration restrictions.[30] Open borders would be particularly beneficial for the world's poorest. Economist Michael Clemens writes, "[M]igrants from developing countries to the United States typically raise their real living standards by hundreds of percent, and by over 1,000 percent for the poorest people from the poorest countries."[31] A global free market in labor would enable labor to flow to where it is most economically valuable, just as a free market in tradable goods tends to allocate those goods to their most highly valued uses.[32]

My point here is that one major part of the libertarian policy platform—a global free market in labor—is likely to do far more good for the poor than domestic redistribution. This is not to say that some domestic redistribution is unwarranted or that domestic redistribution and open borders are incompatible as some

[30] Lant Pritchett, "The Cliff at the Border," in *Equity and Growth in a Globalizing World*, ed. Ravi Kanbur and Michael Spence (Washington: World Bank, 2010), pp. 263–86; Michael Clemens, "Economics and Emigration: Trillion-Dollar Bills on the Sidewalk?" *Journal of Economic Perspectives* 25 (2011): 83–106.

[31] Michael Clemens, "The Biggest Idea in Development That No One Really Tried," *Annual Proceedings of the Wealth and Well-Being of Nations*, ed. Emily Chamlee-Wright (Beloit, WI: Beloit College Press, 2010), pp. 25–50, 29.

[32] For a discussion of the effect of location on wages, see Michael Clemens, Claudio E. Montenegro, and Lant Pritchett, "The Place Premium: Wage Differences for Identical Workers across the U.S. Border," Center for Global Development Working Paper no. 148, July 2008.

allege, just that standard utilitarian critiques of libertarianism tend to oversell the merits of redistribution relative to other policy proposals.

Implementation Issues

Even with open borders, there still might be room for happiness-maximizing redistribution from rich to poor. But as discussed earlier, it's important to use a clear-eyed, unromantic model of how institutions work. We might be tempted to think of state-administered redistribution as analogous to the sort of effortless and effective microlevel redistribution that occurs every time we transfer money from our savings account to our checking account. But real-world economic redistribution need not simply *transfer* resources. It can reduce the total amount of resources available because it reduces the incentives for labor and capital investment.

Here's a simple case. Robinson Crusoe lives on an island and spends his time fishing. Friday comes ashore and requests that all resources on the island be equally distributed for the sake of social happiness maximization. So Friday gets one of every two fish Crusoe catches. Consequently, Crusoe spends less time fishing and building fishnets because the value of those activities to him has been cut in half. In brief, Crusoe's supply of labor and capital declines under increasing rates of taxation. Before Friday's arrival, Crusoe would fully reap the benefits of his fishing expeditions. Now, half of Crusoe's catch is transferred to Friday for the sake of egalitarian redistribution. Crusoe chooses to fish less because he expects to benefit less from additional labor and capital investment.

Redistribution can also disincentivize labor by decreasing the expected costs of leisure. When Friday is guaranteed half of Crusoe's fish, he has an incentive to do less foraging (for example). He expects to get fish regardless of whether he gathers berries to trade with Crusoe for some fish. He concludes that his time is better spent in pursuits other than berry picking, so he elects not to pick the berries. Friday's change of heart isn't a reflection of an unwillingness to work, but rather the change in the *opportunity cost* of doing things other than working. Before the redistribution, if Friday went surfing instead of picking berries, he didn't get fish from Crusoe. Now, he expects to get fish *and* time on the waves, meaning that he has a much weaker incentive to pick berries.

As a result of a program of egalitarian redistribution, both Crusoe and Friday see a drop in their incentive to produce their respective kinds of food. In this case, redistribution does not simply transfer goods from one person to another; it decreases the total number of goods available for everybody.

Lastly, real-world redistribution isn't a simple rich-to-poor transfer. A good slice of the pie that gets redistributed goes to people other than the poor, such as the middle class and the rich.[33] Think of programs like Social Security and "corporate welfare," both of which involve tax-funded transfers of wealth. It shouldn't come as a surprise that groups with substantial political power are able to reroute the flow of politically administered redistribution toward themselves.

---

[33] See Tyler Cowen, "Does the Welfare State Help the Poor?" *Social Philosophy and Policy* 19 (2002): 36–54, sec. 2.

The Philosophical Issue

Enough hedging. So far I've covered some practical problems surrounding real-world redistribution, but what can be said by way of a philosophical treatment?

David Schmidtz argues that the very assumption of the diminishing marginal utility of wealth that motivates the argument for redistribution simultaneously *de*motivates redistribution.[34] The key point to recognize is that resources can be used for consumption *and* production. Given diminishing marginal utility, production becomes a more highly valued use of resources than consumption as income rises. Thus, transfers that equalize resources may decrease production and social happiness along with it.

To illustrate, Schmidtz imagines the case of Joe Rich and Jane Poor.[35] Corn is the sole good to be distributed. Rich has one unit of corn; Poor has none. One unit of corn is enough to eat; two units are too much—trying to eat two units of corn will make one sick. Without corn, Rich and Poor would have to eat something terrible—something they certainly would not eat in the presence of adequate corn. Thus, consuming the first unit has high marginal utility for both Rich and Poor; consuming a second unit has relatively low marginal utility. So far, so good for the DMU argument for equality.

Yet as Schmidtz observes, matters look different when we consider production. Given one unit of corn, Poor will immediately

---

[34] David Schmidtz, "Diminishing Marginal Utility and Egalitarian Redistribution," *Journal of Value Inquiry* 34 (2000): 263–72.

[35] Ibid., p. 266.

consume it—that is, she will put the corn to its most highly valued use. Rich's appetite, however, is satisfied, given that he has already consumed a unit. Thus, he will put the corn to a use other than consumption, namely, production. Schmidtz explains:

> Poor eats the corn, whereas Rich, already having eaten enough, has nothing better to do with his surplus than to plant it. . . . Precisely because of diminishing marginal utility, production becomes a higher valued use as income rises. If a community does not have significant numbers of people out that far on their utility curves, such that they have nothing better to do with marginal units than plant them, then the community is facing economic stagnation at best. . . . Therefore, unequivocal utilitarian support for egalitarian redistribution is not to be found in the idea that wealth and consumption have diminishing marginal utility.[36]

It is precisely the assumption of DMU that grounds the objection to redistribution. When you have lots of resources, you get less and less value from consuming an additional unit. So the value of productive investment relative to consumption rises.[37]

The broader point is that concern for social happiness in general and poverty alleviation in particular should prompt us to care about economic production in addition to consumption. Reducing investment for the sake of near-term consumption will

[36] Ibid., p. 268.

[37] Although Schmidtz notes that this point might also support other productive endeavors, such as education. Ibid., p. 270.

slow economic growth, a result that can bring about enormous losses in material wealth over time.

It is *very* easy to underestimate the power of economic growth. Let me quote from an economist, Paul Romer:

> In the modern version of an old legend, an investment banker asks to be paid by placing one penny on the first square of a chessboard, two pennies on the second square, four on the third, etc. If the banker had asked that only the white squares be used, the initial penny would have doubled in value thirty-one times, leaving $21.5 million on the last square. Using both the black and the white squares would have made the penny grow to $92 million billion. People are reasonably good at forming estimates based on addition, but for operations such as compounding that depend on repeated multiplication, we systematically underestimate how quickly things grow. As a result, we often lose sight of how important the average rate of growth is for an economy. . . . For a nation, the choices that determine whether income doubles with every generation, or instead with every other generation, dwarf all other economic policy concerns.[38]

To take a specific case from Tyler Cowen: "If a country grows at a rate of 5 percent per annum, it takes just over 80 years for it

[38] Paul M. Romer, "Economic Growth," *The Concise Encyclopedia of Economics*, Library of Economics and Liberty, 2008, http://www.econlib.org/library/Enc/Economic Growth.html.

to go from a per capita income of \$500 to a per capita income of \$25,000. At a growth rate of 1 percent, that same improvement takes 393 years."[39]

Growth can drive up the real income of the poor by driving down the real price of goods—the same amount of labor buys more (and better) goods over time. For example, to buy a half gallon of milk in 1950 required someone to work for 16 minutes at a typical wage but only for 7 minutes about a half century later.[40] During that same time, the work-time cost of a basket of a dozen staple foods declined significantly, from 3.5 to 1.6 hours.[41] The microwaves we use to cook that food have become vastly more affordable as well. In 1984, only 12.5 percent of households below the poverty line owned microwaves.[42] In 2011, 93.4 percent did.[43] Let's also not neglect the *quality* improvements that new microwaves offer over previous ones. Finally, we shouldn't forget about the products that are available for purchase today that did not exist in the past (e.g., smartphones, Netflix, etc.).

[39] Cowen, "Does the Welfare State Help the Poor?" p. 45.

[40] W. Michael Cox and Richard Alm, "Time Well Spent: The Declining *Real* Cost of Living in America," *Federal Reserve Bank of Dallas Annual Report* (Dallas: Federal Reserve Bank of Dallas, 1997), p. 4.

[41] Ibid.

[42] United States Census Bureau data reported in W. Michael Cox and Richard Alm, "By Our Own Bootstraps: Economic Opportunity and the Dynamics of Income Distribution," *Federal Reserve Bank of Dallas Annual Report* (Dallas: Federal Reserve Bank of Dallas, 1995), p. 22.

[43] United States Census Bureau, "Extended Measures of Well-Being: Living Conditions in the United States, 2011," http://www.census.gov/hhes/well-being/publications /extended-11.html.

One advantage that the growth strategy for poverty alleviation has over the redistribution strategy is that it works with, rather than against, our moral limitations. I've emphasized that one of the market's great virtues is that it channels self-interest toward the public interest. By contrast, citizens' self-interest will often undercut the efficacy of politically administered redistribution. If people work less as taxes increase, the effectiveness of redistribution is lessened. Redistribution is also less effective when the rich lobby for a big slice of the pie being redistributed or invest resources in crafty methods of lowering their tax burden.

Now, consider the growth strategy. Instead of spending $1 million on her third Olympic-size swimming pool (from which she will derive little satisfaction thanks to DMU), a billionaire can invest that money in a game-changing technology that will enable the production of cheaper and better microwaves. She needn't make microwaves more affordable out of an altruistic concern for the poor but out of a self-interested concern for her bank account. She benefits the poor without *intending* to benefit to the poor.

By no means am I claiming that growth is a perfect solution to poverty. But at a minimum, we should be on guard against a tendency to overestimate redistribution's benefits for the badly off and underestimate its indirect costs from its adverse effect on economic growth. Given just how staggering the effects of a drop in the growth rate can be, we shouldn't dismiss the harm redistribution can do to the poor. To its credit, utilitarianism tells us to make the alleviation of poverty and suffering an urgent moral priority. But we should be careful here. The most intuitive way of helping the poor may not be the best way. Markets are deceptively powerful instruments of humanitarianism.

Utilitarianism, despite initial appearances, is a natural fit with libertarianism. It is a moral theory that can have a robust respect for rights and one that values good results over good intentions. The great virtue of the market, from a utilitarian perspective, is that it leads us to promote the happiness of others without demanding that we prioritize their happiness or even know *how* to make them happy. No institution is perfect, but the market does the best job of extracting social benefits from people's limited supply of impartiality and information.[44]

---

[44] Thanks are extended to Adam Lerner and Aaron Ross Powell for helpful comments on an earlier version of this chapter.

Natural Rights

Eric Mack

> Individuals have rights, and there are things that no person
> or group may do to them (without violating their rights).
> —Robert Nozick, *Anarchy, State, and Utopia*

Introduction

Natural rights are moral claims that each individual has against
all other persons and groups. Natural rights allow each individual
to demand that all other individuals and groups not subject her
to certain untoward treatment—not subject her, for example, to
being killed, enslaved, or maimed. Natural rights do not arise
out of the decrees of political authorities or calculations of social
interests or through the particular processes by which individuals may acquire specific property rights or contractual rights.
Natural rights are our *original rights*—rights that each individual
possesses against all other agents, unless those rights have been
waived or forfeited. If there are such natural rights, they must
be grounded in some morally seminal feature of each person.

Moral rights—both natural and acquired—are absolutely central to *political* philosophy. For, since individuals may *demand* that their rights be respected, individuals (or their agents) may use force to ensure compliance with their rights; and political philosophy is about the acceptable use of force.

In this chapter, I explain and recommend the natural rights approach to political philosophy. I will dispel the idea that there is something mysterious or spooky or old-fashioned about this approach. I indicate how this approach captures certain of our most central moral insights and how it connects with further moral insights about the separate importance of each individual and each individual's well-being. Moreover, I will indicate how the natural rights approach that I will be articulating has strongly libertarian implications. Indeed, most of the powerful articulations of classical liberal and libertarian doctrine have issued from natural rights theorizing—from the founding father of classical liberalism, John Locke, in the 17th century to the most highly regarded libertarian philosopher of recent decades, Robert Nozick.

The reason for this striking overlap of natural rights thinking and classical liberal or libertarian conclusions is that properly articulated natural rights doctrine yields the demand for *principled* respect for individual freedom that is at the core of libertarian political convictions. Properly articulated natural rights doctrine underwrites principled respect for *individual* freedom precisely because it begins with the ultimate value of *each individual's* life and well-being.

The general strategy that I employ for the defense of natural rights is to appeal to a broader moral individualism. The root idea of this moral individualism is the separate, ultimate, freestanding value of each individual's life and well-being.[1] Moral individualism has two main facets. The first, *value individualism*, deals with what goal individuals have reason to pursue in their lives. According to value individualism, each has reason to attain his or her personal well-being; that is what each person ultimately has reason to promote.

The second facet, *rights individualism*, deals with what rights individuals must comply with in the course of their pursuit of their goals. According to rights individualism, each individual has a natural right to pursue her own good in her own chosen way; each individual has an original (baseline) right not to be subordinated to the ends of others. In addition, through various actions and interactions with others, individuals can acquire specific property rights and contractual rights. All these rights must be respected by other individuals in the course of their pursuit of their own ends.

So, the basic view of moral individualism is that each individual has a distinct ultimate goal or end of her own—the attainment of personal well-being. However, each person is *morally constrained* in the means that may be used in the pursuit of those ends. An individual may well have reason to seek wealth but is morally precluded from doing so by enslaving others. An individual may well

---

[1] This root idea is at work in different ways in Locke and Nozick. Also see Loren Lomasky, *Persons, Rights, and the Moral Community* (Oxford, UK: Oxford University Press, 1987); and Douglas Rasmussen and Douglas Den Uyl, *Norms of Liberty* (University Park: Pennsylvania State University Press, 2005).

have reason to pursue aesthetic creativity but is morally precluded from doing so by lopping off others' ears to create a wall decoration. These moral side-constraints on *how* individuals may pursue their ends correspond to people's natural and acquired rights. Such rights—rights, for example, not to be enslaved, not to have one's ears lopped off, not to have one's justly acquired property expropriated—provide each individual with a morally protected domain within which she may pursue her ends as she chooses (as long as she abides by the constraints established by others' rights). This chapter focuses on people's natural (i.e., original) rights and not on acquired property or contractual rights. Its key thesis is that individuals have natural rights to pursue their own ends in their own chosen ways precisely because each individual has, in her own well-being, a goal worthy of her own pursuit.

The next section sets the stage for the rest of this essay by describing one particular bit of evil-doing and what we naturally think about it. The following three sections articulate value individualism and the way it undermines common conceptions of social justice. The next section provides the transition from value individualism to rights individualism and is followed by an explanation of the "deontic" character of rights individualism. The penultimate section deals briefly with some otherwise unaddressed issues. The final section sums up and concludes.

One Horrible Example

In Cleveland between 2002 and 2004, Ariel Castro kidnapped three young women. Until the escape of one in May 2013 led to the rescue of the other two, Castro held them in captivity, beat and raped them repeatedly, threatened to kill them, and—in one woman's case—used violence and starvation to induce miscarriages.[2] If we know anything at all about right and wrong, we know that Castro's actions were deeply wrong. This is not a judgment about the *illegality* of Castro's actions. It is a judgment about the *moral* criminality of Castro's conduct. It is because we think this sort of conduct is *morally* criminal—antecedent to and independent of its *legal* criminalization—that we favor its *legal* criminalization and would find it scandalous for such conduct not to be legally forbidden.

Consider some further things we know about Ariel Castro's conduct. We know the wrongfulness of his action was fundamentally a matter of the wrong he did *to* those young women themselves. Certainly, their relatives and friends were severely, albeit indirectly, harmed. Nevertheless, the core victims were the three young women. Legal proceedings were properly brought against Castro for the violations he inflicted upon those three particular human beings, not the indirect harm done to their friends and families.

Insofar as it makes sense to talk about overall social utility or overall balance of happiness over unhappiness across society, we can confidently say that Castro's actions lowered overall social

---

[2] See "Ariel Castro Kidnappings," *Wikipedia*, https://en.wikipedia.org/wiki/Ariel _Castro_kidnappings. Also see John Glatt, *The Lost Girls: The True Story of the Cleveland Abductions and the Incredible Rescue of Michelle Knight, Amanda Berry, and Gina DeJesus* (New York: St. Martin's Press, 2015); and the Lifetime television movie, *Cleveland Abductions*, 2015.

utility or worsened the overall balance of happiness or well-being. However, Castro's moral criminality *did not consist in* his lowering overall net social utility or in his worsening the overall balance of happiness over unhappiness. First, if his criminality consisted in his lowering overall social utility or in his bringing about a less favorable overall balance of happiness over unhappiness in society, his victim would have been *society at large*. But his victims were those specific young women, not some conjured-up social abstraction. The criminality of Castro's conduct resided *within* his treatment of those women. Second, Castro's treatment of those women would remain morally criminal even if—assuming again that it makes sense to speak in this way—his treatment of them actually raised overall social utility or the overall balance of happiness over unhappiness.

Suppose that Castro would have been profoundly miserable had he not kidnapped and beaten and raped his victims and that kidnapping and beating and raping them provided him with enormous enjoyment. Suppose that the total gain for Castro was greater—if it makes sense to speak in this way—than the total suffering he imposed. Or if you doubt that anyone could have been such an efficient converter of others' misery into his own enjoyment, suppose that Castro shared actual or virtual access to those women with 20 or so of his closest friends and the total gain for himself and his friends exceeded the total loss for the women. The truth of that supposition would not *in the least* overturn our judgment that Castro's conduct was profoundly wrongful. Our moral condemnation of Castro is based on the nature of his *acts*. That is why this condemnation is not hostage to further information about the gains for Castro or for his friends that his conduct might have engendered.

Nor does the wrongfulness of Castro's behavior depend on its sordid purpose. Suppose Castro's real purpose was to bring vivid attention to the failure of police departments to search conscientiously for missing young women. Suppose that he was actually himself repelled by what he had to do to wake up the nation to the need for more rapid and persistent searches for mysteriously missing young women. Despite this repulsion, he carried on— even arranging for the escape of the women and his subsequent attention-getting trial (and never revealing his true and noble purpose). This secret purpose would not at all mitigate the moral transgressions he committed, even if he succeeded in lowering the long-term incidence of the sort of conduct in which he engaged.[3]

Nor was Castro's conduct wrongful because it ran contrary to his having agreed to eschew such conduct. Castro's behavior was profoundly wrong, even though he never entered into any such agreement. In short, the wrongfulness of Castro's conduct did not depend on that conduct's being condemned by any political authority or on that conduct's diminishing overall utility or happiness in society or on its contravening some agreement or contract into which Castro had entered.

A good deal of what is meant by saying that Castro's three victims had *natural rights* against Castro's kidnapping, raping, and

---

[3] Our perception of him would change from his being a low-minded monster to his being a high-minded monster.

beating them is simply that they had moral claims against such treatment that were antecedent to and independent of any declaration by political authorities, any social inexpediency of that treatment, and any agreement to eschew that treatment. The general assertion of natural rights is the ascription to all individuals of such antecedent and independent moral claims against being subjected to certain forms of treatment (e.g., being killed, enslaved, abused, or maimed).

What is it about the nature of his conduct toward those women that makes Castro's behavior so obviously wrongful? We can, of course, provide a list of the natural moral rights of the women that Castro violated—rights to liberty, rights to bodily integrity, and so on. But here we are looking for something deeper that will help explain our ascription of those rights to those women and to all persons. Here are some plausible, overlapping answers to our question. Castro subordinated those women to his will; he made them into instruments for his purposes in ways that radically interfered with their living in accordance with their own purposes. He treated them as beings existing merely as means to his ends, rather than as beings who are, morally speaking, ends in themselves.

Value Individualism as a Necessary Condition for Rights Individualism

It seems that individuals will have robust moral rights against one another if and only if impressive value attaches to individuals and their ends. It would be strange for morality to include robust protective rights for individuals and their pursuits if individuals *as individuals* do not have great importance. Loren Lomasky correctly ties protective individual rights to the distinct and separate value of each individual:

> [L]iberalism has traditionally recognized an irreducible plurality of incommensurable values . . . . Liberalism accords to each individual a unique and irreplaceable value, and because individuals are many, so too are [ultimate] values. Rights are consonant with individualism because rights provide the most morally stringent protection of the worth that each individual exemplifies.[4]

If persons possess robust protective rights, they must somehow be underwritten by the *separate, ultimate* value of each person as a pursuer of ends. Or to put things slightly differently, those rights must somehow be underwritten by each individual having in own well-being an end of separate, ultimate value. Any adequate defense of natural rights that promises robustly libertarian conclusions must begin with value individualism.

To explain what is involved in each person's having in her own well-being an end of separate and ultimate value, we need to use a somewhat difficult philosophical distinction between *agent-relative value* and *agent-neutral value.*[5] I start here by explicating agent-relative value, but the contrast may not be fully clear until I also explicate agent-neutral value. Consider the value of

---

[4] Lomasky, *Persons, Rights, and the Moral Community*, p. 52.

[5] See Eric Mack, "Moral Individualism: Agent-Relativity and Deontic Restraints," *Social Philosophy and Policy* 7 (1989): 81–111.

Jennifer's personal well-being. On the agent-relativist view, just as the realization of Jen's well-being will be a realization of well-being *for Jen*, and just as the benefit of that realization will be a benefit *for Jen*, so too will the value of that realization of personal well-being be *value for* Jen. Neither the realization, nor the benefit, nor the value is free-floating. They each exist *in relation to* Jen. The value of this realization of personal well-being is not free-floating value but, rather, *value-for-Jen*.

Another individual, for example, Benjamin, can readily recognize that the realization of Jen's well-being is beneficial for Jen without thinking that any abstract beneficialness is associated with this realization and without thinking that *he* has reason to promote said abstract beneficialness. Similarly, Ben can readily recognize that the realization of Jen's well-being is *valuable for* Jen without thinking that there is a type of depersonalized valuableness associated with this realization and without thinking that *he* has reason to promote this depersonalized valuableness.

Of course, on the agent-relativist understanding, the realization of Ben's well-being is beneficial *for Ben* and has *value for Ben*. Just as Jen and Ben can recognize that the value-for-Jen of her personal well-being provides Jen with reason to pursue *this* end— and yet may provide Ben with no such reason, Jen and Ben can likewise recognize that the value-for-Ben of his personal well-being provides Ben with reason to pursue *that* end—and yet may provide Jen with no such reason.[6]

---

[6] Each will have reason to promote the well-being of the other to the extent that the well-being of the other is a component of his or her own well-being.

So on the agent-relativist view of the value of well-being, this value is deeply individuated. There is the value-for-Jen of Jen's well-being, the value-for-Ben of Ben's well-being, and so on for each person. There is no value of depersonalized well-being as such. When Jen's well-being is realized, things are better *along the value-for-Jen dimension*. Similarly, when Ben's well-being is realized, things are better *along the value-for-Ben dimension*. Prospective value-for-Jen provides Jen with reason—*agent-relative reason*—to promote what will realize that value, while prospective *value-for-Ben* provides Ben with agent-relative reason to promote what will realize that value. However, the fact that *Jen* has agent-relative reason to promote that which has value-for-Jen does not at all imply that *Ben* has reason to promote that valuable-for-Jen state of affairs.[7]

In contrast, on the view that each individual's well-being has agent-neutral value, depersonalized human well-being as such has value. Each instance of human well-being has value *full stop*. The value of any given individual's well-being is not essentially tied to that individual as *value-for-that-individual*. Rather, each individual is a location at which the agent-neutral (i.e., depersonalized) value of human well-being can be engendered. Individuals provide the warehouses in which this agent-neutral good thing, human well-being, can be accumulated and stored. And the *agent-neutral value* of any given prospective bit of well-being provides everyone equally with *agent-neutral reason* to promote

---

[7] Jen's well-being may *also* be a constituent of Ben's well-being. In that case, things are *also* better along the *value-for-Ben dimension* when Jen's well-being is realized.

that instance of well-being, that is, to add to the world's inventory of the value of well-being.

On the agent-neutralist view, each agent will have reason to do his particular part in the program of action that on net maximizes human well-being even when doing so involves sacrificing his own well-being or the well-being of some other individuals. Although it may be psychologically natural for each agent to hope to be a location at which well-being is realized rather than eliminated, each agent will have no more *reason* to favor his being a location for well-being over anyone else's being the recipient of that agent-neutral valuable state.

The agent-neutral understanding of the value of human well-being cannot accommodate the root idea that each individual has in her own well-being an end of separate ultimate value. For, on the agent-neutral construal, an individual's own well-being has no distinct standing as a rational end; each individual's prospective well-being is merely a possible instantiation of generic human well-being. There is no pluralism of final ends, and there is nothing morally irreplaceable about any individual or her well-being. Rather, there is a single measure—human well-being as such—applied to all rational discussions about which outcomes to pursue.

The only ultimate end is the single centralized end of attaining the socially optimal tradeoffs of some people's well-being for others' well-being. In the final analysis, given the agent-neutralist understanding, each individual has reason to sacrifice well-being that would be located within her life whenever that sacrifice would yield more extensive well-being located elsewhere. The only way a true pluralism of ultimate values can exist, the only way in which the separate importance of each individual and her well-being can obtain, is if the value of well-being is agent-relative, not agent-neutral.

Recall the thought experiment about a socially conscientious Ariel Castro who correctly judges that his seizing control over and physically and sexually abusing young women (combined with his eventual trial and conviction) will on balance markedly decrease the number of young women subjected to such treatment. On the agent-neutral construal, if those women recognize the effectiveness of Castro's scheme, reason requires that they *volunteer* to participate. Moreover, if they decline Castro's invitation to join in his scheme to maximize agent-neutral value (or minimize agent-neutral disvalue), it seems that reason requires that he proceed as the actual Castro did, that is, to force their participation.

Morally speaking, on the agent-neutral construal of the value of human well-being, everyone (including those women) is a means toward the end of fostering human well-being at large. If, morally speaking, individuals are means to a comprehensive shared end beyond their own lives and well-being, it is difficult to see how they could possess moral rights that protect them against being forced to serve that end.

Further Considerations on Behalf of Value Individualism

All versions of value individualism maintain that each individual has ultimate reason to advance a realization of genuine well-being. Different versions of value individualism reflect different conceptions of individual well-being. But the core common feature of every version is an individualization of—and, hence, a radical pluralism of—ultimate rational ends. According to the value individualist, if I seek to convince someone to adopt a particular goal, I need to show her that *her* life will be enhanced by her achieving that goal. I may merely have to persuade her that the proposed goal fits into or complements her current understanding of her well-being. Or, instead, I may have to persuade her to modify her view about what sort of outcomes will contribute to her flourishing. For instance, I may have to persuade her that cultivating relations of friendship and mutual appreciation will contribute greatly to her living well.

Value individualism starts, therefore, with the most basic and noncontroversial claim about practical rationality—that it is rational for each agent to pursue what is genuinely, personally advantageous. Reasons are considerations on behalf of acting or forbearing in certain ways. That an action or forbearance will promote an agent's well-being seems to be an obvious—indeed, *the most obvious*—candidate for a reason *for that agent*. It is nonproblematic—not at all mysterious—that what is *beneficial* to an individual is valuable for that individual, and its benefiting that individual supplies her reason to attain the beneficial condition. So if Jen's happiness is beneficial to her, she clearly has reason to promote her happiness. However, if Jen's happiness is not (also) beneficial to Ben, it is at least very difficult to see why he should have reason to promote it. Indeed, it can seem quite mysterious how the bare fact that a certain state of affairs is beneficial for Jen provides a reason for Ben to strive to bring it about.[8]

---

[8] It does not help to say that some state's being prudentially good for Jen does not explain why Ben would strive to bring it about, whereas that state's being morally good does.

One piece of indirect testimony that value individualism is the most basic and noncontroversial claim about practical rationality is that moral theorists who want to reject this contention often feel the need to start with it and then somehow transcend it. For example, many utilitarian theorists start with the rationality of individual utility or welfare promotion and attempt to move from that to the rationality of promoting aggregate utility or welfare. Most notoriously, John Stuart Mill moves with great rapidity from each person's happiness being the good for her to the aggregate happiness being the good for everyone: "[E]ach person's happiness is a good to that person, and the general happiness, therefore, a good to the aggregate of all persons."[9] Mill's quick inference seems to involve a jump from the modest claim that each person's happiness has value for him or her (i.e., has agent-relative value) to each person's happiness having agent-neutral value and, hence, everyone's happiness beckoning everyone to promote it.

In *A Theory of Justice*, John Rawls's starting point is the basic rational choice proposition that "[a] person quite properly acts, at least when others are not affected, to achieve his own greatest good, to advance his rational ends as far as possible."[10] Rawls rejects the utilitarian view that, when others are affected, each person should be as concerned about gains and losses to others as he is about his own gains and losses. However, Rawls does

---

[9] John Stuart Mill, *Utilitarianism* (Indianapolis, IN: Bobbs-Merrill, 1957 [1861]), p. xx.

[10] John Rawls, *A Theory of Justice* (Cambridge, MA: Harvard University Press, 1971), p. 23. This rational choice proposition is the starting point for most other versions of contractarianism.

hold that, when others are affected, rational agents seeking their own good will subject themselves to very demanding principles of justice.[11] The latter sections of this essay indicate how, within moral individualism, individuals are subject to constraints far less demanding than those proposed by Rawls on how they may treat others in the course of their pursuit of personal value.

Like Rawls, Robert Nozick considers whether one can transition readily from the basic and noncontroversial claim that it is rational for individuals to maximize benefits over losses *within* their own separate lives to the utilitarian claim that it is rational for individuals to maximize benefits over losses *across* persons:

> Individually, we each sometimes choose to undergo some pain or sacrifice for a greater benefit or avoid a greater harm . . . . In each case, some cost is borne for the sake of a greater overall good. Why not, similarly, hold that some persons have to bear some costs that benefit other persons more, for the sake of the overall social good?[12]

Why aren't tradeoffs across persons for the sake of net gains akin to individuals rationally advancing the net good within their own individual lives? Nozick's response is this:

> But there is no *social entity* with a good that undergoes some sacrifice for its own good. There are only individual

---

[11] For a devastating critique of Rawls's nonutilitarian case for those demanding principles, see Robert Nozick, *Anarchy, State, and Utopia* (New York: Basic Books, 1974), chap. 7.

[12] Ibid., p. 32.

people, different individual people, with their own individual lives. Using one of these people for the benefit of others, uses him and benefits the others. Nothing more. What happens is that something is done to him for the sake of others. Talk of an overall social good covers this up.[13]

Here, Nozick seems to make things too easy for himself by holding that the utilitarian stance depends on a mistaken belief in a social entity with a life and well-being of its own. A more generous reading sees Nozick's denial of such a social entity as a dramatic way of denying the existence of a single dimension along which the value of the gains and the disvalue of the losses of all persons register. It is his way of denying the existence of a master axiological ledger in which all gains and losses for all persons are added and subtracted to yield a master moral assessment. Rather, for each individual I, there is a separate ledger—labeled "value- and disvalue-for-I"—in which costs and benefits for that individual are registered: gains and losses can be combined within ledgers but not across them. This method of accounting affirms the separateness of persons.

Throughout this chapter, I seek to be neutral between different conceptions of human well-being, and hence neutral between different versions of value individualism. Nevertheless, one substantive truth about human well-being needs to be emphasized to guard value individualism against what would otherwise be an obvious attack. That substantive truth is that, at least for almost

---

[13] Ibid., pp. 32–33.

all people, an important and deep component of individual well-being is standing in relationships of mutual perception, appreciation, responsiveness, and concern with some other people. For almost all people, connectedness with other people, empathy, benevolence, generosity, friendliness, mutual respect, and the like contribute to living well. At least in almost all cases, the pursuit of individual well-being importantly includes the pursuit of these forms of sociality. It is (almost always) good for one to be the sort of person who, of course, will jump into the pool to save the proverbial drowning child.

Value Individualism Undermines Social Rankings and Social Tradeoffs

Suppose Ben proposes to engage in some treatment of Jen that will diminish Jen's well-being by five units yet will result in an enhancement of Ben's well-being by seven units. Ben seeks to provide a value-promoting justification of his action by saying that, according to his favorite formula for such matters, the outcome will be *socially better* than the status quo. Ben's proposed treatment of Jen will yield a more highly ranked social outcome. Jen does not challenge Ben's factual assertions about how many units of well-being will be lost or gained. However, as an insightful value individualist, she rejects Ben's value-promoting justification by insisting that the outcome of Ben's proposed action will simply be a gain for Ben and a loss for Jen. "Nothing more," Jen insists, because there is no common scale of value on which the seven units of gain for Ben outweigh the five units of loss for Jen. She even profitably quotes Nozick's remark that "no moral balancing act can take place among us; there is no outweighing of one of our lives by others so as to lead to a greater overall social good."[14]

One of the ways in which value individualism lends support to rights individualism is that it *clears the way* for rights individualism by undermining all consequentialist proposals—not just utilitarian ones—to assess actions, policies, or institutions on the basis of whether they yield or fail to yield the most highly ranked of the available social outcomes. Suppose that three overall social outcomes—I, II, and III—are available, each one resulting from one of three actions (or policies, or institutional structures), and each outcome involves payoffs (in units of well-being) for three individuals—*A, B,* and *C.* We get the following matrix:

	A	*B*	*C*
Outcome I	42	23	7
Outcome II	9	25	9
Outcome III	8	10	10

Which social outcome is best? Advocates of different formulas for ranking overall social outcomes provide different answers. According to the advocate of well-being maximization, outcome I is best. According to the advocate of maximizing the minimum well-being payoff,[15] outcome II is best. According to the advocate of equal well-being, outcome III is best.

---

[14] Ibid., p. 33.

[15] This is Rawls's "difference principle" applied to well-being rather than income.

However, according to the value individualist, the question about which overall outcome is best has no valid answer. According to the individualist, all that can be validly said is that outcome I is *best-for-A*, outcome II is *best-for-B*, and outcome III is *best-for-C*. (When the value individualist hears the claim that some overall outcome is best, he immediately asks, "Best for whom?") No "best overall" judgment is available because the gains to one or two individuals from the realization of any given outcome cannot be weighed against the losses to one or two individuals from the nonrealization of some other available outcome. This is because gains and losses for *A* take place along the *value-for-A* dimension, while gains and losses for *B* take place along the *value-for-B* dimension, and gains and losses for *C* take place along the *value-for-C* dimension. Since these are distinct dimensions of value—since *value-for-A*, *value-for-B*, and *value-for-C* are *sui generis*—the gains and losses for any one of those individuals are incommensurable with the gains and losses of the other individuals. There is no common currency (e.g., agent-neutral value) for these gains and losses; there is no exchange rate between these distinct currencies.

From Value Individualism to Rights Individualism

We have been focusing on a negative function of value individualism, namely, its use to rebut value-promoting justifications for imposing sacrifices on individuals for the sake of some supposed optimality of social outcome. Nevertheless, it is crucial to see that such rebuttals of these diverse value-promoting justifications do not *in themselves* do anything to establish that the proposed conduct is *wrongful* or *in violation of the rights of* those targeted by that conduct. It is one thing to debunk a proposed justification for a course of conduct; it is another thing to show that the conduct in question is wrongful or in violation of rights. Something further needs to be said to ground the judgment that the imposer of sacrifices wrongs or violates the rights of the persons on whom the sacrifices are imposed.

To get a sense of what that something further might be, let's consider how Nozick's argument moves beyond the debunking of imposing losses on some for the sake of social optimization. Recall that in the debunking phase (discussed earlier), Nozick maintains:

> There are only individual people, different individual people, with their own individual lives. Using one of these people for the benefit of others, uses him and benefits others. Nothing more. . . . Talk of an overall social good covers this up. . . . [The person who is used] does not get some overbalancing good from his sacrifice, and no one is entitled to force this upon him.[16]

The fact of our "separate existences" implies that "no moral balancing act can take place among us; there is no moral outweighing of one of our lives by others so as to lead to a greater overall *social* good."[17]

[16] Nozick, *Anarchy*, p. 33.
[17] Ibid., p. 33 [emphasis in original].

However, Nozick moves on with an implicit distinction between what strictly *follows* from the fact of the separateness of persons—that there can be no moral balancing—and what is *reflective* of this fact. Moral side constraints are *reflective* of the separateness of persons and of the groundlessness of moral balancing. This separateness *underlies* those side constraints. As Nozick puts it (with my underlining added):

> The moral side constraints upon what we may do, I claim, reflect the fact of our separate existences. They reflect the fact that no moral balancing act can take place among us; there is no moral outweighing of one of our lives by others so as to lead to a greater overall *social* good. . . . This root idea, namely, that there are different individuals with separate lives and so no one may be sacrificed for others underlies the existence of side constraints.[18]

In sum, the separateness of persons and the impossibility of moral balancing underlie and are reflected in the existence of moral side-constraints. Intuitively, the thought is that the very fact of the separate value of each person's life and well-being that undermines moral balancing and moral outweighing also underwrites the proposition that imposing losses on a (nonconsenting) individual to provide gains to others wrongs that individual.

Nozick goes a bit beyond the terms "reflects" and "underlies" when he says that to use a person by way of imposing a cost on him in order to provide a benefit to another "does not sufficiently

---

[18] Ibid.

respect and take account of the fact that he is a separate person, that his is the only life he has."[19] If we sufficiently take account of the fact that "he is a separate person, that his is the only life he has"—that is, if we are respectful of (responsive to) that fact—we will be circumspect in our conduct toward that individual. We will treat that individual as a possessor of rights. Nozick thereby advances toward a claim that I will be making, namely, the fact that "he is a separate person, that his is the only life he has" is a *reason* to be constrained in our conduct toward him. More specifically, it is a reason to avoid treating this individual as a means to our own ends.

It is a serious defect in Nozick's own argument that he does not explicitly recognize that it is one thing to debunk justifications for the imposition of sacrifices and another thing to ground the wrongfulness of imposing those sacrifices. Still, I think the ease with which one moves from the debunking phase to the conclusion that the debunked impositions *wrong* the individuals who are imposed upon strongly suggests that Nozick is correct.[20] A sufficient appreciation of the value individualist basis for rebutting consequentialist arguments in favor of impositions also supports the judgment that such impositions are moral transgressions against those who are subjected to them.

---

[19] Ibid.

[20] In his separateness-of-persons critique of utilitarianism, Rawls also moves immediately from debunking the utilitarian justification for imposing sacrifices on individuals to the conclusion that it is unjust to impose a sacrifice on *A* for the sake of bestowing a greater gain on *B*. The conflation of persons "subjects the rights secured by justice to the calculus of social interests." Rawls, *Theory of Justice*, p. 30.

So I turn now to my own reasoning on behalf of the proposition that one's having in one's well-being an ultimate end of one's own provides all others with *reason* to be circumspect in their conduct toward one. This is the proposition: the separateness of persons and the impossibility of moral balancing provide reasons for moral side-constraints. Ben's being under certain moral side-constraints in his conduct toward Jen—and Jen's having correlative natural rights against Ben that he abide by the same constraints—*is* simply a matter of Ben's having such reason to be circumspect in his treatment of Jen. The idea of Jen's possessing such natural rights against Ben is no more mysterious than the idea of Ben's having such reasons to be constrained in his conduct toward Jen.

Standard discussions of the bases for ascribing natural moral rights to persons cite such features as self-consciousness, purposiveness, capacity to form and commit to long-term projects, and the capacity to live meaningful or self-determining lives.[21] I believe that features like these are paradigmatic necessary conditions for the reasonable ascription of rights to persons precisely because those conditions are themselves necessary for the morally seminal fact about persons, namely, that they each have in the attainment of their personal well-being—in the flourishing of their lives—an ultimate end of their own. Why believe, though, that this fact provides all other individuals with reason to constrain their treatment of everyone else?

Suppose Ben agrees that Jen has an ultimate end of her own in the realization of her well-being. This fact has obvious directive

[21] Nozick, *Anarchy*, pp. 48–51.

import *for Jen*. It tells her what final goal it is rational for her to promote—what guiding outcome she has reason to seek. But does this fact about Jen have *any* directive import for Ben? There seem to be three possible basic answers. The "no directive import" answer is that this fact about Jen *as such* provides Ben with no reason to engage in or eschew any conduct toward Jen. The "addition" answer is that the directive import of this fact about Jen is that her well-being is to be added to Ben's well-being to form a more comprehensive end that Ben is to promote. The "constraint" answer is that the directive import of this fact about Jen is that Ben is not to preclude Jen from pursuing her own well-being (in her own chosen way).

Here is the case against the "no directive import" answer. The value individualist affirms the reality of a multiplicity of individuals, each of whom has rational ends of her own. Ben is not the only independent source or center of value. He is not the only being who has purposes of his own to fulfill. Normative solipsism is false, and Ben knows it to be false. So when Ben looks out on the world, he sees entities of two strikingly different sorts. He sees objects that have no ends or purposes of their own and that he naturally assumes are morally available for his (or others') use, and he sees entities who, like himself, properly devote themselves to their separate and distinct ends. It would be incredible for this striking difference between those entities not to provide Ben with reason to treat entities of the two sorts differently.

Consider some examples. As Ben is walking along, he notices a stick lying in his path. Not breaking his normal stride, he steps on the stick and breaks it. As Ben continues to walk along, he notices a person's neck lying in his path. Breaking his normal stride, he steps over the neck and avoids breaking it. An observer asks Ben why he behaved differently in the second case. Ben answers that in the second case, his breaking of the neck would have amounted to destroying the life of a being with rational ends of her own, with a good of her own that she properly pursues. Ben's response does provide a reason—a consideration on behalf of—his discrimination between the stick and the neck. If Ben had not discriminated between the stick and the neck, we would think that he had not appropriately processed—had not sufficiently taken into account—the difference between a mere object and an entity with ultimate ends of its own. If Ben honestly professes not to see how anything about the person whose neck is on the path provides him with reason not to step on it, we will take him to have the cognitive processing defect characteristic of psychopaths.

Suppose nonpsychopathic Ben enters what he believes to be a *Westworld* sort of amusement park. Such a park is populated by brilliantly programmed automatons who appear to be dangerous human beings who seek in clever ways to maim and kill visitors. Ben seeks the enjoyment of simulated life-or-death contests with the inhabitants—who, when bested, "bleed" and "expire" convincingly. After his 48-hour adventure, which included "killing" or "maiming" a good number of the inhabitants he encountered, Ben exits the arena. He is met by a rescue squad who inform Ben that they are about to enter the area to free the inhabitants who really are innocent human beings who have been kidnapped and deposited in Westworld by agents of the Federal Department of

Entertainment (headed up by Ariel Castro). At this point, Ben recalls that a number of those who he destroyed yelled out something about having been kidnapped and about how they would not hurt him if he would not hurt them. Unfortunately, he construed those pronouncements as just part of the clever automaton programming. Ben now is aghast at what he has done, and he has good reason to be.

The circumstances of Ben's homicidal actions—especially the degree to which he was assured he would be encountering automatons—might substantially excuse Ben. But notice that we all—and, very likely, especially Ben—will believe that in such circumstances Ben will desperately *need* excuses. For, what he has done has wronged those he has killed or maimed. They were wronged precisely because they were in reality persons with lives of their own to lead. When he testifies in the hearing to determine whether he will be excused, Ben says: "If I had known they were people like me—beings with lives of their own, not objects available for my amusement—I would have known not to attack them. I would have known that to attack them would not sufficiently respect and take account of the fact that each of them was 'a separate person' and that 'his is the only life he has.'"[22] I conclude that the "no directive import" answer is mistaken.

That leaves us with the "addition" and the "constraint" answers. Recall that according to the former, the directive import of the fact that Jen has in her well-being an end of ultimate value is that her well-being is to be combined with Ben's well-being to form a

[22] Ibid., p. 33.

more comprehensive end that Ben is to promote. The friend of the addition answer is not merely saying—as the value individualist might—that when particular individuals with ends of their own encounter one another, they will sometimes incorporate aspects of one another's well-being into their own and, hence, acquire reason to care about one another's well-being. Rather, according to the additionist, the bare fact that Jen's well-being has value requires that Jen's well-being be joined to Ben's to constitute a more comprehensive end that Ben has reason to promote. The bare fact of the value of Jen's well-being (along with the value of everyone else's well-being) calls upon Ben to serve Jen's well-being (and everyone else's) under some formula for ranking over-all social outcomes. On the addition view, the import of the bare fact of the value of each person's well-being is that it is rational for each to serve everyone's purposes (in accordance with the favored formula for ranking overall social outcomes).

But that, in effect, is a denial that each person has reason-generating purposes *of her own*. Indeed, the addition answer must be mistaken, because the value of each person's well-being is essentially value-for-that-person. The directive import of the morally seminal fact that Jen has in the realization of her well-being an end of ultimate value cannot be that Ben (and everyone else) has reason to promote that realization. Hence, the directive import of that fact must be that Ben (and everyone else) has reason to be constrained in his conduct toward Jen. That is, that fact about Jen provides Ben (and all others) with reason not to interfere with her pursuit of her good by her own chosen means. (Those means are themselves constrained by the like restriction on Jen that she not interfere with others' pursuit of their ends.)[23] We *respect* or *honor* others as agents with separate ultimate ends and purposes of their own not by promoting their ends as we do our own but, rather, by not sacrificing them to our ends and, more generally, by not interfering with their chosen pursuit of their own ends and purposes.

Rights individualism is the affirmation of such rights on the ground that the appropriate response to the separate moral importance of others as beings with ultimate ends of their own is noninterference with others in their (similarly noninterfering) pursuit of their own ends in their own chosen ways. To exploit the prestige of Kantian terminology, it is because each person is an end-in-herself in the sense that is central to value individualism that each person is an end-in-herself in the sense that is central to rights individualism.

Moral Rights as Deontic Claims

I will say a bit more about the substance of the moral constraint that one has reason to abide by in one's interactions with other persons shortly. But first we need to highlight the contrast between goals one has reason to advance and constraints (or principles or rules) one has reason to abide by. The requirement on Ben that he not interfere with Jen's (similarly restrained) pursuit of her own personal ends is a moral side-constraint on Ben rather than a mandated goal. For the requirement does not at all tell Ben what outcome he must promote (or hinder). It simply restricts the means by which Ben may pursue his chosen ends. Even though it will almost certainly be valuable-for-Jen that Ben abide by this

---

[23] For a more technical argument from value to rights individualism, see my "Prerogatives, Restrictions, and Rights," *Social Philosophy and Policy* 22 (Winter 2005): 357–93.

side-constraint, that prospective value is not the basis for the constraint. Similarly, even though it will likely be valuable-for-Ben to abide by the constraint, that prospective value is not the basis for the constraint. Rather than being ruled out because of their disvalue for the subject, the agent, or society at large, certain ways of transacting with Jen are ruled out because of their very nature—as acts that interfere with Jen's pursuit of her own ends.

Since moral side-constraints (and the rights correlative to them) do not depend on the disvalue (to the subject, the agent, or to society at large) that arises from their violation, the side-constraints (and the rights correlative to them) remain in place even if their violation would have value (for the subject, the agent, or society at large). That is why the rights can stand as fundamental principles for ordering human relations among diverse individuals who may well not endorse each other's chosen ends or conceptions of well-being. In the standard philosophical language, moral side-constraints and the rights correlative to them are *deontic*, rather than *consequentialist*, moral claims.

Consequentialist theorists are wed to the idea that all rightness and wrongness in actions must be a matter of the good or bad consequences of those actions—however goodness or badness of consequences is measured. They reject the idea that some sorts of actions can be wrong in virtue of their character rather than in virtue of their results. It is a major problem for this stance that we constantly reasonably condemn actions on the basis of their character rather than on the basis of an investigation of their consequences. We condemn Ben's enslaving Jen without any inquiry into whether or not that enslavement (like most enslavements) has on net bad consequences. Discovering that within some particular slavery system, the ratio of happy slave owners to unhappy slaves is much higher than we thought does not lead us to revisit our condemnation of that system of slavery. We condemn Ben's securing the conviction and punishment of Jen, who he knows is innocent of the crime, whether or not that conviction and punishment on net has bad consequences. Consequentialist theorists desperately try to show that all false convictions and punishments will on net have bad consequences and, hence, can be condemned by them. But as consequentialists, why not go with the consequentialist flow and happily embrace socially expedient false convictions and punishments? The answer is that consequentialists themselves implicitly recognize the wrongful, rights-violating character of false convictions and punishments.

The consequentialist view that actions can be assessed as right or wrong only on the basis of their consequences depends on the antecedent view that all action is performed for the sake of its (anticipated) consequences. If that were correct, the only way to assess an action would be to determine whether it effectively promotes desirable consequences. However, it is false that people act only for the sake of consequences. Every minute of the day, people perform or eschew actions on the basis of their perceived character. This is what it means to be a rule follower. As F. A. Hayek points out, "Man is as much a rule-following animal as a purpose-seeking one."[24] This is why moral inquiry has two

---

[24] F. A. Hayek, *Law, Legislation, and Liberty*, vol.1 (Chicago: Chicago University Press, 1973), p. 11.

discrete dimensions: the search for goals that we are rational to promote and the search for rules (and rights) that we have reason to comply with in the course of our goal seeking.

Further Steps in Natural Rights Theorizing

The natural right against interference with one's pursuit of one's own ends in one's chosen ways is highly abstract; it needs to be more finely articulated for it to provide more determinate guidance. A natural way to proceed is to identify different fundamental ways in which individuals can be interfered with and ascribe to all persons a natural right against each of these modes of interference. Probably the most central and important way in which individuals can be precluded from devoting themselves to their own ends is to deprive individuals of discretionary control over their own persons, that is, over the exercise of their own mental and physical faculties. Moral protection against this mode of interference has traditionally been articulated as the natural right of self-ownership.

However, interferences with persons' pursuit of their own goals are not exhausted by violations of the right of self-ownership. Because persons need to use extrapersonal material and exercise ongoing discretionary control over such material in order to effectively advance their ends, persons can be impermissibly interfered with by barring them from using material (that is not already being used by others) and from acquiring and exercising discretionary control over extrapersonal resources. Moral protection against this mode of interference takes the form of a natural right of property—a right to use and acquire ownership rights over extrapersonal portions of the world.

Persons can also be precluded from advancing their own projects by way of deception. Moral protection against this mode of interference takes the form of a natural right to have agreements that others have entered into with one fulfilled. Of course, the precise way in which these basic rights will be codified in different places and at different times will depend on customary understandings and social conventions. So, for example, the exact conditions under which one is guilty of a trespass or violation of a contract will vary from one place and time to another.

Individuals operate within a moral structure in which their advancement of their own goals is constrained by a medley of rights possessed by others—relatively finely codified forms of others' natural rights and acquired property rights and contractual rights. The deontic insistence that each individual has reason to respect the rights of others *independent of whether particular instances of respect are beneficial to that individual* may suggest that the individual would be better off if morality did not cramp and burden him with a requirement that he respect others' rights. Yet for each individual, this moral structure also includes all the protective instantiations of *her* own natural rights and acquired rights. Moreover, a social order centering on mutual respect for one another's rights has the attractive feature of being an order in which each acknowledges the high moral standing of each other person and receives a like acknowledgment from others.

Furthermore, widespread belief in the moral force of the rules associated with people's rights—for example, do not seize or destroy the property of others, do not welsh on contracts—is crucial to the widespread existence of voluntary cooperative interaction. Jen and Ben will each generally desist from plundering the other and will each generally perform as she and he have contracted only if each is confident that the other will reciprocate. And that confidence will often depend on each party's believing that the other is committed to the relevant rule and, therefore, will desist from calculations about how much she or he could gain by inducing the other party to follow the rule while she or he defects from compliance.

Widespread belief in the moral force of the relevant rules sustains mutually beneficial cooperation by directing people away from the usually self-defeating attempt to benefit from another's compliance while also not bearing the cost of one's own compliance. Thus, rather than cramping individuals and limiting their attainment of personal well-being, these restrictive rules facilitate increasingly elaborate and advantageous forms of voluntary cooperation.

I have not addressed many crucial questions about the implications of the present natural rights approach for libertarian doctrine. Here, I will mention a few that are likely to occur to the reader. The first is the importance of moral rights construed as deontic claims for principled anti-paternalism. Principled anti-paternalism is the view that an individual can be wronged when she is forcibly prohibited from proceeding with some voluntary action *even if* her well-being is promoted by that forcible prohibition. Such successful paternalist intervention—intervention that is actually good for its subject—can be condemned only on the deontic grounds that it fails to honor the subject as an agent with a life of her own to live.

Natural rights theorists from Locke to Nozick have correctly endorsed a "Lockean proviso" according to which property holders may not (singly or jointly) use their holdings in ways that make Jen's economic environment less receptive to her bringing her self-owned powers to bear in the pursuit of her ends than her economic environment would be in the absence of private property. The theoretical basis for such a proviso is that one can be denied the discretionary use of one's own powers both by direct interference with one's person and by deprivation of one's opportunities to deploy those powers. The Lockean proviso makes explicit the requirement that property owners not use their holdings in ways that on net diminish others' opportunities. As an empirical claim, such a proviso will rarely be violated because the free development of private property economies tends strongly to increase economic opportunity for all.

Natural rights theorists from Grotius[25] to Nozick have correctly endorsed a necessity (or catastrophe) clause according to which an individual in dire circumstances that are not of her own making may permissibly escape those circumstances by using the property of another without the owner's consent. The theoretical basis for such a clause is the value individualist grounding for rights individualism. The deontic honoring of each individual as a being with separate ultimate ends of her own—which takes the form of ascribing strong moral rights to all individuals—cannot plausibly impose obligations on such individuals to freeze to death in a

---

[25] Hugo Grotius, *The Rights of War and Peace* (Indianapolis: Liberty Fund, 2005 [1625]), bk. II, chap. II., sec. VI.

freak blizzard rather than to break into an unoccupied wilderness cabin. However, the precise structure of such a necessity clause cannot be addressed here. Finally, I mention the obvious fact that this essay has not at all explored the implications of natural rights theorizing for the legitimacy or illegitimacy of states.[26]

Conclusion

I have defended the natural rights approach to political philosophy by situating the affirmation of basic natural rights within a broader moral individualism. The argument begins with value individualism—the view that individuals each have in the realization of their own well-being an end of ultimate value. This value individualism undermines tradeoffs between gains for some and losses for others. It undermines formulas for achieving social justice that call for the interests of some to be sacrificed for the interests of others. However, the undermining of those tradeoffs and social justice formulas does not as such explain the wrongfulness of imposing sacrifices on some for the sake of others. What explains that is the fact that each individual's possession of

---

[26] I offer my natural-rights take on these topics in "Self-Ownership, Marxism, and Egalitarianism—Part I: Challenges to Historical Entitlement," *Politics, Philosophy, and Economics* 1 (February 2002): 119–46; "Self-Ownership, Marxism, and Egalitarianism—Part II: Challenges to the Self-Ownership Thesis," *Politics, Philosophy, and Economics* 1 (June 2002): 237–76; "The Natural Right of Property," *Social Philosophy and Policy* 27 (Winter 2010): 53–79; "Non-Absolute Rights and Libertarian Taxation," *Social Philosophy and Policy* 23 (Summer 2006): 109–41; and "Nozickan Arguments for the More-than-Minimal State," in *Cambridge Companion to Anarchy, State and Utopia*, ed. Ralf M. Bader and John Meadowcroft (Cambridge, UK: Cambridge University Press, 2011), pp. 89–115.

ultimate personal ends provides all other agents with reason to be circumspect in their conduct toward that agent. More specifically, it provides all other agents with reason not to prevent such individuals from pursuing their own ends in their own chosen ways (except for ways that involve like interference with others).

Hence, all individuals have natural rights not to be interfered with in their (noninterfering) pursuit of personal well-being. More specifically yet, all individuals have natural rights of self-ownership, natural rights to acquire and exercise discretionary control over extrapersonal objects, and natural rights to the fulfillment of agreements made with them. Such rights provide the fundamental moral framework for a society in which free individuals can engage in voluntary cooperative efforts to their mutual advantage.

Kantianism

Jason Kuznicki

Immanuel Kant (1724–1804) is one of the most influential philosophers of all time. His work was both exemplary of the Enlightenment and, in some ways, deeply critical of it. He made important contributions to all major subfields of philosophy, and few philosophical inquiries since his time have been able to side-step the questions he raised. Summarizing the work of such a figure may be difficult, but it must be said first that Kant was above all a champion of free inquiry and of the power of human reason. Although he identified certain well-contained topics about which he believed reason was obliged to remain silent, he did not deny its power in any other cases. On the contrary, he affirmed it.

Kant was moreover an ethical individualist who supported free trade, private property, and an objective standard for right and wrong conduct. He looked forward to a future of ever-improving legal regimes that would more and more respect the autonomy and dignity of every human being, and he urged all nations toward a just peace with one another.

In short, Kant was a classical liberal. Not only that, but even in those places where Kant diverged from what we now would call libertarianism, one might argue that he did so in spite of his deeper philosophical commitments, rather than because of them. With the help of further reflection, we might even say that a somewhat better Kantian would be significantly more libertarian than Kant himself ever was. Importantly, Kant's own system was explicitly open to this kind of development and growth, and it is a mark of his philosophical acumen that he left the door open for those sorts of future improvements.

Let us begin with Kant's ethics. What is it, Kant asked, that enables us to think about ethical questions in the first place? Can anything be found that conceptually underlies all, or nearly all, claims about morality? In other words, is there a *groundwork* on which ethics rests? And if we do find a groundwork, how can we know it is objective and lasting?

Kant considered the contemporary answers to those questions unsatisfying. He demonstrated that most other ethical systems rested on what he termed *hypothetical imperatives.* Hypothetical imperatives are statements of the form "If you want x, you must y." Statements of this type inevitably derive their moral force from the listener already preferring the stated outcome, x.

Hypothetical imperatives may tell us a good deal about the means to attain a particular end, but they can tell us nothing about, for example, why we have ends in the first place. They also won't be useful in all times and places. Some people, faced with different circumstances or possessing different values, will not find *x* a compelling reason to act. How can we ever find common ground, not just with some people, but with all people?

For example, if you want to understand physics, you must study mathematics. But this presupposes that physics is worth understanding. It might be—but if so, why? And for what? Such questions might be answerable, at least for some people, but the sheer fact that we *can* answer them tells us that physics is not an end in itself. We have answered them only by invoking other ends, and so we must continue our search.

Kant carried this objection to remarkably great lengths: for example, if we want to be happy—a common goal in ethics—then there might be found various courses of action that will make us so. But, Kant argued, happiness in all cases consists simply of getting what we want—so we must be more specific. What *is it* that we want? And on what basis do we want it? We ought to name the object that we desire, rather than obfuscating about the emotional state that comes from getting it.[1] That is not merely an abstract objection either, because clearly not everyone is made happy by

---

[1] See Julie Lund Hughes, "The Role of Happiness in Kant's Ethics," *Aporia* 14 (2004): 61–72. As Kant wrote, equating good with pleasure "is opposed even to the usage of language, which distinguishes the pleasant from the good, the unpleasant from the evil, and requires that good and evil shall always be judged by reason, and, therefore, by concepts which can be communicated to everyone, and not by mere sensation, which is limited to individual subjects." Immanuel Kant, "Critique of Practical Reason," in *Kant's Critique of Practical Reason and Other Works on the Theory of Ethics*, 4th rev. ed., trans. Thomas Kingsmill Abbott (London: Longmans, Green and Co., 1889), p. 111, http://files.libertyfund.org/pll/pdf/Kant_0212_EBk_v7.0.pdf. Note also that I have preferred online, public domain translations because of their easy availability.

the same things. Some people are even made happy by the attainment of what appear plainly to be wicked things: the murderer who takes pleasure in killing may be motivated by happiness just as well as the poet who takes pleasure in verse. So what is that thing that we should *all* desire, in *all* circumstances? What is the thing that it's *never* wrong to want?

The answer, Kant said, was a good will. The cultivation of a good will, and the subsuming of all other desires to the development of a good will, was for Kant *the* work of ethics, the end toward which all other ends pointed. Conscious, rational inquiry about the good was *in itself* the highest good we might have, and all acts that tended to encourage or manifest a good will were for this reason to be counted good as well.

Crucially, the good will is premised on our capacity for *autonomy*, a word that Kant used to denote our capacity to set forth ethical rules for ourselves. Ethical agents are all those who seek to supply their own conduct, and their own will, with a reasoned law. Good ethical agents will express and act on the will to impose those laws upon themselves; this project is the one thing that we may, and should, desire as an end in itself. (Kant took yet another step and argued that the human faculty of *reason* existed for the sake of expressing this ethical law, though that step is not relevant for our purposes, and it is highly contested among philosophers down to the present day, who tend to doubt that nature imbues any faculties with built-in purposes.)

In any case, a truly fundamental ethical law would have at least three important attributes: (a) it would be objective in nature, and thus not subject to arbitrary whims or desires; (b) it would be based on reason alone, and thus intelligible to all ethical agents; and, (c) it would be of a type that we could deliberately subject ourselves to it. As Kant wrote in the *Groundwork of the Metaphysics of Morals*, "The basis of obligation must not be sought in the nature of man, or in the circumstances in the world in which he is placed, but *a priori* simply in the conception of pure reason."[2] Reason itself would be the groundwork of ethics.

Kant's ethical theory, then, is neither a *consequentialist* nor a *natural law* account, but it is what philosophers call a *deontological* account. It is not consequentialist, because its laws are not derived from any consideration of what may happen after we attempt to follow them. And it is not a natural law account, or at best it is only very weakly such, because it does not elaborate a theory of human nature on which its morality is necessarily based. Kantian ethics purports to be based on our duty to reason alone. The capacity for reason may be an attribute of mankind, and Kant certainly believed that it was, but reason for Kant is universal and objective and not merely one of mankind's attributes. As such, no claims about human nature are necessary for Kant's ethical groundwork to be established, and no changes of time, place, or circumstance can alter it.

A Kantian might even say that natural law accounts that refer to human nature are by this very fact composed of *hypothetical imperatives*: they all implicitly take the form, "If I am human, then I must . . . ," a form that renders them hypothetical. Whatever follows after

---

[2] Immanuel Kant, "Fundamental Principles of the Metaphysic of Morals," in *Kant's Critique*, p. 29. Note that the title of the *Groundwork* is here translated as "*Fundamental Principles . . . .*"

that statement may be wise practical advice; it may be true for all humans; it may even make the practitioner euphorically happy. But it would not be a *fundamental* moral law. Ethics must consider, but it must not be founded upon, any such hypothetical imperatives.

Indeed, the agents in a Kantian account of ethics need not be biologically human at all. They must simply be capable of reasoning and of apprehending reason, and desire to give themselves a reasoned law to govern their actions. Such a being could be a space alien, a hyperintelligent computer, or a god, and it would make no essential difference. One potentially appealing feature of Kant's ethics, then, is that it is open to the inclusion of new species of moral agents, should any be contacted or created in the future. Natural law accounts, and to a lesser extent consequentialist accounts, are not necessarily so open.[3]

This discussion brings us to a fairly urgent question: What does this foundational moral law look like, anyway? Beginning with the necessity that reason must not contradict itself, Kant arrived at what would come to be known as the first formulation of the *categorical imperative*—called "categorical" because it was to apply to all ethical agents, in all circumstances whatsoever. It ran as follows:

Act as if the maxim of your action were to become by your will a universal law of nature.[4]

---

[3] This appeal to a transhuman form of reason is entertained more or less explicitly in "Fundamental Principles of the Metaphysic of Morals," in *Kant's Critique*, p. 51.

[4] Immanuel Kant, *The Metaphysics of Ethics*, 3rd ed., Henry Calderwood, trans. J. W. Semple (Edinburgh: T. & T. Clark, 1886 [1796]), p.34, http://oll.libertyfund.org /titles/1443#kant_0332_338.

As with all reasoned laws, the moral law must be consistent. As a result, we must be able to will that its maxims should be enacted *for all moral agents*. If I cannot will that a maxim *should* apply to all, then I should reject whatever maxim I am considering.

For example, I cannot reasonably will that all people should steal, for this maxim cannot be universalized consistently. It is not merely that a world full of thieves would be a miserable place, although certainly it would be. Rather, theft presupposes the concept of legitimate property ownership, and I cannot consistently will *both* the existence of legitimate ownership *and* its occasional, ad hoc violation. We are now able to understand, through reason alone and without appeal to consequence, that the moral principle underlying theft involves a willful contradiction. It must therefore be rejected. Many similar principles of conduct are likewise ruled out, as reflective readers will quickly appreciate.

It is important to remember that the first formulation asks us to consider maxims, or principles, and *not* individual actions: if I awaken at 6:00 a.m. and eat a bowl of oatmeal, I should certainly not insist that everyone else in the world do exactly the same. But by the first formulation, I must still consider what maxims, if any, lie behind my actions. I might say that the maxims are things such as "strive to be punctual in your work" or "eat so as not to harm the self." I can readily will, without contradiction, that either of them should be followed by everyone.

Note that I cannot will similarly for those maxims' opposites. It is not simply that bad consequences would follow from being late or gluttonous, although perhaps they would. The real problem is that attempting to fashion a maxim of either lateness or gluttony would entail setting up an inconsistency somewhere in my maxims. How can it be that I *should not* arrive to work at the same time when I *should*? And how could I will to eat in ways that tend to injure the only unquestionably good thing, which is the good will? Neither can be universalized; the first contradicts itself, whereas the second contradicts the cultivation of the good will.

The need for universalization also forbids several things that Kant has often and wrongly been accused of advocating, particularly in libertarian circles.[5] For example, there can be no possible duty of self-sacrifice purely for the good of others. This is so for at least two reasons. First, such a duty cannot be consistently universalized. Formulating a consistent maxim that would command pure altruism for all moral agents is clearly impossible. The simple reason is that someone else must always exist who will stand as the beneficiary. Of the beneficiary, no comparable sacrifice is asked. And second, to act purely for the anticipated good of another, or for that of a collective, would be to act for a merely consequentialist reason, which is forbidden. As Kant himself wrote:

> Benevolent wishes may be unlimited, for they do not imply doing anything. But the case is more difficult with benevolent action . . . since our self-love cannot be separated from the need to be loved by others (to obtain help

---

[5] Ayn Rand famously despised Kant. It may be that her quarrel with Kant arose not from his ethics or politics, but from his metaphysics and epistemology. This analysis, although plausible, would sit badly with the few relatively clear places in which Rand attempted to critique Kant; in them, she makes primarily ethical objections. Metaphysical and epistemological concerns, meanwhile, are beyond the scope of our inquiry.

from them in case of necessity), we therefore make our-selves an end for others; and this maxim can never be obligatory except by having the specific character of a universal law, and consequently by means of a will that we should also make others our ends. . . . [But] that one should sacrifice his own happiness, his true wants, in order to promote that of others, would be a self-contradictory maxim if made a universal law. This duty, therefore, is only indeterminate; it has a certain latitude within which one may do more or less without our being able to assign its limits definitely.[6]

In short, Kant condemned unlimited altruism, while recom-mending a limited, well-reasoned helpfulness. It's good to be helpful, because one day you too might desire help, and the moral title to help will come from your own fidelity to the maxim of helpfulness. But do not imagine that this maxim is unlimited in scope. We can prove, by sheer logic, that it can't be.

Kant did, however, reserve a central role for the concept of *duty*. As we have already seen, actions that outwardly conformed to the moral law were not sufficient to make an agent moral. One must do them because one knows that they are right, and not merely in the hope of securing a gain or avoiding a loss, whether to oneself

---

[6] Kant, "Critique of Practical Reason," p. 199; just previously, on p. 198, Kant insisted that *our own perfection* was a duty of a similar type. A field opens up for the practice of virtue, one that is governed neither by pure altruism nor by pure egoism, for both of those extremes are logically untenable.

or to anyone else. Our duty is ultimately an impersonal one, a duty owed to reason alone, and neither to self nor others.

The first formulation can thus be understood as a kind of test for interior moral maxims. These maxims stand to be refined over time as they are reconciled with one another and increasingly clarified. We might even think of the first formulation as describing a sort of ongoing research project, combined with the ethical command that all who are capable of understanding the categorical imperative are by this very fact obliged to continue searching and reasoning.

It may seem, however, that the first formulation gives little clear guidance about politics in particular. Kant's second formulation of the categorical imperative may help us a bit more:

> So act as to treat humanity, whether in thine own person or in that of any other, in every case as an end withal, never as means only.[7]

Closely related to this second formulation is his third formulation:

> [E]very rational being must so act as if he were by his maxims in every case a legislating member in the universal kingdom of ends.[8]

Philosophers have puzzled for more than two centuries over precisely what Kant meant in claiming that these three formulations were all restatements of one another. (Unfortunately, Kant never

[7] *Kant's Critique*, p. 68.
[8] *Kant's Critique*, p. 75.

fully explained this claim.) One way of thinking about it may be simply that our *maxims* will always sooner or later implicate *rational beings*—at the very least, they implicate our selves—and as a result, they must always proceed from a correct understanding of the attributes of rational beings. If our maxims fail in this regard, they will be *inconsistent* and thus impossible to universalize. As we honor the ethical search in ourselves, we must do so for others; we must recognize that they are on a similar search to our own. That search requires us to seek and be bounded by universality—and to recognize that all other rational beings should do the same. We are all to consider one another as legislating members in a universal kingdom of ends. Thus, reason and the capacity for reason imbue human beings with a dignity that makes us something more than mere tools or animals.

The political implications now come into sharper focus. In common with Aristotle, Kant held that the search for the good *is* an end in itself, regardless of where one might find oneself in the search. As a result, we should not use any ethical seeker merely as a tool for our own purposes. Those latter purposes will undoubtedly rest on hypothetical imperatives. By definition, they will be particular to us, in our narrow lives, and thus they will be less important than the quest for the good. In an attempt to fulfill our particular goals, we will have trampled others' autonomy, which is a necessary part of *their* search for the good. This we must not do.

Here, then, is the basis (a) for the *commonality* of human dignity and (b) for laws that treat individuals with an equal initial respect. An Aristotle or an Einstein may be superlatively intelligent, but this intelligence entitles him to no greater share of human dignity—and to no inherent preference in law—when compared with a person of average or below-average intelligence. Those of exceptional talent are *not* to be accounted supermen, because it is the capacity to undertake the ethical project itself that confers human dignity, rather than any particular attainment along the way.

Now we begin to see how Kant's ethics might lead to something like libertarianism. Could some baseline set of requirements necessary to treat other persons as ends in themselves—and never merely as a means to some particular end—be instantiated in law, to the exclusion of all other types of law? Such a regime could demand—admittedly perhaps quite often—that individuals refrain from behaving in certain ways; that is, they must refrain from behaving in some of the ways that entail treating others merely as a means to an end. Plausibly, they must refrain from theft of legitimately held property. A fortiori, they must not murder or enslave. They must not deal with one another dishonestly or constrain the free intellectual and moral inquiry of others. And so on.

It is likely not possible to legislate in a way that rules out *all* violations of the categorical imperative, particularly because, as we have seen, so many of its violations are interior and imponderable. "Did you *really* act with a good will?" is a question that in many cases we can effectively ask only of ourselves, and even then, we may not have a ready answer. It is also a question we might prefer, on prudential grounds, not to entrust to any external agents.

Still, at least a rough, outward set of prohibitions on the use of other moral agents merely as tools is in many ways congruent to familiar classical liberal aims. A classical liberal might likewise say that the positive duties commanded by the categorical imperative—such as the duty to treat others as ends in themselves—are not capable of being furthered by legislation: if one treats another as an end merely because the civil law has commanded it, then one has certainly not become a more moral person.

The regime in question would potentially face many limits: plausibly, it would never be permitted to order individuals to build a bridge, or go to war, or even pay taxes. Doing so would itself constitute a violation of the categorical imperative, because it would treat the citizens merely as a means toward a greater end, the end desired by government planners. Just as no individual could consistently possess a moral power to command others, so too no government could possess it.

The argument above follows closely the justification that Robert Nozick gave for his own form of libertarianism in his 1974 book *Anarchy, State, and Utopia*, one of the most important and widely read works of libertarian political philosophy.[9] It is quite wrong to claim, as some have, that Nozick's libertarianism was "without foundations."[10] Nozick's foundations were Kantian. Regrettably, his treatment of Kant in Chapter 3 of *Anarchy, State, and Utopia* is fragmented and unsystematic. Nozick generally preferred questioning to expounding, and in this chapter he appears to have presumed a familiarity with Kant's work that academic

---

[9] Robert Nozick, *Anarchy, States, and Utopia* (New York: Basic Books, 1974).

[10] See Thomas Nagel, "Libertarianism without Foundations," *Yale Law Journal* 85 (1975): 136–49, http://www.jstor.org/stable/795521?seq=1#page_scan_tab_contents.

philosophers would certainly have, but that libertarian activists perhaps might not. Nonetheless, it can be shown that Nozick began with a Kantian respect for persons as ends in themselves and concluded that this respect would necessarily entail a politically libertarian social order, one with robust negative rights that must not be violated. Let us now recapitulate his argument.

Nozick first drew a distinction in ethics between *constraints* and *goals*. Goals are those things that agents try to attain or maximize; constraints forbid certain methods that agents could otherwise use in the pursuit of their goals. Nozick observed that utilitarian moral philosophy concerned itself almost entirely with goals, such as the maximization of happiness, and that utilitarianism generally failed to consider constraints. As a result, utilitarian accounts of individual rights tended to be either lacking or unpersuasive: it is commonly much easier to articulate rights as constraints on other agents' behavior than as goals to be maximized. For example, one cannot easily quantify the freedom of worship, a step that would be necessary for freedom of worship to be treated as a goal to be maximized by rational agents. Yet it is altogether simple to say that agents shall be morally constrained from coercively imposing a particular form of worship. No quantification is necessary, or even helpful.

Nozick next observed that utilitarianism is commonly thought deficient in that it seems to bless the use of individuals toward its goals in ways that clash with strongly held intuitions. For example, a utilitarian might knowingly punish an innocent man merely to appease an angry mob, provided that punishment would cause more aggregate happiness than abstention.

Common sense would ask us to consider where justice lay in this situation, and a Kantian would claim to have discerned the reason for this commonsense request: the punishment would have been undertaken without a thought to ethical duty, or, in other words, to the universalization of one's maxim. One can't possibly will that *all* innocent people should be punished, or that punishments should always be arbitrary with regard to guilt. Either of those factors would be inconsistent. The only thing one could consistently will here would be that the innocent must *never* be punished. Utilitarianism would have to operate on inconsistent maxims, in that it would apparently *sometimes* punish the innocent, in pursuit of the mirage of happiness.

Nozick's objection to utilitarianism forms a clear parallel with Kant's objection to similar systems in his own day. Both Kant and Nozick complained in effect that the systems unsatisfyingly rested on merely hypothetical imperatives, like the pursuit of happiness. As a necessary consequence, systems that advocated maximizing happiness as a goal—with no side constraints—would soon bring their advocates to recommend, in effect, using people merely as tools. This is precisely the sort of action that the second formulation most clearly prohibits.

Nozick then speculated on how a society might be set up to prohibit the use of people as tools more generally. He noted that political philosophy is concerned "only with *certain* ways that persons may not use others; primarily, physically aggressing against them."[11] (Moral philosophy, presumably, would remain free to

[11] Nozick, *Anarchy,* p. 32.

range across all of human conduct, but in doing so, it would often remain a private endeavor.) But although the scope of political philosophy is narrow, invoking Kant's second formulation might threaten to eliminate politics entirely. Nozick wrote:

> The moral side constraints upon what we may do, I claim, reflect the fact of our separate existences. They reflect the fact that no moral balancing act can take place among us; there is no moral outweighing of one of our lives by others so as to lead to a greater overall *social* good. There is no justified sacrifice of some of us for others. This root idea, namely, that there are different individuals with separate lives and so no one may be sacrificed for others, underlies the existence of moral side constraints, but it also, I believe, leads to a libertarian side constraint that prohibits aggression against another.[12]

States *routinely* break this side-constraint. Constantly, in all times and places, states use people merely as tools. Quite possibly they are incapable of doing otherwise. To speak more precisely, *the agents of states* set goals that they wish to attain, and they compel citizens to try to attain them, the citizens' dignity and autonomy notwithstanding. States as we know them therefore stand under a severe moral indictment. Far from commanding our respect, our political leaders should be held in contempt. It would seem that the entire point of their existence is to treat people merely as tools and not as moral agents.

---

[12] Ibid., pp. 33–34 [emphasis in original].

Those who wish to defend the actions of the state are thus obliged, as Nozick argued, either to deny all side-constraints (perhaps by denying Kantian moral philosophy itself, and by substituting some more pliable rule); or to offer a different explanation of side-constraints that is less libertarian; or to argue that the individuality and dignity of persons are compatible with initiating coercion against them, a coercion *not* tantamount to treating them as tools, or things, or beasts of burden. Perhaps we are permitted to treat humans as tools but only in *some* senses. It is hard to understand, however, how this treatment might be the case without a wholesale denial of the first formulation of the categorical imperative. Failing that, though, a strict Kantian must regard the modern state as illegitimate.

On the whole, Nozick was prepared to accept that outcome, and much of the rest of his book is devoted to proposing and defending visions of social life that did not entail using people as tools. Nozick's exploration of the alternatives was subtle, thoughtful, and notably attentive to *process*. That is, he was uniformly suspicious throughout his work of theories that moved quickly toward—or that merely described—a static end state that was to be regarded immediately as just. As we shall see, this attention to process—to history and to development—was another trait he shared with Kant.

Famously, however, in one footnote Nozick did suggest an exception to the need for individual rights understood as side-constraints. Perhaps because that exception is so singular, it has been dear to statists ever since. Nozick wrote, "The question of whether these side constraints are absolute, or whether they may be violated in order to avoid catastrophic moral horror, and if the latter, what the resulting structure might look like, is one I hope largely to avoid."[13]

We who propose to defend more systematically a Kantian foundation for individual liberty must not avoid Nozick's question; if we did, it might become yet another "little gap" through which "every man's liberty may in time go out."[14]

Yet if we are being strictly Kantian, it is unclear exactly how fidelity to the categorical imperative in our political side-constraints could ever cause a catastrophic *moral* horror to arise—that is, a horror that depends for its existence on our moral commitments alone. Two other possibilities seem much more likely. Although both are awful, in neither of them can we fairly say that our morals are to blame.

The first is that we have made the nonmoral error of proceeding from mistaken hypothetical imperatives. For example: *if* we wish to prevent plague, *then* we must punish witchcraft. This is, of course, a terrible mistake, but it is not an error of morality. It is an error of knowledge, because it proceeds from the mistaken belief that witches cause plagues. The categorical imperative can direct us to study such empirical matters, but it cannot supply us with conclusions, no matter how elementary. Those we must find for ourselves.

As reasoning beings who have apprehended the categorical imperative, yes, we are obliged never to knowingly violate it.

---

[13] Ibid., p. 30.

[14] John Selden, cited in F. A. Hayek, *The Constitution of Liberty* (Chicago: University of Chicago Press, 1960), p. 205.

But merely grasping the categorical imperative does not endow us with all the knowledge needed to act in ways that avert every bad consequence. Nor does it even promise to. The best the categorical imperative can do for us is to command us to learn better and better ways of proceeding, given the constant play of contingency around us. Lived morality may and should be guided by the categorical imperative, but it will always be justified at least partially with reference to hypothetical imperatives as well. And some of them, alas, may be tragically mistaken. None of them is a reason to abandon the categorical imperative itself. Kant himself seems to have been well aware of this fact. He termed the ability to select well among possible hypothetical imperatives *prudence*, and he saw nothing per se wrong with obeying the counsels of prudence. On the contrary, it was a key part of his moral system.[15]

The second possibility occurs when we are mistaken in our belief that a set of events actually constitutes a catastrophic moral horror. Such events may not be catastrophic moral horrors at all, but rather false positives. For example, the social equality of women was once thought a moral horror. And yet today, it looks like one

---

[15] Kant writes, "Hence it follows that the imperatives of prudence do not, strictly speaking, command at all, that is, they cannot present actions objectively as practically necessary; that they are rather to be regarded as counsels (*consilia*) than precepts (*præcepta*) of reason, that the problem to determine certainly and universally what action would promote the happiness of a rational being is completely insoluble, and consequently no imperative respecting it is possible which should, in the strict sense, command to do what makes happy." We may pursue happiness, but we must not understand this pursuit to be based on a categorical command. Kant, *Fundamental Principles of the Metaphysic of Morals*, p. 47.

of the clearest possible implications of the categorical imperative itself. If the history of catastrophic moral horrors is any indication, our ability to identify them is far outrun by our propensity to generate false positives. The mixing of the races, love between people of the same sex, in vitro fertilization, vaccination, anesthesia, marijuana, jazz music, and countless others have been characterized, in effect, as catastrophic moral horrors, and none are anything of the kind. Once again, deontological ethics can't be blamed for these things, because nothing in them is blameworthy.

Before we leave Nozick's mostly Kantian treatment of libertarian political philosophy, we should admit that Nozick himself had some further qualms. In his book *Philosophical Explanations*, Nozick appears to have doubted some relevant aspects of Kantianism. Following a suggestion from Walter Kaufmann, Nozick questioned whether Kant's categorical imperative should be termed categorical at all. Was it not, he asked, just another hypothetical imperative, one bearing the implicit condition to do this *if you want to be rational*? What if you *don't* want to be rational? Nozick asked. "Only a philosopher would think that this is a clincher," he quipped. "Who else would think that the ultimate insult is to be called irrational?"[16]

Various ways exist to escape this difficulty. One of the simplest is to point out that any interlocutors proceeding along these

---

[16] Robert Nozick, *Philosophical Explanations* (Cambridge, MA: Harvard University Press, 1981), p. 354. But he had qualms upon qualms; the imperative that Nozick settles on, some hundred pages later, nonetheless has an admitted "kinship" to Kant's, and it's a fair question whether Nozick did not in fact slouch back to a restatement of the categorical imperative. See p. 462.

lines would in so doing have forfeited their claim to our reasoned consideration. Persons who deliberately renounce reason are *not* entitled to give us their reasons and expect us to pay heed to such reasons. Because such people have declared that they are not deploying reason, no useful conversation can take place between us. Still less may they legislate for those of us in the kingdom of ends, of which they claim they are not even a part.

Let us now return to Kant, who was not so politically radical, even if Nozick's work suggests that he should have been. Kant's own politics were a distinctly moderate classical liberalism, one that even approved of involuntary taxation, on the grounds that it alone made civil society possible. Kant's political theory included a significant social contract aspect, but it was also sensitive to the fact that human societies are subject to change in the course of history, for either better or worse. Kant viewed it as the ongoing task of enlightened philosophy to gradually ameliorate the defects found in the societies of his day. Modern libertarians are apt to find his approach deficient, but among the deficiencies, they will find much to praise and to ponder.

In keeping with his ethical thought, Kant proclaimed that the supreme principle of law should be as follows:

> Every action is right and just, the maxim of which allows the agents freedom of choice to harmonize with the freedom of every other, according to a universal law.[17]

---

[17] Immanuel Kant, *The Metaphysics of Ethics*, 3rd ed., ed. Henry Calderwood, trans. J. W. Semple (Edinburgh: T. & T. Clark, 1886 [1796]), http://oll.libertyfund.org /titles/1443#Kant_0332_338.

We can immediately appreciate that the preservation of practical choice—which allows the prospect of social harmony—was central to Kant's conception of justice. He moved from this principle very quickly to a formula quite resembling the later law of equal freedom, variants of which are found in Herbert Spencer, John Stuart Mill, John Rawls, and others. As Kant wrote:

> So act that the use of thy freedom may not circumscribe the freedom of any other.[18]

The formula is not as capacious as Spencer's, who accorded each individual the *maximum* liberty compatible with a like liberty in others. But we can discern here a sharp distinction, as is common in the classical liberal tradition, between *liberty*, which is respectful of the same in others, and *license*, which is not. But why do laws exist that are socially enacted and thus (obviously) exterior to the will? Kant's answer reveals much about his social theory in general, and particularly that theory's evolutionary character:

> The very notion of law consists in that of the possibility of combining universal mutual co-action with every person's freedom.[19]

Law exists to facilitate cooperation—but only on the condition that we do not at the same time obliterate anyone's freedom. Law exists not to achieve a given outcome in society but to allow both

---

[18] Ibid., p. 179.
[19] Ibid., p. 180.

voluntary cooperation and individual liberty, with which many different projects might be realized.

In his "Idea of a Universal History from a Cosmopolitan Point of View," Kant even suggested that both freedom and cooperation were necessary for mankind *to achieve its destiny as a species*— an idea that we can forgive our readers for shrinking from, at least at first. It certainly sounds profoundly unlibertarian. Yet on closer examination, the destiny that Kant imagined may not be so threatening. What Kant had in mind by the destiny of the species may even resemble what F. A. Hayek termed a spontaneous order:

> The means which Nature employs to bring about the development of all the capacities implanted in men, is their mutual Antagonism in society, but only so far as this antagonism becomes at length the cause of an Order among them that is regulated by Law.[20]

It is irrelevant whether "Nature" causes this order to emerge, or whether the order emerges of its own accord, or even whether those two possibilities are just different ways of saying the same thing. What is key is that mankind can develop to the fullest only in the context of an ongoing social order, one that lasts across many lifetimes and permits a measure of peaceful competition. One form of peaceful competition will spring to mind

---

[20] Immanuel Kant, "Idea for a Universal History from a Cosmopolitan Point of View," 4th proposition, in *Kant's Principles of Politics, Including His Essay on Perpetual Peace: A Contribution to Political Science*, trans. William Hastie (Edinburgh: T. & T. Clark, 1891 [1784]), http://oll.libertyfund.org/titles/358#Kant_0056_39.

immediately for classical liberals, namely, the market process. Others, however, do exist, and it is worth inquiring how at least two social systems, the market order and socialism, might fare from a Kantian perspective.[21] Let us consider Kant's attitudes toward the market process, or at least what we can infer about them, before moving on to what a Kantian libertarian might have to say. Following that, we will consider some of the objections of a Kantian socialist.

One cannot properly belong to the classical liberal tradition without a robust account of private property that entails its relatively unrestricted usage and transfer. To be called liberal in any sense, this account must also give solid reasons to reject a similar usage and transfer of persons. And indeed, Kant had just such an account. Kant's theory of the institution of property was in many ways more historically grounded than Locke's, or even Hume's. It also sat well with the intellectual and ethical project we have outlined above—the gradual apprehension of the ethical laws of reason, and the reconciliation of the will to reason's dictates.

Kant believed that property rights typically arose gradually, out of repeated claims, counterclaims, adjudications, and reaffirmations, rather than from any one definitive act of settlement or assignment, whether by the state or by individuals.[22]

---

[21] Competition is indeed possible under socialism, albeit outside the market process. Competitions in the arts, athletics, and the like certainly have existed under socialist regimes. Whether they are preferable to their capitalist counterparts is a question we need not explore, though I suspect that socialists may be thankful for our silence.

[22] This summary closely follows Marcus Verhaegh, "Kant and Property Rights," *Journal of Libertarian Studies* 18 (Summer 2004): 11–32.

This process-oriented view helps us gain new perspective on several vexing problems, including compensation for historical wrongs. It may prove, for example, that, contrary to the common-law maxim concerning improperly acquired property, legitimacy *can* arise over time. Given the initially arbitrary (and often criminal) origin of nearly all title to land, there is no other way forward in any case. We must either concede that all the world is stolen, after which we must establish an institution to redistribute everything, or we admit that past errors are better corrected gradually. Institutions that redistribute everything are too dangerous in practice ever to be trusted, and thus our choice becomes clear.

From an unowned condition, land in Kant's theory might first be appropriated by anyone with the means to defend it. No mixing of labor was required to stake a claim. This provisional claim, however, was in no sense an absolute right. In this Kant differed from Locke in two ways. Locke, recall, would insist that the mixing of labor was necessary to establish ownership. And from that point on, Locke held that ownership was settled and absolute.

On neither point would real life appear to correspond well to the Lockean account. On both, Kant's account seems to describe initial appropriation with greater historical accuracy. There is at best a *limited* obligation not to interfere with land that is in this manner only provisionally controlled by others. But this obligation may be breached if a land claimant refuses, for example, to enter into a state of civil society with his neighbors. It will not do to have barbarians on our borders. Indeed, this very consideration brought Kant to believe that implementing a social contract was morally obligatory, that contract's relative justness notwithstanding. Anything at all would constitute an improvement over the lack of civil society.

This move is certain to be rejected among libertarians, but it is unclear to me how foundational it is to Kant's social thought. After all, contracts of this type may be exceptionally rare.[23] In any case, the provisional obligation to respect property rights solidifies with the entry into civil society, which rational beings should recognize as desirable. It solidifies further with time and usage under a just regime of laws.[24] As the modern scholar Marcus Verhaegh has written:

> The best metaphor for Kant's account of movement out of the state of nature is one of disarmament—staged, negotiated disarmament. We are all duty-bound to reduce violent conflict and the potential for violent conflict by moving toward a scenario in which ownership disputes are decided by the rule of right law, rather than ongoing, competing military power. But prior to full disarmament—the fully cosmopolitan globe—military force plays a significant role in setting the bounds of right ownership.[25]

Alas, military force is still necessary. And it would remain necessary, Kant believed, until a worldwide regime of perpetual peace had been established, one in which all countries enjoyed a

---

[23] See Kevin E. Dodson, "Autonomy and Authority in Kant's Rechtslehre," *Political Theory* 25 (February 1997): 93–111.

[24] Verhaegh, "Kant and Property Rights," p. 20.

[25] Ibid., p. 21.

republican form government, as well as the renunciation of war and standing armies. This cosmopolitan social order would be one of the crowning achievements of human civilization. Kant also thought it would take many generations to accomplish. In the meantime, governments should do their best to move toward it.[26]

In contrast to his strong claims about the interior necessities of reason, Kant was relatively modest in his claims about the nature of history and its unfolding. He did *not* claim to have discerned a set of historical laws that will operate as of necessity, even if, at first glance, he may seem to have done so, and thus to stand condemned as a historicist. On the contrary, Kant was deliberately vague about the institutions of the future cosmopolitan society, which neither he nor any of us could discern in their entirety. Unlike Marx or Hegel, Kant also left room for—and indeed assigned a central place to—the liberty of individual action, which will, if allowed to operate, *eventually* instantiate the cosmopolitan society of the future. The active agents here will be free individuals, not social classes, national spirits, or impersonal social forces, and the claims that Kant made about the future were few and qualified.

---

[26] Kant's vision of a gradual transition—from violent appropriation defended violently toward a cosmopolitan civil society defended by reason alone—anticipates much of subsequent German liberalism, particularly the anarcho-capitalist vision of the early 20th-century sociologist Franz Oppenheimer. Oppenheimer's "free citizenship" bears a strong resemblance to—and would seem to share all the essential qualities of—Kant's cosmopolitan law, with the sole exception that Oppenheimer believed in the eventual obsolescence of government itself. Thus, although it is not often appreciated today, a significant strain of market anarchism was directly inspired by Kantian social theory. See Franz Oppenheimer, *The State: Its History and Development Viewed Sociologically*, trans. John M. Gitterman (Indianapolis, IN: Bobbs-Merrill, 1914; repr., London: Forgotten Books, 2012).

How then do property rights and cosmopolitan law relate to Kant's ethical project? Neither will necessarily make us good people; nothing prevents the propertied individual from having a bad will. Nor are property rights even necessary for possessing inward ethical freedom, for one *always* has the capacity to will the good—or not—regardless of how unfree or poor one may be. A good person may live, and be good, under a bad government, or in destitution. The traits are in this sense quite independent.

But property rights in things alone—and never in persons—can help us obey more perfectly the negative duties that are most clearly implied by the second formulation of the categorical imperative: by granting individuals each the capacity to acquire, modify, and alienate property, we also allow them to use property to their own ends, and we declare, as it were, our maxim that only unreasoning things are to be used as tools—and never people. A cosmopolitan regime of private property that excludes slavery thus draws a bright line between the kingdom of ends, which is reserved for people, and the kingdom of means, which largely overlaps the legal category of property. This outward conformity, Kant believed, could lead people to the inner apprehension of the moral law.[27]

---

[27] That is, Kant did *not* really think that external conformity to the moral law was completely valueless. Although it could not be called ethically foundational, external conformity did have a didactic and instrumental value. In the second section of the *Critique of Practical Reason*, Kant described a method of teaching ethics that began with commonsense intuitions about ethical actions and motivations and proceeded socratically toward the categorical imperative. Along the way, the student would learn to distinguish merely outward conformity from the goodness that inheres in the good will. It is evident that properly formulated laws could aid considerably in following this method. Kant, "Methodology of Pure Practical Reason," in *Critique of Practical Reason*, pp. 209–17.

Under a cosmopolitan, property-holding regime, we likewise obtain a similar type of outward autonomy for ourselves. Much of the cosmopolitan project seems aimed at making the *outside* more closely resemble the *inside*. It aims at expanding our freedom of action in the phenomenal world, that is, the world of exterior experiences, to more closely resemble the freedom of action in the interior world of the mind. What we do with our property, do note, may be good or bad, but we will at least have secured one of the foundations of leading a morally good external life, which is the capacity for self-rule. (For Kant, the growing capacity for an adult-like self-rule, a rule independent of the state, was also the essence of the Enlightenment.[28]) Under free institutions, obedience to the written law and obedience to the moral law may now begin to harmonize, even if, as Kant warned, our current property claims may not be fully settled or just. In time, they can be, if only we continue to will it.

So far, we have said much about property ownership but little about trade. A classical liberal might even wonder, hereabouts, what the point of ownership might be, if it were not that ownership allowed for transfer and for the market process to operate. Our silence, though, is for a fairly strong reason: Kant himself would appear to have cared little for economics. He rarely deployed examples that proceeded from what we might term economic behavior in the narrow sense, that is, those involving buying and selling. His thoughts on the matter would appear to have been few, and we are left to draw inferences from a meager data set.

---

[28] Immanuel Kant, "What Is Enlightenment?" trans. Mary C. Smith [1784], http://www.columbia.edu/acis/ets/CCREAD/etscc/kant.html.

When Kant did write about market exchange, however, he certainly did not write to condemn the practice in all cases. Instead, he condemned only specific types of exchange, including instances of fraud; price discrimination; and the sale of organs, such as teeth, a common practice at the time. (Of those three, it is not at all clear that the last two condemnations must stand.) Kant was also aware of the writings of Jean-Jacques Rousseau, who did condemn commerce, often quite explicitly, and it is evident that although Kant had every opportunity, he declined to agree.

In all, however, much work remains to be done in theorizing the market process from the standpoint of Kantian ethics. Important groundwork has been laid by the contemporary philosopher Mark D. White, who suggests that Kant's *negative duties*—those things that we are obliged, in an absolute sense, to refrain from doing to others—and Kant's *positive duties*—those things that we are obliged, in a limited sense, to do out of benevolence to others—are both compatible with a market society. The former make a market society possible, and the latter make it agreeable. White has even loosely paralleled these two types of duties with the worlds described in Adam Smith's two great works, *The Wealth of Nations* and *The Theory of Moral Sentiments*. The former considers the realm of merely negative duty, whereas the latter examines our positive duty of beneficence. Although Smith's ethics were not deontological like Kant's, the approach still seems promising.[29]

---

[29] See Mark D. White, "Adam Smith and Immanuel Kant: On Markets, Duties, and Moral Sentiments," *Forum for Social Economics* 39 (April 2010): 53–60. See also Mark D. White, *Kantian Ethics and Economics: Autonomy, Dignity, and Character* (Stanford, CA: Stanford University Press, 2011).

Against all this, however, it has sometimes been suggested by socialist students of Kant's ethics that the categorical imperative actually forbids all, or at least many, market exchanges. In buying and selling, do I not treat my counterpart merely as a means to an end? Have I not made a mere object of the baker? Have I not treated him precisely as I might have treated a vending machine, which is undoubtedly a tool? (It hardly seems that the scripted, almost mechanical conversations that take place in the course of a typical business transaction would constitute much of an improvement, then, over someone talking absentmindedly to a vending machine!) Things seem to stand even worse in regard to the buying and selling of labor, in which the capitalist would appear to weigh the choice to employ a laborer against the choice to "employ" a machine, one that might constitute, for his purposes, a perfect substitute. Is this not a fatal flaw in the project of justifying the market process in Kantian ethics?

If it were a flaw, then the fact that market exchange would seem necessary to us would indicate no more than a failure of our own will, with the corresponding need to rectify it. Perhaps we must even resign ourselves to the catastrophic moral horror of advocating socialism (which, we would have to concede, we had misclassified). So might say Kantian socialists and some others.[30] Indeed, no less an authority than Ludwig von Mises argued that "out of

---

[30] The signal figure for this interpretation of Kant is Hermann Cohen, though it must be conceded that it seems to suggest itself almost immediately to all libertarian skeptics of Kantianism. Hermann Cohen, *Ethik des Reinen Willens* (Berlin: Bruno Cassirer, 1904; repr. Charleston, SC: Nabu Press, 2010).

Kant's mysticism of duty . . . it is easy to trace the development of socialist thought."[31]

Readers should already appreciate that Kant's allegiance to duty was at least not openly mysticism, even if they do not follow or agree with his argument. At no point does Kant appeal to the unknowable or to a higher mind; the appeal is, purportedly, to one's power of reason alone. There are several further reasons why Mises was simply wrong in this passage, and why Kant's cosmopolitan social order need not be—and perhaps should not be—a socialism.

First, as Kant himself argued, the only perfect duties that we owe to other autonomous moral agents—that is, the only duties that are absolute, or categorical—are negative in character. They are actions that we must be certain of refraining from. We have already seen that we do not have a perfect duty to help others, much less to provide them with any particular set of resources, categorically and without regard to circumstance. Kantian socialists must therefore reckon with the fact that all forms of nonvoluntary socialism will entail duties of exactly this improper type. In common with every other form of modern state, socialist states necessarily use people as tools.

Second, for Kant himself, the provision of economic goods appears to have been a matter not of ethics but of prudence and skill. The question of which economic system—(a voluntary)

---

[31] Ludwig von Mises, *Socialism* (Indianapolis, IN: Liberty Fund, 1981), p. 388. Mises's analysis of the Kantian socialist Hermann Cohen is insightful and correct, I believe, but I do not agree that Kant should share the blame, for reasons that will soon become clear.

socialism or (a voluntary) capitalism—would best supply the world's material needs, is not therefore a matter to be settled with reference to the categorical imperative alone. Rather, economic science can and should settle it independently, albeit guided by the side-constraints that arise from the imperative.

Third, we should consider reciprocity: If I am treating the baker as a tool—well, is he not doing precisely the same to me? Does he not treat me as a means of getting rid of his surplus bread? Might I just as well be replaced by a *purchasing* machine? Maybe so. But how can it be that we both treat each other *merely* as tools? If I am treated as a tool, then I am robbed of my autonomy. But if I am robbed of my autonomy, how can I also treat my counterpart, who allegedly masters me, as a tool? It is hard to see how I can act in the ethical sense at all, let alone act badly, when I have been deprived of my agency. The presence of reciprocity, then, suggests that neither party's will has been violated by the other.

Fourth, if we grant that market exchanges treat at least one agent involved merely as a tool, how do we differentiate market exchanges from nonmarket forms of cooperation, which seem to stand similarly accused? In what sense do participants in a voluntary socialism *not* treat one another as merely a means to an end? The categorical imperative does not require us all to live as hermits; indeed, Kant enthusiastically recommended cooperation of many different kinds.

We must now look for some way to formulate the essential act of cooperation that does not depend on maxims that fall victim to the categorical imperative. Note that it will not suffice simply to say that our cooperative dealings concern only the disposition of tools, and that, as a result, only hypothetical imperatives are in play. The very question at hand is whether we have impermissibly treated our counterparts in the exchange as tools in themselves.

Cooperation of all types might be said to take the following form, whether in the market or out of it: together, two autonomous agents agree to formulate a plan, according to which they will use their combined resources. Both agents equally desire that the plan be enacted *over any available alternatives*. Given that the plan represents each agent's first choice, it would appear difficult to claim that the plan does not represent what the participants will. Note that this conclusion holds true whether or not a market exchange has taken place; note also that both buyer and seller get their first choice of all available options, even when the sale does not go through.

In this reconstruction, a vending machine is still a tool, but it is a tool that both buyer and seller agree to use together to realize an agreed-upon distribution of resources. A baker is still an autonomous agent, one who proposes a plan of action to all who enter his shop. And a capitalist, who must choose between human labor and machine labor, does not necessarily treat a laborer merely as a machine. Rather, he chooses between two different plans, both of which at various points entail human beings voluntarily working for pay: either the laborer does it directly, or else the laborer(s) who made the machine play that role indirectly. In every case, there is a cooperation of wills.

Much work remains to be done here, in part because of modern classical liberals' deep aversion to Kantian ethics and in part because of Kant's neglect of economics. But the Austrian school owes much to Kant in spite of this neglect, above all in epistemology. As a result, the project of further reconciling Kant's ethics to libertarianism is likely to prove fruitful to scholars who are so inclined.

The project will not always be easy. Kant flatly denied one right that classical liberals have generally emphasized, the right of resistance to the state. But as with the question of whether one may compel obedience to an initial social contract, it is possible to argue that Kant's dismissal of the right of resistance is a peripheral part of his social thought. Is it really, as Kant thought, always the subject who has broken the social contract? And never the state? A contract that one party is incapable of violating would be highly unequal, and might even violate the categorical imperative. A better Kantian should perhaps reject it out of hand, exactly as Robert Nozick did.

Finally, freedom of expression played a special role in Kant's social theory. Whereas modern libertarians are apt to collapse the freedom of expression into simply another aspect of one's property rights—albeit perhaps a psychologically important one—for Kant, the ability to exercise one's reason publicly as it regarded current affairs and government was more than a special use of one's property. It was also a key part of living in a civil society. The capacity was vital for two reasons. First, Kant believed that it was the citizens' only substantial defense against the sovereign power in cases where the sovereign acted wrongly. And second, good government itself could arise only through a process of deliberation, in which all views were heard, candidly and without fear of punishment.

Now, we need not hold, as Kant did, that individuals have no proper right of revolution against a sovereign in order to believe that the right to air our grievances commands a special status in a governed society, as opposed to a stateless one. Even a slight regard for consequence will allow us to reach that conclusion anyway. This regard for consequence may *not* form any part of the groundwork of the moral law. But it is also not forbidden by the moral law, and entrance into civil society may require it in the manner of a hypothetical imperative.

Much work remains to be done in grounding libertarian social thought in Kantian ethics, but it is clearly a viable and ongoing project, one that already promises to free libertarian social thought from many of the problems that have beset it in certain of its other formulations.

4

Contractarianism

Jan Narveson

The general idea of the social contract theory has been around for a long time. There is a clear shot at it in Plato's *Republic*, for example, long before the more recent and famous efforts of Hobbes, Locke, Rousseau, Kant, and later John Rawls and David Gauthier. What is this general idea, and what is it an idea *of*? And how does it relate to libertarianism? Those questions will be discussed in this chapter.

Social contract is a theory about the foundations of a certain class of normative theories—moral and political. We begin by explaining the point of a *foundational* theory, and of the advantages of this particular theory of that type. We then move on to the specifically moral and political nature of the resulting theory, concluding with the argument for libertarianism as the basic output of the theory. Theories of this type accomplish something important—but not nearly everything, and we will recognize its limits as well.

Social Contract as Normative Foundation

The very subject of the "foundations" of a normative theory has long been and continues to be disputed by philosophers. As its name would suggest, the term refers to the basic premises on which the theory rests. It would take a very full discussion to explore the many byways of such a theory over the years, a project we can hardly undertake here. But several basic points may be noted. The first is that many theorists think that there are no "foundations." A foundationist theory holds that there are certain (one or a few) basic general premises, or kinds of premises, that *support* a theory about what's just and unjust, right and wrong—support in the sense that the truths of the theory derive from those few or that one normative premise, plus relevant factual premises, those being subject to empirical test.

A separate question is whether those basic normative premises are themselves sui generis—or can they in turn be derived from facts of some sort? The latter view, of course, invites charges of committing the "naturalist fallacy" that obsessed moral philosophers in the 20th century. Any theorist who attempts this latter route must respond to that charge. We will, in fact, do so in this exposition.

As said, philosophers have a tendency to deny foundationism in moral and political theory. And that attitude produces a general response: if no foundations exist, then how do you get anywhere in discussion when we disagree, as we so often do, about such topics? If nothing you can say clearly counts, and can be *shown* to count, in favor of or against anything, then the prospect of resolution is nil. Is that bad? Yes, says the social contract theorist. And probably everyone would agree that *if* it can be done, that would be nice; what they deny is that it can.

The next thing to say is that a foundation is evidently useless if it is no better, no more "solid" than what it purports to "found." We must not build on sand. This observation is especially important in relation to almost all current proposals about foundations. A major and highly pertinent example is a type of theory called "intuitionist," according to which there are indeed "basic" moral claims in the sense that *no* further reason can be advanced on behalf of such claims. People may even assert that those claims are "self-evident." The trouble with that, however, is that it is impossible to find any moral statements that have not been rejected by some. Indeed, there are "amoralists," moral skeptics, who claim that there is no such thing as morality. What does the intuitionist say to them? What, that is, that might make some impression—might appeal to the *rational* faculties of the skeptic? The social contract theorist holds that there *is* something we can usefully say. That theorist likewise has a reply to the "relativist," who insists that morality is merely "relative," such as to culture or personality, and so on.

If a social contract theory is going to work, it must be founded on facts—real features of human and social life. There must be enough generality and similarity so that the theory clearly reaches to everybody, not just a few. And it must make a prescription that makes rational sense to everybody—everybody must be able to see why *this* prescription, this principle, is the way to go. Is this possible? We'll see.

Social contract theory holds that morality, viewed rationally, is founded on, in some sense, *agreement* or at least *rational* agreement—agreement of the kind that any rational person can see reason to make. And this provides major resources for replies to skeptics and dissenters (if it works): if you *agree* that something or other is or would be right, then you are not in a position to turn around and deny it. We would have to distinguish between actual historical agreements, typified by commercial contracts, treaties, and so on, and *hypothetical* agreements—agreements that one *would* make on reflection. And, especially important, we must look for agreement *in action*. Anything merely done on paper or in words is of no interest unless it somehow bears on actual action, and the disposition to act.

Such an agreement obviously cannot be a sort of panhuman Constitutional Convention in which we all get together and sign some formal document. It can, however, be a recognition of an underlying rational structure. We come to agreement in action as the result of commonsense appreciation of our condition. David Hume is the source of a great example: when two men row a boat, they fall into a rhythm and a level of effort that gets them going in one direction. No initial discussion and no "contracting" are necessary.

As a widely recognized more modern example, consider the "rule of the road": when driving on a two-way street or road, keep to the right (or the left, if that is the locally recognized rule). Here, the merit of following the rule is that we avoid the damaging or fatal collisions that we can otherwise expect. It is a merit that anyone can understand, and in actual conditions, virtually everyone virtually always adheres to. The rare exceptions are discussable: passing a slower vehicle, which is fine when it's safe. Then the question "*Is* it safe in this case?" becomes relevant. That might be a matter of disagreement, but now there are clear criteria to appeal to in deciding it—we are not just at sea. Another merit of the example is that it explains what can be "relative," even though that doesn't upset the normative output. What is relative is which side of the road we are to drive on. Get a bunch of people together where they are driving or walking or horseback riding, and soon enough you find them adhering to one side or the other; once they do, it is irrational for a newcomer to go against the rule.

A far more serious structure, which has come in for an immense amount of discussion in mathematical, social-scientific, and philosophical circles for most of a century, is the now-familiar prisoner's dilemma. In the two-person cases that are the norm in discussion, this little graph schematizes the idea (let A and B be the two parties, and the numbers then rank-order, by their own preferences, the outcomes for that pair of choices). So (a) we each face a choice between two alternatives, x and y, and what happens to each of us depends on what we each choose; (b) if we both choose alternative x, each gets his or her second-best outcome; if we both choose y, we both get the third-best outcome, which is much worse for each. (c) But if I choose x and you y, I get my best and you your worst; and if you choose x and I choose y, then vice versa. We assume that we are both free agents, choosing as we will. What do we do?

		B	
		x	y
	x	2, 2	4, 1
A			
	y	1, 4	3, 3

The problem is that where we choose differently, one gains greatly—at the expense of the other. So we choose the same—but which? In the absence of any sort of trust or further consideration, each is impelled to choose the "safer" option, y: this avoids the worst outcome, fourth, yes—but the outcome for both of us, third, is much worse than the second, which we could have if only we could rely on the other to choose that way. That's the dilemma: each goes for the best and in doing so ends up badly—in a way that could have been avoided.

Avoiding that worse outcome, says the contract theorist, is the object of morality. It tells us to cooperate rather than disagree, thus leading to better outcomes for us both. Morality's rule is cooperate, if the other party is willing to reciprocate. But if he doesn't, you are entitled to withdraw your cooperation.

The prisoner's dilemma appears to be at work in innumerable situations in real life. And one very general case of it, the social contract theorist argues, is the most basic one of all. To see what it is and why it is important, we move to the great philosopher who, more than any other, has brought this kind of theory into prominence: Thomas Hobbes (1588–1679)—supplemented in contemporary times by David Gauthier.[1] The problem concerns liberty—yours and mine (A's and B's). Liberty is the absence of interpersonal violence or coercion; more generally, of *negative intervention*—intervention to worsen the life, or situation, of the person intervened upon. We are at liberty (of the "social" kind that is the subject of these chapters) when no such negative intervention is threatened.

---

[1] David Gauthier, *Morals by Agreement* (Oxford, UK: Oxford University Press, 1986).

Hobbes and the "Natural Condition of Mankind"

If a social contract is to have much range of application, what is it about humans and their interactions that would make it so? That question has a general answer. On innumerable occasions in life, people might be able to gain at other people's expense. The most salient way is by actual physical violence. A hits B over the head and walks off with B's load of vegetables. And there are other ways, familiar to all, in which somebody can "do someone else down" —lying, cheating, and defrauding are among the most important—and walk away with gains at his or her expense.

What makes them so ubiquitous is a certain general similarity or comparability among people. Hobbes puts his finger on it when he asserts a sort of human equality, saying that "as to strength of body, the weakest has enough to kill the strongest."[2] As it can take very little strength to kill someone, what he says is obviously plausible. Only infants, the decrepit, or the severely disabled—or special local cases where one has the other "in a corner"—offer cases where that kind of "equality" doesn't pretty obviously hold. It is true that our relative levels of strength vary enormously. But it is almost never literally *impossible* for A to kill B if A is really determined to do so. And in social situations, of course, we can make life miserable for certain other people—or even for a great many of them—in many other ways.

That's what is possible. But is it *likely*? Some reflection on this question is needed. Most of us nowadays live in relatively safe social circumstances. And yet, even here and now, newspapers daily report violence, by people near or far. Such violence occurs despite

[2] Thomas Hobbes, *Leviathan* (New York: Dutton, 1953 [1651]), chap. 13, p. 101.

our living in societies with, usually, pretty good moral senses, and government agencies—notably the police—attempting to make the lives of the violent difficult as well. But what if we had neither of those—neither governments with laws and police nor people brought up to be decent and civil?

Hobbes's claim to theoreticians' fame is very strong, though the relation of his actual arguments to the more fundamental game-theoretical reasoning of contemporaries is inferential and conjectural, of course, rather than explicit—because game theory didn't come into existence as a formal study until the mid-20th century. The nub of the matter is this: Hobbes, appealing strictly to individual deliberative practical reason, and in a quite uncontroversial understanding of reason, develops a picture of how things would be in the absence of the state—awful, he holds. He then asserts a "Law of Nature" with a number of subordinate laws (which should count as theorems rather than further laws, since he claims, plausibly, that all the later ones follow from the first one), according to which rational men will seek peace. However, in the absence of the state, he argues, peace will be unavailable. So rational men will create the state, granting authority to a government whose laws will then inherit the authority of the Law of Nature. It's a brilliant idea—if it works. Whether it works—and, if not, then what if anything might work instead—is the question.

The Baseline Issue: States of Nature and Others

If we are to deal with one another in the game theorist's way, we need to reckon our gains and losses from some point of departure. If we think in terms of a "grand social theory," one that shows how morality derives (perhaps evolves) from a previous condition in which it did not obtain, then the natural thought is to start with the "natural condition of mankind"—Hobbes's words, which we now normally rephrase as the "state of nature." What Hobbes very famously claims is that in this "natural" condition, people will perceive that they have no protection against the violence of others and will turn to it themselves, in self-defense if nothing else, and we will thus have the terrible condition he describes as a "war of all against all."

Several questions arise about this idea, of which two are especially pertinent here. First, the phrase "natural condition of mankind" could refer to a hypothetical historical condition. If so, which condition? We can discuss that in tandem with the second question: Is the "of nature" component specifically *political*, as Hobbes tends to treat it? Or is it *moral*? The correct answers to these questions, I will here suggest, are that the condition in question need not be historical, and that it must be moral rather than specifically political. To explain:

If the idea was to tell a sort of universal history of prehistorical man, then the Hobbesian project runs into heavy weather. For anthropologists overwhelmingly agree that most primitive human communities do *not* have governments, strictly speaking.[3] And yet, contra Hobbes, they *do* have (rudimentary) moralities, and moreover are predominantly peaceable. Locke, in short, is more nearly correct than Hobbes. To argue for the necessity of *government* as the needed specific remedy, the case must be refined, as by George Klosko[4]—and will be controversial.

[3] Carles Boix, *Political Order and Inequality: Their Foundations and Their Consequences for Human Welfare* (New York: Cambridge University Press, 2015).

[4] George Klosko, *Political Obligations* (New York: Oxford University Press, 2005).

But the argument can be reformulated in a much more powerful and fundamental way. We can imagine, without having to theorize very much, how social life might be if we were devoid of any sense of morality. As Hobbes puts it, "The notions of Right and Wrong, Justice and Injustice, have there no place." He does indeed go on to say,

> Where there is no common Power, there is no Law; where no Law, no Injustice. It is consequent also to the same condition, that there be no Propriety, no Dominion, no *Mine and Thine* distinct; but only that to be every man's that he can get; and for so long, as he can keep it.[5]

But note that those inferences are not *consequent*, as Hobbes has it, of the "natural condition": they are, rather, a *definition* of that condition. We are not surmising how things might be, but drawing attention to certain familiar features of social life that we can—with effort—imagine away, and then plausibly see that such a social condition would be so difficult to imagine as to be all but impossible. The "natural condition" is that in which no widely recognized social *rules* as yet exist.

And what would be the problem? Here, Hobbes puts his finger on it: the basic problem is *violence*. It is certainly not the absence of a state, with its infinite further potential for more violence. People *can* often gain (or suppose they can gain) by taking advantage of others, taking their possessions or their very lives to serve our own purposes. How are we to prevent such things? The beginning of an answer, at least, is to adopt *rules*—literally to

[5] Hobbes, *Leviathan*, chap. 14, p. 105.

rule them out. Instead of evaluating our actions purely in terms of their likelihood of advancing our ends, we instead ask what our fellows *have reason to put up with* from us, and we from them. And to this, Hobbes has a brilliantly simple answer: we are to go for peace, not war; the methods of war (violence) are to be reserved for defense, against those who refuse to respect others. All else is peace, which is simply the absence of war.

The Here and Now

What's going on here? And especially, how does this apply, not in the hypothetical vacuum we have imagined, but in daily life *now*? Although this is a question leading to many complications, there is still a relatively plausible and straightforward way of working out the implications of Hobbes's idea.

First, we are not in the primitive "state of nature." We confront each other against the background of much that we agree on.

In the here and now, we will face, roughly, two sorts of people: (a) peaceable ones who are ready to respect the lives, persons, liberties, and properties of others; and (b) people who are ready to "invade and despoil," to use Hobbes's colorful language—that is, to cheat, lie, steal, and perhaps inflict physical wounds or even death in order to get their way. What do we do about the latter? How do we behave toward the former?

Answering the second question is easy: they respect our persons, we respect theirs. The first three Hobbesian Laws say, essentially:

1. *Don't* make war on the peaceable, but be peaceable in return (and *do* feel entitled to counter violence with defensive measures, possibly including violence, in return).

2. *Don't* "reserve liberties for yourself that you won't grant to others." So insofar as we have agreed rules among us, do what those rules call for; and insofar as we don't, then seek out those with whom you would like to cooperate more substantially than just by refraining from killing or damaging them, and work out the agreements you want. Thus, for example, we can buy and sell in the "marketplace"—stores, real estate, and all the myriad services of modern life, where we can "pay our money and take our choice." Here, it is a matter of understanding the terms and living up to them. And so:

3. In general, we are to *keep our agreements* when we make them. Note that there is no requirement to *make* any particular agreements. There is only the fundamental one that makes social life possible, as already sketched—the first Law, calling for peace. But if we do make a given arrangement with someone else, then we do have duties: we *owe* it to that person that we fulfill the terms, and the person *owes* it to us to do what has been agreed to. (The second and third Laws can be shown to be deducible from the first, but we won't pause to go through the exercise here.)

These are all precepts that are not normally difficult to interpret in modern life—with one very big class of exceptions: the "laws" of the states we live in. Now here, the problem is that we did *not* agree, in any detail, to the vast majority of them and indeed, don't even know more than a tiny fraction of the thousands of laws our various levels of government have passed. When the power of the state has been employed to create a certain institution or set of ways of doing things, and we see serious defects and problems in the systems it has worked out—well, what now?

For by far most of us most of the time, that issue is dealt with by knuckling under, "sucking it up," and accepting, provisionally, the laws as they are in order to keep the authorities away, so far as possible, from our door. But clearly, we cannot, as did Hobbes, simply go along with the state's rules as if they were due to an agreement that we had really *made* with particular people to select one person or small group of persons as the "ruler," the authority on all details of our lives, followed by lifelong subordination to his decrees.

The moral status of the state is rendered a huge problem by its ambiguous status. Many, of course, talk as though what the laws of one's state say to do is actually, morally *right*. One can be forgiven for wondering whether those who say this have actually thought it through. We look at Nazi Germany, Stalinist Russia, pre-Civil Rights Alabama—and then into the myriad problematic cases in modern life. And we can hardly swallow the Hobbesian dictum, that what the government says *is* in effect, truly "law"—truly has the force of Hobbes's Law of Nature. "Like h--- it does!"—must be our reaction.

But because we do live here and because so many people do follow those rules, we by and large have to live *with* those rules and complain as best we can in letters to the editor, books and papers, public meetings, and so forth—those of us, that is, who live in the better contemporary states where we can do such things without serious consequences, such as jail terms or being poisoned by an agent of the government, or . . . and of course, vote in elections in hopes of improving things.

This short excursion on the state is simply intended to illustrate why there is a clear answer to our question of the status and character of any fundamental agreement: it is moral, *not* necessarily political. It underlies, is antecedent to, legislation and edict.

The "Circumstances of Justice"

Let's now go back to basics once more and ask, what is it about human life that makes the Hobbesian Laws of Nature so plausible as a set of rules for social living? This question is answerable, in general, and Hobbes and his successor Hume have worked out the answers with power and clarity. They are as follows:

1. The only possessors of rational decisionmaking powers via deliberation are individual persons.[6] Each person proceeds in the light of his or her *own* perceived interests (or "values"—for present purposes, the terms are the same) and powers. We choose among the options in action that our bodies, environments, and social circumstances make available, on the basis of our perceived, felt desires or interests, and try to do our best by them.

2. Those interests and powers are enormously variable from one to another. The *powers*, crucially, typically include

[6] We table here the large subject of animal life "below" the human level, where the massive barrier is at least that of ready communication. We, in general, simply cannot literally talk with animals, whereas we can literally talk with virtually any other adult humans, at least via fairly reliable translation. And if we can't even *make* an agreement with some animate being, there obviously isn't much of a case for requiring us to *keep* that agreement.

sufficient strength and will to inflict serious injuries on just about any of our fellows, along with much else. And our *interests*, given both our power and our environmentally available options, are such as to sometimes lead us into at least tentative conflict with at least some others.

3. We are all dependent on our physical environments for food, warmth (insulation from extreme heat), and (clean) air, at a minimum. Especially, the requirements of sustenance and rough ambient temperature control can be met only by eating enough of a certain range of organic material from time to time and by fashioning clothing and some sort of shelter. Nature doesn't take care of those requirements on its own: our exertions, and cognitive involvement, are needed as well.

   The requirements *can* lead humans into conflict, where, as Hobbes puts it, we both desire the same thing that we cannot both have ("have" enough of to keep us "content"); this is what it is to say that resources are "scarce." Crucially, however, our environmental situation is such that the human input to resources enables us, with suitable levels of cooperation *if* available, to expand supply to overcome these scarcities. Scarcity, in other words, is not fixed and zero-sum, but amenable to more or less control at the hands of humans—especially to cooperating ones.

4. Although all humans, probably, have *some* sympathies with others, most have relatively limited sympathy: when push comes to shove, we cannot expect people routinely to "love their neighbor."

5. And finally, morality is not "natural" either: at the least, not of sufficient natural power to cope with the potential difficulties stemming from the first four conditions.

These together show us that humans have something to gain from peaceable cooperation, and much to lose without it. Condition 3 especially, given the others, leads us to the brink—of war or peace. Which way shall we go? Hobbes, mankind in general, and libertarians in particular, say *peace* is the way to go. The output is "negative": "seek peace" means, simply, don't aggress, don't use violence; more generally, *don't* seek to make yourself better off *by* making some other people worse off. You may do that only if those people have already done something to merit defensive action by you.

Conversely, this fundamental rule does *not* immediately direct us to feed the starving, help the needy, or rescue the endangered. Whether and why those are things we ought to do are a matter for further inquiry. But whether we ought to kill people whenever it serves our interests is *not* a "further item." To keep that on your list of options is indeed to head us down the road to the "war of all against all." That we may make war on the warlike is rational. Making war on the peaceable, however, is another matter: even if it seems rational to do it, it is clearly not rational to subscribe to a general morality that allows it.

Note that contractarians are not saying that all rational persons will always be nice guys. We are saying that it is rational for people to publicly accept and support a general program of approval of the peaceable and disapproval of the warlike. The mark of acceptance of this is, first, that we live up to it by *being* peaceable; and, second, that we preach what we practice, encouraging others to be peaceable as well. Morality is partly action and partly promotion of an "agenda"—a program of public education, inculcation. Social contract proposes to identify a uniquely rational view of morality, one based on individual practical reason reacting to the fact of social life.

Self- and Other-Regarding Interests

The social contract theory is usually characterized as basing morality on "self-interest." That is a misunderstanding, and an important but also understandable one. Rational action consists in choosing the best means to one's own overall set of ends, indeed. But among those ends, are all of them exclusively concerned with the agent's *own* benefit? Certainly not. Typically, as has long been recognized (e.g., by Bishop Joseph Butler[7]), we have interests in various other persons, especially loved ones such as a spouse and children, but also friends, fellow workers in favored causes, and more. Indeed, people are often ready to make major sacrifices, including even of their very lives, for those persons. The idea that rationality as such is self-interested in the sense that words like "selfish" conjure up is quite mistaken.

What is not mistaken is that our interests are *ours*. A does not act in order to promote B's interests, or C's, but A's, even if A in fact chooses to promote the interest of B or C. That is the element of truth in the characterization.

---

[7] Joseph Butler, *Fifteen Sermons Preached at the Rolls Chapel* (London: J. and J. Knapton, 1726).

But social contract calls on us to adopt principles that would be acceptable to everyone, not just to oneself. And for that reason, morality cannot be devoted to any one person or proper subset of persons, such as the adherents of a particular religious outlook. And since any proposal by one person to promote the good of another would be contingent on that other's agreement, insofar as it figures as a *moral* requirement, the elements of regard for others in particular persons' outlooks do not affect the overall result. Just as I cannot simply give you a certain gift without your acceptance, so I cannot include you as a beneficiary of some provision in the social contract unless you are prepared to accept it.

Hopefully, this clears up the issue about self-interest. But it does raise a different and very important question: that of motivation. The question is, why would I accept a moral requirement that might sometimes require me to sacrifice some interest of mine? It is here that the social contract scores over all other theories about the foundations of morals. I accept such a requirement because if I don't, you and others will be at liberty to disregard it in your behavior toward me. If I feel free to murder you, then you are free to murder me. Am I ready to accept that implication? Not likely!

It is important that the answer could conceivably be yes. Every theory has to face the prospect that some people will claim to have no use for morality. With those people, all we can say is that we, the rest of mankind, are in principle *at war* with them—because they, after all, are at war with us. We can hope—and often really expect—that we will make life worse for such people. Social contract respects all interests that are compatible with the pursuit by others of their interests as well. Thus—and *only* thus—do we all get along, and progress, as a community.

Value Pluralism and the Social Contract

People differ. They differ in their physical and mental makeup, and that difference includes the particular profiles or complexes of values that they are inclined to pursue. This is *value pluralism*: recognition of the diversity of values among people. It is often called "moral pluralism," but that expression is ambiguous. The basic social contract is not plural, but unitary, the same for all—that is its point. It does not permit a variety of conflicting *moral* requirements. On the other hand, the lifestyles, practices, tastes, and pursuits of people—their "philosophies of life"—are indeed plural, and they are precisely what morality *does* permit. In a sense, we each have one such profile, a distinct particular profile unique to the individual. (To illustrate the point, your hunger is a desire for food in *your* stomach, not *mine*, even if the particular kind of food we desire is exactly the same. But of course, it is usually different in that way, too.)

Social contract is designed to accommodate the widest possible array of interests compatible with the pursuits of everyone else. Thus, for example, the tolerance for diverse sexual behaviors, or religious beliefs, and so much else, for which liberalism in general is noted, is part and parcel of the outlook of social contract. And that, in fact, is the source of its universality. Everyone has the same requirement: to refrain from *compelling* his or her fellows to conform to any particular lifestyle, religion, or whatever other element of values that individual is interested in. We may attempt to persuade by argument or by example, but we may not *force* others to do things *our* way.

Political or Moral?

As was noted earlier, the social contract tradition has mostly been expounded in specifically political terms. All of us, on that account, agree to accept one government—a monarch, in most versions until recently—and to live in accordance with that government's requirements. But then the question arises: Are you sure you'd want to go along with *that* ruler? Do we accept Adolf Hitler's rules? It is surely obvious that this is questionable in the extreme. Not just government, but *good* government, is surely what we'd choose if we had our choice. (Do we? That's actually a puzzle—see more below.) And that choice implies that we have some criteria for "good" government.

What is a government supposed to be trying to do that would make it choiceworthy? Any answer to that has to be a *moral* answer. We will all agree that what governments are for is *this* or *that*. Once we see that that's what the choice has to be about, it becomes obvious that social contract must be viewed in moral terms, rather than necessarily or specifically in political terms. It is a logically open question whether, in the words of Thoreau, "that government is best that governs not at all."[8] Government, if it is to be legitimate, must respect our rights. It is not the *source* of those rights, at base; instead, it is—if it's doing its job—obligated to protect them, for all of us.

---

[8] Henry David Thoreau, "Civil Disobedience," in *Collected Essays and Poems*, ed. Elizabeth Hall Witherell (New York: Penguin/Library of America, 2001), p. 203.

Morality

In order to determine whether government is moral, we first have to understand what the concept of morality entails.

Morality—Rational and Otherwise

So, what is morality? There are several types of answers to this rather ambiguous question. First, of course, morality is a social phenomenon: it is a community's set of generally accepted and generally imposed behavior controls. People address one another's actions and respond—verbally and otherwise—along certain general lines, varying from one community to another.

Second, morality may be thought of as a set of rules, requirements, and principles—expressed as "Such and such is right," or "You are to do so-and-so!"—where "you" is essentially everyone, and the people, the "we" who make the assessments and deliver the "commands," are, likewise, also pretty much everyone. However, we want to use the sense of morality as *that set of rules or principles, if any, that passes the tests of reason*: the philosophically best such set, rather than just any old set that people may happen to have. And here, "best" is—we hope—thought of as "true" were it not that the applicability of the notion of "truth" is one of the questions philosophers discuss, at length, in their reflections on the subject of morals. But all we need to mean is this: a "true" or "right" morality is the one that all rational individuals can accept as the general canon for regulating interpersonal relations.

Clearly, social contract, like the other prominent theories of the subject, is mainly an entry in the third category. Every moral philosopher supposes that the favored set of precepts he or she endorses is also found, at least in some measure, in actual practice. But in view of the diversity of moralities among human communities, this supposition can hardly be maintained in a very thorough way. Social contract, if I and my predecessors in this vein are right, will be reflected very widely in almost all communities, even if such moralities are found along with accretions whose credibility we may have our doubts about. Every community disapproves of sheer murder, even while practicing stoning of premarital lovers or women who expose more than two inches of ankle, and so on. Every community disapproves of lying and cheating, even though its leaders lie and cheat extensively. Much of everyday morality, especially when we move very far from the philosopher's home, doesn't fare too well at the court of reason. But this observation doesn't mean that moral theory is either pointless or impossible. Rational criticism is possible and is important.

Better for Everyone

Everyone has some idea of what's good or bad in the way of day-to-day life, some idea of what's better and what's worse. If, then, we ask what we would ideally like from our surrounding society, there's an obvious answer: each person, A, hopes that the actions of others that affect A will make for A's own good (meaning what that person fundamentally values) rather than the reverse. Of course, that conclusion means that others hope the same from A. And so an obvious thought about a proposed morality is this: Does it conduce to *everyone's* good? If so, then everyone would have reason to go along with it.

Utilitarianism is the theory that our actions—or at least our set of concrete moral rules—should as a whole conduce to the "maximum good" of society, where that is understood as the sum of goods and bads over the whole community. That definition of utilitarianism identifies a feature that makes the theory vulnerable, for it appears the theory could sanction the imposition of severe evils on *some* people in order to promote the good of some *other* people, so long as the number of the latter times the degree of good in question outweighs the weighted sum of evils to the former. So strong is this criticism that utilitarians are sure to devote a good deal of theorizing to show that the problem can somehow be avoided.

The social contract view, by contrast, does not have that particular problem. Because all have a veto, the basic rules do not sanction the evils of some as a price to be paid for the good of others. Either those sacrificed willingly go along, in which case they see the good of the others as part of their own good, or else they don't go along and the action is overruled.

Social contract, then, calls for rules such that they are expectedly *better for everyone*. But that approach is misleading too. Very few of any human actions literally affect everyone, or could. And all human actions, insofar as they are deliberate and intentional, work expectedly for the good of the agent, at least. No one could rationally insist on *universal* benefit from anyone. But we *can* insist on universal *nonharm* from everyone. Usually, harm to others is easy to avoid, whereas benefit for others is not so easy to achieve; nor do we have much motive to produce such benefit.

Rather, we seek our good and therefore would promote it in cooperation with others who seek theirs, and so we find ways in which to advance our benefit mutually: acts on each person's part that benefit some in some way and others in different ways, both being agreed upon by the other. In that way, we reconcile the diversity of human nature with the need for moral restraint. And this, we hold, is "the way to go" for society in general. If we insist only on refraining from intervening negatively in the lives of others, the way is open—in multifarious directions—for benefit to many. And because everyone is subject to both the same rule and the same general motivation, we can expect that the ideal of universal benefit is actually achievable—not a utopian dream, but an everyday expectation.

That is, it is so long as people are not malignant. But some of them are; against those, the theory insists on our universal right of defense—of and by oneself in the first instance, and in concert with our fellows who are under threat or are ready to help out in the second instance. What those who agree to nothing else agree to is disagreement—ruling nothing out. If they are dangers to others, then those others will perforce do their best to be at least similarly dangerous to them. They have, as we say, "asked for it." The only things we can rule out for society as a whole are things we each want to avoid on our own behalf.

The reason the object of the social contract is not in the first instance government becomes, as we reflect on it, clear, in two ways. In the first place, there are any number of governments, and nations to be governed. If there were a single supercontract, would its object be an ideal world government? Or would it underwrite every government there is, warts and all? The second has to do with contract. Morality is about peace, but government is about war—coercion, violence, social control. Agents of the state are of two types: Machiavellians or—far more frequently—dissemblers who claim that *they* are using all this coercion for excellent reasons, even as they line their pockets at our expense. The "agreements" governments want are not social contracts, but alliances with some other governments against still others, and agreements among potential friends who will assist in supporting this particular government's program of extraction.

Liberalism to Libertarianism

"Liberalism" is a much-discussed and much-contested notion. Much of the discussion, however, is due to lack of definition—even an insistence that clear definition is impossible. But a reasonably clear, fairly definite understanding of the idea enables us to make sense of it and to see what's right about it. It goes as follows:

Liberalism is exemplified by normative systems that hold two points: (a) that the sole acceptable purpose of rules, laws, and in general interventions must be the *good of those intervened upon*; and (b) that it is those persons themselves, rather than any supposed authorities, who fundamentally embrace those values. Individuals, then, are the basic holders of the values that interventionist institutions and personages are to respect. (We might say that they are the "originators" of value, but that statement is misleading and gets us into unnecessary metaethical discussions.) Both are essential. So-called liberals of the present day tend to think that they, the pundits or the theorists or the elected politicians, know what people want better than those people themselves.

On the first point, liberals contrast with Thrasymachus in Plato's *Republic*, who declares for Kleptocracy: the purpose of government, says he, is to extract the maximum from the governed. Government is for the sake of the governors, rather than the governed.

The second contrasts with Plato himself and with all whom we may refer to as "conservatives" (a term whose popular usage is related to but not identical to this) who would insist that someone else knows what's good for us better than we do. Our good is not what *we* say, but what *he* (or *it*, where "it" refers to some supposedly authoritative institution or group) says.

The liberty and dignity of the individual follow from those two basic features. And they, in turn, lead to the social contract theory. For if we each fundamentally pursue our own values, and yet we wish the protection of restrictions against the interventions of others, then we shall have to secure them on the basis of mutually agreeable arrangements: those that leave each of us better off and no others worse off. And by far the main respect in which we can expect this improvement is to forgo the method of promoting our benefit that consists in forcibly extracting it from others. Not, then, imposed slavery, but *free exchange*. That is libertarianism.

Libertarianism

To understand how the libertarian principle can be applied to social contract theory, we first need to clarify and define the basics of libertarianism.

Libertarianism: What and Why

The essence of libertarianism is that we declare peace: each person has a right to the *nonaggression* of others. So there is a general duty of nonaggression. (It is tiresome, but necessary, to remind readers that justified defensive actions are *not* "aggressive"—they are rational responses to others' aggressions.) Note that this security is not *based on* "self-ownership" as is often said; for it *is* self-ownership. To own oneself is to have the right to decide what one is going to do, which is the same as others being required to refrain from the aggressive interventions of others. But it *is* literally based on our capacity to promote our own good, plus the perceived capacity of others to interfere with that promotion, and of our own to interfere with theirs. Thus, we all benefit from mutual peace.

Pareto

The social contract presumes a general sort of equality. But it is not equality in the capacity to produce goods; it is, rather, a rough equality of broadly aggressive capabilities—of our capacities to make life worse for others. It is that capacity that is, socially speaking, our chief problem. And it is that that leads us to adopt the Pareto criterion of exchange. An exchange is said to be Pareto superior if at least one party is better off, and all others no worse. Of course, in a one-on-one exchange, *each* party acts to promote his *own* benefit, and so each is or at least supposes himself to be better off as a result. But meanwhile, there is everyone else, who possibly may be affected by our interaction. And social contract calls on us to respect all those other people's interests as well, namely, by not worsening them through our actions. And so social contract sanctions all and only transactions that leave at least some better off and none worse off than in the status quo before the exchange.

Our broadly Hobbesian perspective is that the fundamental beneficial exchange with all others is *peace for peace*—I don't harm you; you don't harm me—which is better for all than the "war of all against all," in which we cannot expect or rely on the forbearance of others. (It is also better than the war of some against some, if peace is possible.) Nothing about those exchanges, however, requires that the *degree* of benefit we might each obtain from a given exchange be "equal," if we can even measure the quantities whose equality is in question. It has been a stumbling block of utilitarianism since its inception that there is no obvious way to come up with an interpersonally valid such "measure." But that we each, subjectively estimating our situations, reckon that we will improve our lives from the transaction, is by comparison not generally difficult—indeed, the sheer fact that each party voluntarily accepts it is taken to be presumptively sufficient reason to suppose this. Importantly, we can come up with evident, socially transmissible ways of indicating our assent to proposed arrangements. All we need on that score is effective communication. We come up with the language of promises and contracts to do the job, and it generally works. (Where it breaks down, we will need means of negotiation and adjudication to settle possible disputes.)

Rights, Right, and the General Right of Liberty

To say that someone, A, has a "right" is to envisage that there is someone else, B, upon whom this right of A's imposes a duty, which is a *cost* to those upon whom it is imposed. Note that that's *all* that rights are: duty imposers. A supposed right that imposes *no* restrictions on anyone, such as Hobbes's so-called right of nature, is simply not a right at all. Rights, like morality in general, are about our interrelations: people relating to each other. If some theorist purports to be asserting rights of animals, canyons, and so on, what he is attempting to do is to impose duties on *us*. Canyons and seals cannot speak for themselves, and from the viewpoints of those of us who don't see any benefit in accepting the proposed rights of canyons or seals, the advocate has an uphill battle. And since the social contract is strictly notional—it is not a political convention—and everyone has a veto, it's a lost battle at the level of fundamental rights, which is what we seek here. If animals are to have rights, that will have to be well downstream.

Where it is proclaimed that someone has a fundamental *moral* right, B is *everyone else*. Moral rights are rights of everyone against everyone. Libertarianism's proposed fundamental right is that of peace from all others, that is, their refraining from aggressions. Refraining from aggressions is a cost to them insofar as they suppose they might benefit from such aggressions. To get a unanimous agreement of all with all, at least notionally, we therefore need to show that everyone does better on balance by accepting this cost in return for the benefits of security from the depredations of his fellows. What would make it worthwhile to accept this cost must be that peace is seen by the others as better than war. If they don't get it, then we will *of course* have war. That is the bottom line, and the respect in which Hobbes has the right idea. Social life with no constraints is dangerous and likely altogether unprofitable. With them, we can advance—together. Without them, we have the unhappy Hobbesian prediction: life devoid of the benefits of civilization and "nasty, brutish, and short."

And so we may as well admit that the general fundamental right of liberty is had by all and *only* all those for whom peace is preferable to war. We can argue that this liberty is for literally everybody, but against those advancing with guns, argument will have to wait. Still, it is arguable that a consequence of this statement is that immorality as a live option is going to be less profitable as military technology and social organization advance. One hopes that the war of all against all will become, as time goes on, the war of some few against all the rest of us—and, frankly, that we who prefer longevity, comfort, and interesting lives will win.

In going for the simplest principle—Hobbes's first Law of Nature, calling for peace and the renunciation and proscription of wars of aggression—we adopt the rationally most plausible basic morality.

Liberty and Property

Libertarian, and classical liberal, thinkers have been distinctive in proclaiming a right of *property* as part and parcel of the basic array of moral rights to which we should all be entitled. For example, in Locke's version, the Law of Nature calls upon all "not to harm another in his life, health, liberty, or property."[9] (A careful analysis will show that his law is equivalent to Hobbes's first Law as well, but we needn't pursue that here.) What we do need to pursue, however, is his fourth entry, which raises many eyebrows. The basic right of peace is easily seen to forbid attacks on our persons, yes—but why on our *properties* as well? Of course, Locke

[9] John Locke, *Second Treatise of Government* (North Carolina: Hayes Barton Press, 2006 [1690]), sect. 6, p. 8.

rightly points out that our properties include, indeed start with, our *selves,* a claim that, as pointed out earlier, is really equivalent to the liberty principle itself. But external property? Houses, cars, TV sets? Coal mines? 747s? How do those items make it into the protected set?

The beginning of wisdom here is to appreciate that an attack on your property *is* an attack—an attack on *you.* If you try to defend against my attack, then I have to attack not your TV set but your person. The question then becomes, why should you give in to my attacks rather than defend? For that is what a denial of property rights amounts to.

The answer is in the main also supplied by Locke, but as this is not a history of the subject but a theoretical exposition, we won't pursue exegesis here. Instead, we follow the customary division of how we "acquire" things. A can avail himself of *x* for his own use by (a) simply finding it, being there, occupying it (as when it's a bit of land); or (b) by *making x,* in which case it would be requisite that the stuff he makes it out of is also somehow his rather than someone else's; or (c) someone else, B, could just give *x* to A, out of love, say. And then (d) A could get *x* by exchange: A previously has *y,* B has *x,* each would prefer what the other now has to what he or she has, and so they make an agreed exchange. This exchange transfers the property from one to the other in a completely peaceable way. And finally, of course, (e) A might just take it from B. But this fifth way, we hold, is excluded by our principle. The question is, how?

And the short answer is that what is here called "theft," or more accurately *dispossession against the will of the previous possessor* is a case of aggression, because aggression is intervention, against his will, into the life and activities of another person in a way that leaves him worse off. (The liberal idea entitles us to take it that "leaving B worse off" and "against B's will," for such cases, are equivalent, noting that B is always free to change his mind about what is to his benefit.)

Aggression is "making war"—just what the Hobbesian-libertarian principle forbids. If x is previously within B's "possession," *and* it came to be so without any previous aggression by B against anyone else, then forcibly separating x from B is wrongful—a violation of B's right.

Most humans are sympathetic. If the person who attacks us is, say, in desperate need, most of us are ready to help. But we aren't ready to simply turn over our valued and legitimately obtained things (e.g., our incomes) to all comers. And the libertarian principle says that we may not be *forced* to do so at all. In this, the libertarian differs radically from every other political and moral orientation.

A Brief Note about Socialism

A comparison with what we may very broadly term "socialist" theories is useful here. The libertarian principle differs from any socialist idea in the following way. Socialisms in general proclaim *egalitarianism,* in the sense that nobody is to be able to advance *more* than anyone else: the condition of progress for A is that A shares it with B, C, and so on, in a supposedly "equal" degree—of course, thereby inheriting the classic problems of measurement of utilities that has plagued utilitarianism from the start. And so, in its political-economic version, socialists call for appropriation by agents of the public for "redistribution" along the particular egalitarian line being pressed by the version in question—for example, "from each according to his ability, to each according to his need."

By contrast, libertarianism permits any action of A's that advances A's well-being, so long, merely, as it does not *thereby worsen* B's. Particular actions, or specific programs of action, need not literally improve the situations of all, or even anyone other than the individual actor (or whoever that actor is trying to benefit). So consider the hypothetical desperate person described earlier: do we harm him by refusing to help? No. We do not make that person worse off than in the status quo, in which the individual is already desperate. After our refusal, the person is still desperate. But, of course, we meanwhile might have offered a paying job or temporary aid until the person gets on his or her feet. We might even have persuaded a great many people to join in an insurance network to alleviate just such cases.

But the fundamental social contract does in another way meet the egalitarian criterion as stated and, libertarians hold, meets it *better* than any socialism: we are all better off *having libertarian morality in place*, even if we are not necessarily all better off from anyone's doing any particular right action. The reason is that in our hypothetical prior condition of total amorality, people are not forbidden to harm others in any number of ways, including killing.

Clearly, to live in a society where nobody kills is a big improvement. If everyone's having an internalized inhibition against such killing serves in fact to prevent those killings, then having a morality, which is essentially a set of internalized inhibitions, will lead to the safer condition in question. And that is a major improvement. Moreover, says the libertarian—contrary to what you might think—we are all better off living under the libertarian principle than under any seemingly more "generous" principle. A society where we are compelled to do much for others, even when it leads to no benefit to ourselves or those we care for, is more onerous than one in which we are all free to help as much as we care to, but also not to help if we don't care to (not, it should be noted, free from the frowns of others, but free at least from their swords and chains). Whereas, as history so resoundingly attests, societies imposing huge burdens on all remain or become poor—so poor that their typical citizens are worse off than the beggars in free societies. The impositions of welfarist moralities ring hollow—just like the promises of politicians, with which we are all familiar.

"Luck" Egalitarian Libertarianism

Some theorists have argued that because we cannot possibly have *made* the set of natural resources upon which we ultimately draw to make into usable goods to enhance our conditions, then we should take the view that those basic resources are, somehow, *public property*. (Locke himself begins that way, immediately recognizing that so to regard it poses a major problem for any ideas of legitimate acquisition by individuals.) The "luck" egalitarian/libertarian's idea is that we should distribute the value of undeveloped natural resources equally among all, in the interests of fairness, but above that, it's free market all the way. What we cannot do is agree with, for example, the Sharia whose "whole package [according to an Islamic spokesman] would include free housing, food, and clothing for all, though of course anyone who wished to enrich himself with work could do so."[10]

After all, the luck egalitarian reasons, none of us can have done anything to deserve whatever assets we may have, or that our environments offer, by nature. Before we are born, there is no "we" to have done any deserving, and after, it is too late: here we are, having emerged from this particular womb, in this particular natural and social environment, none of which could have been our doing. So how can we "deserve" it?

Now, one may be tempted to go from "no one deserves it any more than anyone else" (which is surely true) to "so it should go equally to all" (which is clearly not). But the reasoning is fallacious. If the idea is that it is a necessary condition of one's legitimately having x that one *deserves x*, and it is then observed that at the outset, *no one deserves anything*, then what should be equally distributed is not *everything*—it's *nothing*. And that way lies madness. And after that, it is but a quick step to realize that we should be regarded as *entitled* (to use Robert Nozick's nice distinction) to whatever just is part of us or attached to us or in whatever way "given" to us by nature or, by our own efforts, somehow carved out of or extracted from nature. For to deprive us of what we possess—however we came to possess it so long as it was not by violence—is to aggress against us. And that deprivation, to remind yet again, is precisely what is forbidden by the basic Law.

---

[10] Quoted by Graeme Wood in "What ISIS Really Wants?" *Atlantic*, March 2015, p. 86.

(Note: one could have been given by nature some horrible physical malady, say. Some of Nature's endowments we would be glad to be without. Forbidding others from taking *those*, if they could, would be otiose.)

Have-Nots? Free Markets on Poverty

Especially here in the Wealthy West, many wring their hands over the plight, as it may be, of their country's or the world's poor. And they ask how those poor are to be ministered to in the absence of state assistance. There are two excellent responses to this, plus a very fundamental third.

1. It is not obvious that the better-off *owe* anything to the poor; if anything, it is pretty obvious that they don't. For it is not the activities of the relatively wealthier that have *made* the poor poor. Bad government, bad luck, and various sheer circumstantial factors account for nearly all cases.

2. By this time, most of the world's poor are poor because of the incursions of governments, usually military—either their own or neighboring ones. Obviously, the first thing to do is to get those armed men off their backs—however that's to be done.

3. State largess is always extracted from taxpayers, many of whom will always be unwilling. A noncoercive solution is always to be preferred. And such a solution is essentially universally available: the poor are ready to work for lower wages, making profitable interaction with them a live option. Whenever world politics *permits* such beneficent

"exploitation," we can expect it to happen. And that will certainly solve the problem, just as it has in the wealthy countries already, as for example in modern China, which has, after abandoning the absurdities of Maoism, effectively embraced market solutions, raising the living standards of a half billion or more from dire poverty to Asian-standard middle class in a very few decades—something that socialism showed no potential whatever for accomplishing.

We add that poverty in the "rich" nations is trivial compared with that in Africa and South Asia. Yet those unfortunate nations are also coming along, despite their desperately awful governments. Those fortunate areas whose governments have reasonably free-market sympathies—South Korea, Singapore, Hong Kong—are far above the levels endured by the citizens of, say, North Korea. They indeed have joined the world's rich economies.

This is the *ultimate* solution to "poverty." Handwringing and sponging off taxpayers are not. We, of course, should and do regard it as a virtue to be helpful to others, including the poorly off, who are naturally likely to be prime candidates for philanthropic assistance. But such assistance is necessarily temporary and occasional—especially useful in response to disasters such as tsunamis and earthquakes. Otherwise, however, the market is our fundamental and sufficient recourse. The poor we need *not* "always have with us"—unless you insist on counting as "poor" those in the lower tenths or fifths or whatever of the actual income distribution, whatever it is. But to do that, however politically popular, trivializes the problem insofar as it is one.

Conclusion

Social contract is misconstrued as an agreement among a particular set of people to establish a government. Properly viewed, as an account of the underlying rationale and genesis of morality, it is the fundamentally rational approach to that subject and, in consequence, to that of government. It is so because it accounts for—derives—morals from the very general facts of human nature and society, in terms comprehensible to all normal people. It proceeds from the obvious premise that we are all possessed of interests and abilities, that we live among others of broadly similar situation in those respects, and that we can communicate and achieve cooperative solutions to serious problems of supply. No other moral theory does so without resorting to mysteries and opacities. And the most natural and obvious reading of our situations impels us to the libertarian view as our fundamental moral outlook. It is that basis that enables us to make progress in social life. No more can reasonably be asked.

Rawlsianism

Kevin Vallier

John Rawls (1921–2001) was arguably the most important political philosopher of the 20th century. His systematic works, *A Theory
of Justice* and *Political Liberalism*, set the stage for myriad debates
within political philosophy.[1] The books also staked out a form of
liberal egalitarianism. Although Rawlsians and libertarians agree on
the basic priority of certain core liberal rights, such as freedom of
speech and freedom of religion, they disagree *dramatically* on the
scope of economic liberties. Rawlsians argue that only the freedom
to choose one's occupation and the right to own personal property
(not capital goods) are fundamental liberties that states must protect.

Libertarians and classical liberals adopt a much broader scheme
of rights, including the right to set one's own prices for goods and
services, the right against government regulation, the right to freedom of contract, and the right to own and operate private capital.

---

[1] John Rawls, *A Theory of Justice* (Cambridge: Harvard University Press, 1999); *Political Liberalism*, expanded ed. (New York: Columbia University Press, 2005).

So what is a chapter on Rawls doing in a book on arguments for libertarianism? The answer is that Rawlsian arguments can be used to defend classical liberalism. In fact, there are two distinct, contrasting, and somewhat incompatible methods of grounding classical liberal institutions in Rawlsian political philosophy. The two methods strongly correlate with the lines of reasoning in Rawls's two books, *A Theory of Justice* and *Political Liberalism*. John Tomasi uses the framework of *A Theory of Justice* to defend what he calls "free-market fairness," which differs from Rawls's theory, "justice as fairness," by expanding the list of economic liberties to include those celebrated by classical liberals. In contrast, Gerald Gaus has pursued the line of argument Rawls set out in *Political Liberalism*. Gaus offers a strong defense of markets within the Rawls-inspired "political liberal" or "public reason liberal" framework.

In this chapter, I will focus on explaining both the Tomasian and Gausian defenses of classical liberalism by comparing them with Rawls's approaches in *A Theory of Justice* and *Political Liberalism*, respectively. Tomasi more directly follows Rawls, whereas Gaus's early versions of public reason liberalism predate *Political Liberalism* but show strong similarities with the Rawlsian approach. Toward the end, I will explore their compatibility. Importantly, I will *not* review libertarian criticisms of Rawls's position. The goal of this chapter is strictly limited to using Rawlsian tools to justify libertarian institutions.

I proceed in five parts. The first reviews the basic features of Rawls's project in *A Theory of Justice*, and the second explains

Tomasi's defense of classical liberalism that revises this project. The third section reviews the basic features of Rawls's transition to *Political Liberalism* and the idea of public reason. The following section outlines the more complex Gausian defense of classical liberalism based in public reason liberalism. In the last section, I offer an argument favoring the Gausian defense, but I also argue that Gaus's theory permits Tomasi's free-market fairness to be the correct theory of justice and to form a basis for political activism in a publicly justified polity.

Rawls's Project in *A Theory of Justice*

Rawls is well known for his prominent role in reviving social contract theory in the United States in the late 20th century. His work followed—and helped displace—nearly a century of political thought, which included, prominently, both utilitarian and Marxist views.

Rawls argues that a society is just when its basic structure is regulated by principles that would be selected through a thought experiment. He imagines people in an "original position," tasked with choosing between different principles of justice. Their choice is constrained by the "veil of ignorance," which denies them information that could bias their selection of principles in ways that we would normally regard as inappropriate, such as drawing on one's race or class. The principles of justice selected will form the rules for distributing what Rawls calls "primary goods" or goods that any person with a rational plan of life would want, such as rights, liberties, income, and wealth. These goods include (a) basic rights and liberties, (b) freedom of movement and free choice among a wide range of occupations, (c) the powers of offices and positions of responsibility, and (d) income and wealth. More elusively, Rawls includes among primary goods (e) the social bases of self-respect, which he understands as "the recognition by social institutions that gives citizens a sense of self-worth and the confidence to carry out their plans."[2]

Critically, Rawls's veil of ignorance prohibits people from choosing conceptions of justice based on deep features of their identities that do not ordinarily seem inappropriate bases for determining what justice requires. For instance, Rawls denies that persons could appeal to their conceptions of the good, such as one's worldview or religion, in selecting principles of justice.

More radical still, Rawls denied that people in a just society could appeal to their natural talents, such as a person's mathematical or musical ability, to claim a greater share of primary goods. For instance, Jane may not claim a larger share of primary goods even if she produced a surplus of goods by using her natural talents. Imagine that Jane invents a computer program that substantially reduces her firm's costs, and that invention leads to her securing a higher income from her job. In Rawls's view, although a society's particular constitution or laws may allow her to keep her income, she has no *basic right* to it in virtue of using her natural talents. The reason is that natural talents are undeserved. Rawls claims that the distribution of natural talents is arbitrary from a

---

[2] John Rawls, *Justice as Fairness: A Restatement*, ed. E. Kelly (Cambridge, MA: Harvard University Press, 2001), pp. 58–59.

moral point of view, meaning that natural talents are distributed by nature at random, and so not in accord with justice or equity. This latter claim has raised libertarian hackles, and rightly so, but the two versions of Rawls-inspired classical liberalism show that the Rawlsian framework can progress even if Rawls's position on natural talents is mistaken.

Central to Rawls's theory is that the parties in the original position are *not* real-world persons. Instead, their choice is a *model* of the process of reflective equilibrium, where persons theorize together in order to harmonize their considered judgments about the requirements of morality and justice. What the parties choose is therefore the best way, or one of the best ways, to identify the conception of justice to which real-world persons are *rationally committed*. Rawls's is not a hypothetical consent theory of politics, where the justification of political order is rooted in what persons *would* agree to under certain conditions but that they have *not in fact* agreed upon. For Rawls, no important normative claim is made true by the consent of hypothetical persons. Instead, hypothetical consent is a *heuristic* for identifying principles of justice that render the broadest, most coherent explanation of the moral and political judgments we share.

When parties choose, their choice is both rational and *reasonable* in the sense that their choice both follows the canons of rational choice and is suitably impartial or unbiased. Also note that the parties do not choose for *us*. Instead, they choose principles to govern a well-ordered society, which models persons *like us* living under favorable conditions. Once the parties select principles of justice, Rawls argues that the principles must be tested against a psychologically and sociologically realistic model of society to see whether the rules can self-stabilize among persons disposed to be just.

Rawls wants to ensure that normally functioning persons can come to comply with the principles of justice because they will recognize doing so as *good for them*. Only then will principles of justice comport with our pretheoretical expectation that the true principles of justice be ones that can survive public scrutiny. Just institutions, that is, need not hide their normative basis. People should be able to access the foundations of their institutions and abide by them on the basis of approving those foundations, given their conception of justice and the good.

The basic idea is that the correct principles of justice should promote social stability in a public fashion, in contrast to views, like utilitarianism, that may require that governments hide their utilitarian principles so as not to discourage citizens from complying with governmental dictates. So again, Rawls's construction does not involve parties choosing principles for us. Instead, the construction attempts to locate principles of justice that satisfy our considered judgments about justice, both our substantive judgments about what is and is not just, and our procedural judgments about the nature of justice, such as whether institutionalizing justice will be stable for normally functioning human beings.

Libertarians sometimes mistakenly construe Rawls as a hypothetical consent theorist. This has led to much confusion. As we can see, Rawls's real view is different, richer, and more plausible.

Rawls then argues that parties will choose two principles of justice, known together as "justice as fairness":

First Principle: Each person has the same indefeasible claim to a fully adequate scheme of equal basic liberties, which scheme is compatible with the same scheme of liberties for all.

Second Principle: Social and economic inequalities are to satisfy two conditions:

1. They are to be attached to offices and positions open to all under conditions of *fair equality of opportunity.*

2. They are to be to the greatest benefit of the least advantaged members of society (the *difference principle*).[3]

The parties choose these principles because the principles will protect and promote the parties' capacity to exercise their two moral powers: their power to be rational and their power to be reasonable. The first moral power is exercised when people form a rational plan of life, whereas the second power is exercised when people formulate and live out a conception of justice.

The first principle ensures that people will be able to claim and exercise the basic liberties required to exercise their two moral powers, by protecting freedom of speech, religion, and press, among others, and by protecting procedural rights, like the right to a fair trial. Citizens must also have the means to realize the "worth" of those liberties, that is, to be able to exercise them in meaningful

---

[3] Ibid., pp. 42–43 [emphasis added].

ways on a regular basis. This principle has lexical priority over the second principle; the second principle never overrides the first.

The second principle ensures that people will be able to enjoy the worth of those liberties on equal terms. Fair equality of opportunity protects against the dominance of any one social group, whereas the difference principle ensures that even the poorest have access to the primary goods necessary to exercise their two moral powers.

Importantly for the entire project, Rawls claims that choice based on our two moral powers derives from our *shared conception of the person*. Reasonable people have different views about what the human person is, but they agree on at least some common features, and those common features form the basis of the Rawlsian project.

Notice how egalitarian Rawls's theory of justice is. Yes, Rawls protects a great many liberties as strongly as he can. But his list of liberties includes only two economic liberties: the right to freely choose one's occupation and the right to own personal property. That means that the state may not order persons to perform jobs; neither may it expropriate the personal—that is, noncapital—goods of persons. But *no* other economic liberties are protected. Therefore, in principle, a Rawlsian can support *vast* amounts of government redistribution, regulation, and even socialist economic production.

Regarding the second principle, libertarian discussions of Rawls's view have tended to focus on the difference principle. But the fair equality of opportunity is in many ways more egalitarian, and it is *lexically prior* to the difference principle in that conflicts between the two principles must *always* resolve in favor of fair equality of opportunity.

Fair equality of opportunity, for Rawls, means that social inequalities can be justified *only* if they promote fair equality of opportunity. The *only* reason the state may allow you to become wealthy, influential or, powerful is if you do so under a system of rules that promotes *equal* opportunity for everyone. Your unequal wealth, influence, and power—no matter how nobly and virtuously achieved or deserved—can be *eliminated*, even if it arises within a social system that *provides great but unequal opportunities to everyone*. Unless the opportunities are equal, they are unjust. Rawls allows but one exception: opportunities used to make the least well-off better off.

The difference principle is, in my view, a bit milder. It requires that inequalities of primary goods maximize the position of the least advantaged members of society. Again, even if you acquire more wealth through productive activities that benefit everyone and exploit no one, the state is not morally required to protect that wealth. Your efforts leading to inequality must occur within a system of rules that *maximize* the position of the least advantaged members of society. Few theories of distributive justice are more egalitarian.

The institutional implications of Rawls's position are similarly egalitarian. Rawls reviews five regime types: (a) laissez faire capitalism with a social minimum (such as a guaranteed minimum income), (b) a capitalist welfare state (with more extensive social insurance, regulation, and government power), (c) property-owning democracy (where the ownership of capital is constantly redistributed away from large capital holders), (d) liberal socialism (basic liberal rights plus government ownership of the means of production), and (e) command-economy socialism. Laissez faire fails to realize the principles of justice because it does not guarantee the ability of persons to enjoy the "worth" of their liberties, especially their political liberties, as the rich and powerful will dominate politics. Although welfare states do better on this score, they are also vulnerable to great political inequalities and so will be dominated by the rich. Command-economy socialism violates basic liberties, such as freedom of occupation. That leaves only property-owning democracy and liberal socialism, both of which involve enormous amounts of government intervention in the economy.

Rawls acknowledges economic problems for capitalism but ignores problems for property-owning democracy and liberal socialism. Capitalism falls victim to inequality, insufficiency, and allows the wealthy to rule. Property-owning democracy and liberal socialism can be assumed to work largely as they are intended. That is because Rawls's work is situated within ideal theory, where we choose a conception of justice for persons living under favorable conditions who are prepared to comply with their political institutions so long as others do likewise. Why Rawls didn't apply the same assumptions to his model of capitalism is an important question, one Tomasi tries to remedy.

In sum, justice as fairness appears to be both highly egalitarian and deeply statist.

Tomasi's *Free Market Fairness*

After all this, you must be wondering how Rawls's apparatus could be used to support libertarian positions. It's a good question.

I will set aside attempts to show that capitalism satisfies the difference principle better than socialism. Some have pursued this line of thought, arguing that the free market in fact maximizes, for instance, the wealth and income of the least advantaged. This is a shallow attempt to use Rawlsian ideas to justify libertarian conclusions. The fix is too easy. Instead, we need to consider again the basic motivations of Rawls's theory of justice and see whether they lead where he believes they do.

Enter John Tomasi's recent book, *Free Market Fairness*.[4] Tomasi takes on many features of Rawls's methodology of justice, such as original position reasoning and the veil of ignorance. He embraces ideal theory, arguing that identifying conceptions of justice requires finding a set of general principles to govern a well-ordered society. This is to say that a well-ordered society contains persons living under favorable conditions who are prepared to comply with a conception of justice. Tomasi also takes on many aspects of Rawls's conception of the person, though he describes that conception as a "responsible self-author," which is not the same. However, because Tomasi spends little time contrasting the two ideas, I will not explore the differences here.[5]

Tomasi also argues that parties will select basic liberties that are based on their shared conception of the person as a responsible self-author. Those basic liberties have a similar special priority over other considerations of justice. Tomasi's major departure from Rawls comes from the *list* of economic liberties he endorses.

---

[4] John Tomasi, *Free Market Fairness* (Princeton, NJ: Princeton University Press, 2012).

[5] Ibid., p. 94.

Tomasi accuses Rawlsian liberals of "economic exceptionalism" that singles out a few economic liberties for protection as basic rights. Tomasi's research program, *market democracy*, of which free-market fairness is a Rawlsian variant, does not endorse "absolute" property rights. Instead, it "affirms a thick conception of economic liberty as part of a broader scheme of rights and liberties designed to enable citizens to exercise and develop their moral powers."[6]

Tomasi's critique draws our attention to Rawlsian arguments for protecting a short list of economic liberties and then attempts to show that these arguments also support expanding the list. In other words, Tomasi claims that thick, libertarian-like economic liberties should be treated on a par with freedom of occupation and the right to own personal property. Tomasi argues, for instance, that if the right of occupational choice is a basic right, "it becomes unclear how the other liberties of working can be excluded."[7] Thick liberties of working include the rights to sell, trade, or donate one's labors. That is, persons have basic rights to determine the conditions of their working lives in general. The right to own productive property can also be justified on the basis of an analogy with the right to own personal property: both ownership rights "can provide a person with personal security" and can serve to express the owner's identity.

One of Tomasi's illustrations of that latter point is "Amy's Pup-in-the-Tub," a small business owned and operated by a woman in

[6] Ibid., p. 69.
[7] Ibid., p. 77.

the Rhode Island area, whose values are expressed in her work. Amy loves animals, especially dogs, and she derives great meaning from making her living caring for them. Tomasi also argues that people should be free to engage in "long-term financial planning" to avoid diminishing "the capacity of citizens to become fully responsible and independent agents."[8] So even persons whose values and commitments are not tied to their work should have the basic right to enjoy the fruit of that work, namely, their income.

Tomasi's second line of argument in defense of libertarian-like conclusions is that respect for responsible self-authorship requires a "distributional adequacy condition," where

> a defense of any version of liberalism is adequate only if it includes the claim that the institutions being endorsed are deemed likely to bring about some desired distribution of material and social goods.[9]

This condition could be egalitarian, if the distribution must satisfy some standard governing the "relative holdings of citizens" where some equalization is required by justice. But it could also be a sufficientarian view where the distribution must ensure that all persons have access to some minimum amount of resources.[10] Or the condition could require the maximization of available resources. Nonetheless, a distributional adequacy condition is required.

---

[8] Ibid., p. 81.

[9] Ibid., p. 126.

[10] Thus, "sufficientarianism" refers to a principle of justice that everyone be given *enough* resources to live minimally decent lives. Contrast this with egalitarianism, which requires equalizing resources even among persons who already have enough.

Lest you think Tomasi is rejecting libertarianism, Tomasi claims that nearly all historical classical liberals and libertarians *accept* a distributional adequacy condition and argue that free-market regimes satisfy the condition.[11]

Tomasi's third basis for classical liberal conclusions is his alteration of the traditional Rawlsian list of primary goods. Rawls argues that primary goods are all and only those essential for persons to develop and exercise the two moral powers that anyone would want no matter his or her rational plan of life. Recall that primary goods include rights and liberties, along with the social bases of self-respect. Thus, Rawls's second principle, which distributes primary goods, has a role in distributing basic rights, liberties, powers, and positions rather than, say, mere money.

However, Tomasi argues that the Rawlsian commitment to maximizing the share of primary goods enjoyed by the least advantaged is ambiguous between different lists of primary goods. Some lists will include major improvements to rights and liberties and minor improvements to the social bases of self-respect. Other indexes will choose the reverse. Some difference principle goods (DP goods, as Tomasi terms them), then, are *rivalrous*, and it is not clear how to trade them off.

Tomasi argues that, in some cases, reasonable people will prefer more wealth to more workplace democracy. That is, reasonable

---

[11] See Tomasi, *Free Market Fairness* (pp. 127–42) for a description of his "hit parade" review of major figures, such as Herbert Spencer, Milton Friedman, and F. A. Hayek, and contemporary libertarian political philosophers, such as Loren Lomasky and David Schmidtz.

people might prefer to have bosses but higher income, whereas others might prefer the reverse. If so, we must attend to levels of social wealth in maximizing the bundle of primary goods. And because, as Tomasi claims, capitalism is such an effective wealth generator, we have an argument that the difference principle requires capitalism (which is not the same as the easy-fix approach mentioned earlier). Tomasi does not mean to claim, however, that free-market fairness requires trading off rights and liberties. Instead, maximizing wealth helps the least advantaged enjoy their rights and liberties.

The alteration and development Tomasi proposes for the list of primary goods will alter the recommendations of the difference principle and fair equality of opportunity.[12] Rawlsian "high" liberals give pride of place to workplace democratic liberties among these goods, but Tomasi argues that free-market fairness focuses much more on the maximization of wealth, combined, perhaps, with a social minimum of some sort.[13] He claims that free-market fairness affirms traditional liberal ideals of formal equality of opportunity and, in doing so, holds that "every citizen, regardless of birth status or economic class, is owed high-quality health care and education as a matter of justice."[14]

[12] Tomasi also argues that Rawlsian emphasis on protecting political liberty can be turned to classical liberal ends, but for reasons of space, I omit that discussion.

[13] Samuel Freeman uses the term *high liberals* to describe social democratic and egalitarian liberals whose conception of liberalism is the most evolved and inclusive of the insights of the liberal tradition as a whole. See Freeman, "Capitalism in the Classical and High Liberal Traditions," *Social Philosophy and Policy* 28(2), pp. 19–55, 2011. Tomasi takes on Freeman's term in his work.

[14] Tomasi, *Free Market Fairness*, p. 241.

But Tomasi denies that justice must be carried out by the "direct" mode of social construction—the form of direct, deliberate government intervention that attempts to design social outcomes. Instead, classical liberals rely on an "indirect" mode of social construction that "emphasize[s] market mechanisms in pursuit of a superior system of education and health care for all."[15] The "market democratic strategy is to create systems with the maximum number of decision points."[16]

Finally, Tomasi uses Rawlsian ideal theory to show that free-market fairness, much like justice as fairness, implies ideal regime types, but ones *very* different from property-owning democracy and liberal socialism. The two regime types are "democratic laissez faire" and "democratic limited government." The former is more radically libertarian; Tomasi associates it with Murray Rothbard–esque opposition to state power.[17] Democratic laissez faire will involve quite limited government and seeks to use market mechanisms as often as it can to satisfy the abstract demands of free market fairness. It "marks the high point of optimism about market mechanisms (and skepticism about political decision making)."[18] Democratic limited government is weaker: although "enthusiastically capitalistic, this regime type allows a greater degree of direct government intervention in economic affairs."[19] Tomasi associates this view with F. A. Hayek and Milton Friedman.

[15] Ibid., p. 242.

[16] Ibid.

[17] This despite Rothbard's well-known hostility to democracy and despite his hostility to the state in general.

[18] Tomasi, *Free Market Fairness*, p. 116.

[19] Ibid., p. 117.

The point of ideal theorizing is twofold. First, it allows us to steer clear of the common failings of human beings that should not pollute our conception of justice, even if these failings should alter our institutional recommendations. Second, it allows us to see how our preferred institutional proposals link up with our commitment to justice under favorable conditions. Satisfying these two commitments allows ideal theorizing to give us inspiring ideals that can establish the moral superiority of some conceptions of justice over others. Many libertarians are wary of ideal theory, seeing it as an escape strategy for socialists. But Tomasi argues that ideal theory favors libertarianism[20]—an important twist.

The Turn to *Political Liberalism*

After the publication of *A Theory of Justice* (*TJ*), Rawls became increasingly convinced that the well-ordered society he described was "unrealistic."[21] In Part 3 of *TJ*, Rawls had assumed that members of a well-ordered society would agree on a partial conception of the good. Consequently, he could demonstrate that *TJ*'s notion of a well-ordered society is stable by showing that this partial conception of the good was congruent with justice as fairness. Such a society would be *inherently* stable because each person believes that compliance with institutions that manifest justice as fairness is compatible with his or her good and the good of others, and so compliance is the best response to the actions of others.

---

[20] Jason Brennan also argues that ideal theory vindicates libertarianism. See his *Why Not Capitalism?* (New York: Routledge, 2014).

[21] Rawls, *Political Liberalism*, p. xviii.

Rawls came to believe that citizens would share in the affirmation of those goods only if they had a shared conception of the person as a free and equal moral agent. But reasonable and rational persons might reject this conception of the person and so reject justice as fairness as an appropriate framework for regulating their behavior. Justice as fairness, therefore, would no longer be stable in the right way, as some agents would be practically rational to defect from the institutions that manifest justice as fairness. True, the state could forcibly impose justice as fairness on an unwilling populace, but Rawls thought that a conception of justice should receive the free support of its members, or else that conception had a significant flaw.

The problem faced by *TJ* is that its notion of a well-ordered society, one regulated by a conception of justice, allows for the free use of practical reason. People can reason freely about what is best and most important in life. But doing so leads people to affirm a variety of incompatible worldviews, philosophies, and religious beliefs. Some of the doctrines will reject justice as fairness and the conception of the person on which justice as fairness is based. And the people who hold those doctrines will begin to dissent from the social order that realizes justice as fairness, and their behavior will follow suit. Stability, therefore, will break down.

The breakdown of stability led Rawls to recast his theory. First, Rawls converted justice as fairness into a "political conception of justice"[22] whose conception of the *citizen* is "free-standing" from the details of the reasonable comprehensive doctrines prevalent

---

[22] Ibid., p. xlii.

in a well-ordered society. A political conception of justice must be compatible with each reasonable comprehensive doctrine so that an "overlapping consensus" can form around the political conception. An overlapping consensus occurs when all reasonable comprehensive doctrines in a society converge on or overlap on a political conception of justice.[23]

Rawls also relaxes the congruence relation. A citizen need not endorse a political conception of justice as part of his or her personal good. Reasonable positions need only be "congruent with, or supportive of, or else not in conflict with" political values, or the values that are part of a shared, political conception of justice.[24] In *Political Liberalism* (*PL*), stability, now called "stability for the right reasons" can occur even if diverse comprehensive doctrines merely fail to provide citizens with sufficient reasons to *reject* justice as fairness. In fact, justice as fairness need only "normally outweigh" each citizen's privately held doctrines and values.

To demonstrate that an overlapping consensus is possible, Rawls tries to show that persons share conceptions of *citizenship* and of political *society* regardless of their reasonable comprehensive doctrines. Reasonable people conceive of citizens as free and equal and of society as a cooperative venture for mutual gain. As a result of sharing those ideals, citizens will want to abide by principles that each reasonable person can accept. The implication of this motivation is that political justification takes the form

[23] Though in later work, such as the introduction to the paperback edition of *Political Liberalism*, Rawls allows an overlapping consensus to form around a set of reasonable liberal political conceptions. See p. xxvi.

[24] Ibid., p. 169.

described by Rawls's "liberal principle of legitimacy," which he defined as follows:

> Our exercise of political power is fully proper only when it is exercised in accordance with a constitution the essentials of which all citizens as free and equal may reasonably be expected to endorse in light of principles and ideals acceptable to their common human reason.[25]

By sharing political conceptions of the citizen and society, citizens of a well-ordered society should all be committed to the liberal principle of legitimacy, which says that state coercion can be justified only by reasons that draw on shared political values. In other words, reasons must be *public*. By using public reasons in discussions about justice and constitutional matters, citizens can assure one another that their political activities are compatible with their shared political conception of justice. Citizens are obliged to cooperate only when others do likewise, so they must have stable expectations that others are disposed to cooperate. The use of public reasons, by virtue of drawing on shared normative resources, becomes not only a sign of mutual respect but also a signal of mutual assurance. Rawls then specifies an ethics of citizenship that is based around his "duty of civility," which requires that citizens, when discussing constitutional essentials or matters of basic justice, offer public reasons for their positions.

The notions of a freestanding conception of the person, a political conception of justice, shared conceptions of citizenship and

---

[25] Ibid., p. 137.

society, the idea of an overlapping consensus, the importance of publicity and public reasons, and the duty of civility all flow from Rawls's attempt to outline the structure of a well-ordered society that is stable for the right reasons. The main ideas in *PL* and their motivation are now in view.

In Rawls's first versions of political liberalism, he assumed that persons endorse the *same* conception of justice, namely, justice as fairness. But the fact of reasonable pluralism, he would later admit, would also lead to reasonable disagreement about justice. Paul Weithman argues that this admission came long after he began to "recast justice as fairness."[26] Pluralism about justice, then, was not an important part of Rawls's political turn. But we shall see that justice pluralism *is* an important part of determining whether the framework of political liberalism is compatible with or even supportive of classical liberalism.

The reason for this is that, for Rawls's last formulations of political liberalism, he recognized that different *liberal* political conceptions of justice could be legitimate for a well-ordered society. Those conceptions must share a "criterion of reciprocity" in social cooperation and recognize the burdens of judgment, or the features of political and moral reasoning that lead rational and informed persons of goodwill to disagree on matters of fundamental import. The conceptions must also have three common features:

> First, a specification of certain rights, liberties, and opportunities (of a kind familiar from democratic regimes);

[26] Paul Weithman, *Why Political Liberalism? On John Rawls's Political Turn* (Oxford, UK: Oxford University Press, 2013), p. 7.

second, a special priority for these freedoms; and third, measures assuring all citizens, whatever their social position, adequate all-purpose means to make intelligent and effective use of their liberties and opportunities.[27]

Notice how broad that range is, at least in principle: Tomasi's free-market fairness fits within the range. Tomasi's view specifies the relevant rights, liberties, and opportunities and gives them lexical priority; and his distributional adequacy condition is meant to ensure that all citizens have access to means to make effective use of their rights and liberties. I suspect Rawlsians will find a way to deny that Tomasi's free-market fairness is a reasonable liberal political conception. But from what Rawls says, there are no grounds to rule it out. Not even *PL*'s special focus on political liberty can do so, as Tomasi draws on the value of political liberty to ground his case for classical liberal institutions. Perhaps Tomasi has the wrong conception of justice, but his view, on Rawlsian terms, is surely reasonable.

Rawlsians will object that Rawls rejected libertarianism in *PL* because it has "no special role for the basic structure" of society, where a basic structure is "a society's main political, social, and economic institutions, and how they fit together into one unified system of social cooperation from one generation to the next."[28] The problem with libertarianism is that it views the state as just one more "private association," and so there is "no uniform public law that applies equally to all persons, but rather a network of

---

[27] Rawls, *Political Liberalism*, p. xlvi.
[28] Ibid., p. 11.

private agreements."[29] In this way, libertarianism "rejects the fundamental ideas of the contract theory."[30]

I will not take on Rawls's criticism of Nozickian libertarianism here,[31] but it should be plain that some versions of libertarianism advocate a uniform public law applied equally to all persons and that makes a special place for the basic structure in its theory. Tomasi's view is one example, but so are most forms of constitutionalist classical liberalism, such as those advanced by Hayek and Friedman. So the Rawls of the later versions of *PL* is likely committed to the position that some forms of libertarianism are reasonable political conceptions of justice. That is an interesting and surprising result.

Gaus's *The Order of Public Reason*

Classical liberals can use Rawlsian tools to bolster the case for classical liberalism in light of Rawls's developments in *PL*. In fact, the line of argument flowing from *PL* concerning the implications of diversity and diverse reasoning may have strong classical liberal implications. Though, as the reader will discover, the reasoning can become subtle and complex.

In *The Order of Public Reason* (*OPR*), Gerald Gaus argues that impartial Kantian reasoning, such as Rawls's original position abstraction, cannot, by itself, generate a uniquely justified set of

---

[29] Ibid., p. 264.

[30] Ibid., p. 255.

[31] But for some of my discussion, see "The Later Rawls's Critique of Libertarianism," *Bleeding Heart Libertarians* (blog), August 3, 2012, http://bleedingheartlibertarians .com/2012/08/the-later-rawlss-critique-of-libertarianism/.

rules or principles, because of reasonable (what he calls "evalua-tive") pluralism. Gaus claims that we should "give up on the hope that we can construct a compelling description of members of the 'realm of ends' that will lead them to agree on the same rule."[32] Instead, we must allow extensive disagreement in personal judg-ments by acknowledging the existence of multiple "optimal eli-gible proposals." Impartial reasoning of the Rawlsian variety can establish only the boundaries of reasonable disagreement; it can-not yield a determinate choice of principles, like justice as fairness.

The bulk of *OPR* tries to explain how free and equal members of the public can converge on a determinate set of social rules. Gaus proceeds by drawing on the tradition of moral thought that stretches "from Hobbes through Ferguson, Hume, and Smith to F. A. Hayek and contemporary game theorists," all of whom claim, in one way or another, that "moralities are social facts with histories."[33] Morality, in this view, is the path-dependent output of cultural and moral evolution. Rawlsian impartial reasoning is indeterminate, so Gaus argues that social evolution is required to lead members of the public to converge on a member of the eligible set of proposals, those proposals for which no reasonable member of the public has sufficient reason to reject.

Importantly, Gaus uses original position reasoning because it helps evaluate whether the rules and principles we've converged on are justified. If we throw out a Rawlsian test of public justification,

---

[32] Gerald F. Gaus, *The Order of Public Reason: A Theory of Freedom and Morality in a Diverse and Bounded World* (New York: Cambridge University Press, 2011), p. 43.

[33] Ibid., p. 44.

"the evolutionary view cannot distinguish authoritarian from non-authoritarian positive moralities."[34] The solution to the indeterminacy of Rawlsian political reasoning, then, is to "evaluate our evolved rules from the perspective of public reason: we must seek to determine whether the outcome of the social evolutionary process is within the optimal eligible set" of rules, principles, and so forth.[35] We can use original position–style reasoning to rule out many proposals for justified laws and policies, and even principles of justice, but such reasoning will not yield a uniquely best choice. Consequently, we must allow nonrational processes, such as social evolution, to converge on one of the undefeated, as in unrefuted, outputs of original position–style reasoning.

Gaus's work drives public reason to classical liberal conclusions in virtue of *six* features of the account: (a) the focus on justifying moral conventions rather than law alone; (b) a moderate account of idealized reasoning by contracting parties, which will generate enormous diversity among the doctrines and reasons persons endorse; (c) the justification of a right to private property; (d) the refutation of socialism; (e) the right against legal coercion; and (f) an emphasis on nonideal theory.

Focus on Justifying Moral Conventions

Unique among public reason liberals, Gaus claims that *social morality* must be justified, in addition to laws. A social morality is "the set of social-moral rules that require or prohibit action, and so grounds moral imperatives that we direct to each other to engage

---

[34] Ibid., p. 46.
[35] Ibid., p. 424.

in, or refrain from, certain lines of conduct."[36] Social morality has several distinguishing characteristics.[37] It structures social interaction and so helps persons coordinate their behaviors and cooperate for mutual gain. Although social morality restrains our aims via social punishment and ostracism, it ultimately extends our ability to achieve our goals. Persons do not comply with the rules that compose social morality—"social-moral" rules—for merely instrumental reasons, but rather because the rules are seen as genuine moral imperatives. Finally, social-moral rules require an individual to defer to the judgment of others who enforce the rules when his or her private judgment conflicts with theirs.

I believe Gaus focuses on social morality for two reasons. The first is that laws and moral norms share critical features and so raise similar justificatory problems.[38] Both law and morality impose demands on individuals that they may well be better off without. The problems of moral and political justification, then, arise for the same reason: norms might restrict individual liberty without cause.

The second reason for focusing on social morality is new to Gaus's work. Gaus notes that the problem with specifically Hobbesian and Lockean solutions to the problem of moral justification is that they are "inherently political" and so "politicize the

[36] Ibid., p. 2.

[37] I describe those features in detail in "OPR, Ch.I.1: Social Morality," *Public Reason* (blog), January 17, 2011, http://publicreason.net/2011/01/17/opr-chi1-social-morality/.

[38] Before *The Order of Public Reason*, *Value and Justification* details his most extensive effort. See Gerald F. Gaus, "Part II. A Theory of Moral Justification," in *Value and Justification: The Foundations of Liberal Theory* (New York and Cambridge, UK: Cambridge University Press, 1990), pp. 251–378.

resolutions of all moral disputes."[39] This theory implies an unattractive form of statism where state authority invades all domains where the content of social morality is disputed.[40] So the focus on social morality is critical to avoid politicizing all moral conflicts— and so to avoid a strong form of statism.

The focus on social morality is critical for Gaus's defense of classical liberalism because it assumes that the ultimate source of social order is not the state but rather the local moral conventions that evolve, as a spontaneous order, from our normal moral agency and routine interaction. Social morality even has a special priority over law because it can resolve social problems without resort to coercion. The purpose of politics is to perform functions that noncoercive social morality cannot. Thus, there is a presumption on behalf of social solutions to social conflict, rather than political solutions.

Moderate Account of Idealized Reasoning

The next feature of *OPR*'s main line of argument concerns the sorts of reasons that can block the justification of coercion and the forms of coercion our objections undermine. Gaus uses the language of "defeat" here, such that refuted justifications are "defeated" and some reasons serve as "defeaters" for coercion.[41] Rawls's account of public justification appeals to coarse-grained concepts, like a political conception of justice and an overlapping consensus of

---

[39] Gaus, *The Order of Public Reason*, p. 24.

[40] Ibid., p. 24, n. 48. Notably, Gaus admits that his "Lockean-inspired account in *Justificatory Liberalism*" falls victim to the same error.

[41] Gaus follows mainstream epistemologists in employing the language of defeat.

reasonable comprehensive doctrines.[42] Political conceptions and comprehensive doctrines are sprawling complexes of norms and rules. Gaus *fractures* these two ideas into much smaller ones: sets of social-moral rules, as we have seen, and sets of diverse, intra-personally related reasons.

Gaus fragments political conceptions into rules in part because he thinks that only rules can solve the problem of indeterminacy. Rawlsian political conceptions of justice are much more general in scope, such that evaluations of social practices depend on appealing to principles that can be justified only by appealing to sophisticated philosophical judgment. Rule-based evaluation does not require such complexities. Consequently, principles are not the primary basis of moral evaluation.[43] Gaus follows Hayek in holding that human beings are as much rule followers as goal seekers. Therefore, a great many of our actions are driven by following rules, far more than are driven by reasoning from principles. Accordingly, our ordinary forms of moral evaluation concern rules rather than principles. In this way rules, not principles, provide "mutually understood guides for social life" available to all normal agents, not merely moral experts.[44]

The move from doctrines to reasons is similar. First, Rawlsian comprehensive doctrines are systematic views of the world, God, right and wrong, good and bad, just and unjust. As such, the doctrines are complex relations of a great many reasons for action. Accordingly, using them to evaluate social-moral rules will

---

[42] Rawls, *Political Liberalism*, p. xxxix.

[43] Though they can help. See Gaus, *The Order of Public Reason*, p. 296.

[44] Ibid., p. 272.

prove overwhelming. Further, most citizens lack comprehensive doctrines because of the cognitive demands of accepting and living by them. Public reason liberals require a more local unit of justification for rules—reasons.

In both cases, Gaus appeals to attractive models of human cognition to set the standards of judgment and evaluation involved in public reason. We evaluate rules on the basis of reasons. An additional implication is that any account of our sufficient reasons must involve *moderate idealization*, where we judge what reasons persons have by appealing to what they would endorse if they had engaged in a respectable amount of information collection and processing.[45] To solve our social problems, we must model agents' reasoning in ways that are realistic, given the bounded nature of human rationality, and that preserve our real-world commitments, which more radical forms of idealization may destroy.

The implication of evaluating rules based on the reasons that persons would affirm under conditions of moderate idealization is that justificatory reasons will vary *dramatically* between persons given their different points of view, histories, and rational commitments. Further, Gaus declines to restrict justificatory reasons to the set of shared or accessible reasons, another departure from

[45] Gaus's *The Order of Public Reason* contains his critique of standard conceptions of idealization (pp. 235–44). For Gaus, an agent has a sufficient reason R to endorse a rule or law if and only if a "respectable amount" of good reasoning would lead the agent to affirm R as undefeated. See ibid., p. 250. A respectable amount of reasoning is determined by the degree of reasoning that members of the public expect of one another, a modest standard often determined contextually.

most public reason liberals.[46] Far more reasons, then, can be used to object to coercion and to successfully defeat the justification for it.

For instance, it is much easier to defeat a law that forces people to take jobs mandated by the state, given all the different reasons that can plausibly override the mandate, and the few reasons that would prove sufficient to justify the mandate to a wide variety of people. Moral rules and coercive laws cannot be justifiably imposed on persons if those individuals have sufficient reason to reject those rules and laws. Given moderate, diversity-preserving idealization, then, different citizens will have sufficient reason to reject a *great* many laws and policies, so much so that we might end up with no justified laws or policies at all (though Gaus thinks that our need to live together is sufficiently strong that concerns about moral anarchy can be answered). That means that an enormous range of laws and policies that Rawlsians propose will be defeated by the diverse reasons of members of the public.

The point of the foregoing, at times technical, discussion is to explain in detail why Gausian public reason tilts in a classical liberal direction. Gausian public reason acknowledges far more sources of *diversity* among citizens, and that diversity brings orders of magnitude more successful objections to coercive laws. Combining accounts of what is to be justified (rules), the group to whom coercion is justified (moderately idealized agents), and their objections to coercion (objections as diverse as the persons who offer them) shows a dramatic shift in the attitude a public

---

[46] See Gaus's critique of the shared reasons requirement. Ibid., pp. 283–87.

reason liberal should have toward coercion. We are now in a position of skepticism of the justification of coercive laws. This will tend to manifest itself in forms of moderate libertarianism.

Justification of a Right to Private Property

So on Gausian public reason, diverse, rational reasoners affirm distinct and conflicting moral rules, and they will not agree on which rules are best to govern their common social life. But Gaus insists that those reasoners do not face a "null" set of justifiable rules. Instead, the reasoners often face the problem of *too many* eligible (undefeated) proposals.

In Part 2 of *OPR*, Gaus uses three conceptual devices to narrow indeterminacy to the optimal eligible set (OES): (a) the abstract deliberative model that maps out the order of public justification, (b) an account of social evolution that will generate social convergence on a member of the OES, and (c) a "testing conception" of public justification that limits the determination of whether a presently practiced rule is in the OES to cases where the rule has become morally controversial.

Let us begin our account of Gaus's right to private property by explaining the idea of the abstract deliberative model, which is similar to Rawls's original position. Gaus's abstract deliberative model holds that diverse members of the public determine what is publicly justified in a series of steps or in an *order* that proceeds from more abstract determinations to more concrete ones.[47] He then argues that members of the public will agree on certain basic

---

[47] The extensive detailing of the deliberative model is developed in ibid., chap. 5.

rights by taking the "perspective of agency."[48] That is, they will endorse a number of rights by reasoning as bare agents, stripped of some of their individuating characteristics. In doing so, members will adopt a presumption in favor of liberty, respect for autarchy (self-directed action, but not full-blown autonomy), rights not to be coerced, freedom of thought, rights against harm, and rights to assistance.[49]

Next in the order of justification are jurisdictional rights, rights that devolve collective choices to individual members of the public. Privacy rights and private property rights are the quintessential jurisdictional rights.[50] In sum, constraints on the optimal eligible set follow an order from the more abstract (formal features of rules) through the relatively abstract (the abstract rights of agency) to the more concrete (jurisdictional rights).

The abstract rights of agency are just that—abstract. They involve rights that all liberals, and indeed most nonliberals, endorse. Among these are rights to assistance, which are a kind of positive right. Libertarians are bound to recoil. But it is important to note that Gaus allows the commitments of libertarian and conservative members of the public to defeat more extensive enforceable duties of aid because of their belief that some persons are undeserving. Even so, here enters an element of Gausian public reason that is not fully libertarian. For Gaus, this is a *good thing*, for his theory should not be coextensive with the comprehensive commitments of a small, sectarian group within liberal orders.

[48] Ibid., pp. 337–41.
[49] Ibid., pp. 341–59.
[50] Ibid., pp. 374–86.

For our purposes, the most important feature of the order of justification is the notion of a jurisdictional right, which assigns individuals and groups rights to govern particular, specific social domains in accord with their own wishes and choices. Public reason derives from more monistic forms of moral reasoning, such as those characteristic of Rousseau, Kant, and the early Rawls. But once we introduce diversity into public reason, it is clear that we will seldom be able to agree when making collective decisions. As a result, we have reason to "partition" moral space so that people can make their own choices when it matters most to them. Jurisdictional rights are moral partitions, "individualized spheres of moral authority in which the rightholder's judgment about what is to be done provides others with moral reasons to act."[51] Thus, jurisdictional individual rights are a kind of public justification, a set of institutional methods that we can use to settle disputes that we cannot resolve collectively.

The most fundamental jurisdictional right is the right to private property, as private property rights "economize on collective justification."[52] To own property, Gaus argues, just *is* to have a legitimate social space in which an agent's evaluative standards not only have free reign but also impose duties on others not to interfere. Gaus denies that the jurisdictional right to private property is fully extensive or absolute; nonlibertarian members of the public will have diverse reasons to defeat such radical authority claims.[53]

---

[51] Ibid., p. 373.

[52] Ibid., p. 374.

[53] Note that socialists make authority claims that are even more likely to be defeated. Gaus does not single out libertarians here.

Nonetheless, Gaus argues that "members of the public will endorse a system of property rights" that, in general, "are not easily overridden and that are extensive, including private property in capital assets."[54] Gaus denies that public reason requires worker ownership of capital because public reason is not meant to promote a controversial ideal of autonomy but rather to preserve the moral agency of diverse persons under conditions of disagreement. Consequently, those who insist upon worker ownership as a condition of autonomy are simply insisting on their own sectarian doctrines.

Rights against Legal Coercion

We now turn to Gaus's case for a right against legal coercion. For Gaus, rights of agency are among our most fundamental rights, and they include a right not to be coerced in the absence of a compelling justification. Libertarians might rejoice here, but not so fast: Gaus claims that reasonable people disagree about which forms of social order are most coercive, so some nonlibertarian views about the coerciveness of the market may present problems for libertarian property rights claims. Nonetheless, there are certain obvious core cases of coercion, such as the forms of coercion used by police, that all recognize as coercive. Legislation is also typically coercive.

Gaus then argues that, insofar as we have a settled scheme of basic liberties (which include a right of private property), these rights set a baseline against which coercion must be justified.

[54] Gaus, *The Order of Public Reason*, p. 377.

If the government proposes to use coercion to force you to wear a motorcycle helmet or evict you from your home and if you have a publicly justified right to make your own decisions with regard to those issues, then the right against legal coercion prohibits state action.

Gaus also notes that publicly justified legislation, despite justifying the use of legal coercion, must be evaluated by counting its coerciveness as one of the reasons to oppose the law (even if those reasons are ultimately overridden). States are not exempt from this standard.[55] Gaus stresses that the right against legal coercion is a right that coercion be prohibited in the absence of a public justification. Further, a law's coerciveness continues to count against it even when the factors favoring the law are stronger.

It should be plain that a right against legal coercion pushes public reason in an even more classically liberal direction. Not only is there a strong right against the state to not be coerced in the absence of a public justification, but also the cost of coercion must still figure into the justification of a law we think is, all things considered, publicly justified. Given the diverse, moderately idealized reasons of the public, the right against legal coercion will be a powerful one, including when it comes to the protection of private property rights.

Refutation of Socialism

Gaus also argues that socialism and strongly egalitarian states are almost always ineligible as systems of political and economic governance. Let's start by considering state socialism. Even if

---

[55] Ibid., pp. 479–81.

substantial redistribution of wealth is justified, "socialist systems would still be outside the socially eligible set,"[56] because socialism necessarily requires collective decisionmaking and so requires consensus about how various parts of the economy should be run. The right of private property is publicly justified because it is a solution to the inability of members of the public to agree on common standards. Socialism, understood as government ownership of the means of production, requires agreement where none can be reasonably expected.

A second argument against socialism is empirical in nature, which is that "extensive private ownership—including capital goods and finance—is for all practical purposes a requisite for a social and political order that protects civil liberties."[57] Rawlsians, Gaus argues, fail to appreciate how difficult it is to divorce the good aspects of markets from private ownership. Gaus states, "There has never been a political order characterized by deep respect for personal freedom that was not based on a market order with widespread private ownership in the means of production."[58]

Rawlsians are apt to complain that such an order allows sufficient economic inequality to undermine democratic freedom. Anticipating this reply, Gaus next appeals to empirical evidence that political freedom and economic freedom are correlated. Gaus argues that little evidence exists to support the claim that the economic inequalities found in liberal democracies today endanger democratic institutions.

[56] Ibid., p. 512.
[57] Ibid., p. 513.
[58] Ibid., p. 514.

Now, against the libertarian, I should stress that Gaus rejects both market anarchist and minimal or small-state libertarianism, because many suitably idealized members of the public will oppose libertarianism and so oppose coercive laws that institutionalize more radical forms of libertarianism. A pure capitalist order would allow for no redistribution of wealth, no government production of public goods, or any regulations other than the regulatory effect of torts and contracts. But many reasonable people, if not the vast majority of them, believe, with epistemic justification, that a less-than-minimal state cannot be publicly justified, because it would coercively prohibit people from collectively deciding to extend state power. As a result, they have respectable objections to the sorts of coercion required to limit the state as much as libertarians would like.

Public reason also cannot prohibit redistribution, since the argument against a more egalitarian state "succeeds only if the justification of property is not dependent on questions about justified redistribution and/or conceptions of social justice within the evaluative standards of Members of the Public."[59] But that is implausible, as these issues are arguably not "even remotely independent issues."[60]

Turning now to egalitarian redistributive liberalism, Gaus argues that, despite rejecting libertarianism, public reason liberals must nonetheless hold that in many contexts, taxation is coercive, and the coerciveness of taxation increases as the tax rate increases.

[59] Ibid., p. 521.
[60] Ibid., p. 522.

Accordingly, the right against legal coercion will provide stronger and stronger reason to oppose taxation as the tax rate goes up.[61] Further, in the production of public goods, the state is bound by a Paretian standard of public finance and public policy. Public programs must be reasonably expected to advance the evaluative standards of all, or they are seldom justified; that is, programs must be *Pareto improvements*.

Further, Gaus argues that evaluating policy requires a clear sense of their benefits *and costs*, which may require bills to contain their own funding directives (a recommendation Gaus adopts following Swedish economist Knut Wicksell), which in practice would substantially limit the public policy process. Gaus then adds supermajority voting rules into the mix, limiting government even more. All of those restrictions are barriers to the public justification of a strongly redistributive state.

In consequence, Gaus concludes that public reason liberalism

> Leads not to socialism, or a thoroughgoing egalitarian liberalism, or to libertarianism [understood as minimal state or anarchist libertarianism—KV], but to the more nuanced approach to legislation we find in the fifth book of Mill's *Principles*, allowing that there are a number of tasks that government justifiably performs, but having a strong overall inclination toward less rather than more "authoritative" (i.e., coercive) government.[62]

[61] Ibid., pp. 523–24.
[62] Ibid., p. 526.

The argument for this position, Gaus claims, rests on five core claims:

1. Individuals are free and equal.

2. Free and equal persons have a moral right not to be forced or coerced without justification.

3. A member of the public will hold that the greater his or her estimates of coercion, the stronger must be the justification.

4. Free and equal members of the public reasonably disagree on many matters involving degrees of coercion, but many reasonable people believe that large states with high rates of taxation and redistributive institutions are more coercive.

5. Only laws that can be justified to all members of the public can reconcile coercion with respect for everyone's freedom and equality.[63]

Consequently, public reason liberalism must "tilt" against coercive states, and public reason liberals are responsible for showing that their favored proposals do not use coercion, at least not in excess of what can be justified *given* the legal right against coercion.[64]

Emphasis on Nonideal Theory

The final feature of Gaus's view that pushes public reason in a more libertarian direction is Gaus's emphasis on *nonideal theory*. Gausian public justification is identified with a "testing conception"

---

[63] Ibid., pp. 526–27.
[64] Ibid., p. 527.

of evaluation, where the aim of a model of public reason is not to reconstruct social institutions from the ground up, but rather to help us evaluate our real-world practices in a way that accords with our real-world normative standards and commitments.

Moral evaluation for Gaus, following Hayek, must begin from our actual social practices and then "test" those practices via the deliberative model.[65] In other words, public justification does not begin by asking whether our entire set of coercive institutions embodies a commitment to general principles of justice. Rather, we test real rules via a test of public justification only when challenges or concerns about the rules arise.

Further, Gaus does not assume that citizens and political officials will fully comply with the law; he limited original position reasoning and allows for far more economic realism than other public reason liberals. Readers of this volume are likely already sympathetic to the claim that formal economic models and empirical data favor libertarianism or alternatives, so by allowing nonideal behavior and real-world data into public justification, public reason liberalism is pushed further still in a classical liberal direction. Libertarians have frequently understood the case for libertarianism as resting in a commitment to nonideal theorizing, where the failures of government are impossible to ignore. In this respect, then, Gaus's emphasis should be welcome.

Which Rawlsian Libertarianism?

The reader will notice that I have spent much more time developing the Gausian position than the Tomasian position. I did so in

---

[65] Ibid., p. 425.

part because Tomasi is not reconstructing public reason from the ground up but is instead modifying justice as fairness to accommodate classical liberal economic liberties and a broader classical liberal outlook on political life.

But I have also focused more on Gaus because I find the Gausian view more plausible. Rawls was right to move from *A Theory of Justice* to *Political Liberalism* because of the problems of reasonable pluralism about the good and justice.[66] Gaus plausibly develops public reason in a diversity-accommodating direction, which I regard as a natural extension of a broadly Rawlsian project. Tomasi's free-market fairness, therefore, will fall prey to the same concerns as justice as fairness. Reasonable people disagree about what justice requires; thus, we cannot use Rawlsian reasoning to vindicate justice as fairness *or free-market fairness*. Ultimately, Gaus has set the stage for the next version of the Rawlsian project, a *Rawls 3.0* that accommodates reasonable pluralism about the good and justice, and other forms of diversity as well. Tomasi's project is associated with *Rawls 1.0*, the Rawls of *A Theory of Justice*.

All the same, the Gausian model does not *rule out* appeals to one's own conception of justice in shaping a publicly justified polity. It is a great good in Gausian public reason for people to appeal to their sectarian conceptions of the good and justice, and not merely to defeat laws that cannot be publicly justified. Appeal to

---

[66] Importantly, Rawls's concerns regarding pluralism about justice postdate the development of *Political Liberalism*, but the recognition of justice pluralism becomes critical in the introduction to the paperback edition and his later article "The Idea of Public Reason Revisited," *University of Chicago Law Review* 64 (Summer 1997): 765–807.

diverse values, Gaus now argues, helps society discover new and better ways of living together.[67] So the advocates of free-market fairness need not give up their view, but they must accept that free-market fairness cannot claim a special status in governing a society's basic structure. Free-market fairness might embrace the *correct* principles of justice, but not the correct principles *in the fully Rawlsian sense*, as they cannot survive public justification due to deep disagreement about justice, and so cannot stabilize a diverse social order in the right way. Thus, these two Rawlsian libertarianisms are in tension. Free-market fairness cannot form the foundation of an order of public reason. But it can form part of that foundation.

---

[67] See Gerald Gaus, *The Tyranny of the Ideal* (Princeton, NJ: Princeton University Press, 2016).

6

Virtue Ethics

Mark LeBar

The task of this chapter is to argue that a moral foundation for libertarianism can be found in virtue ethics. To do so, I must sort out the kind of virtue ethics that most lends itself to this sort of justificatory relation, because many different kinds exist. And I must make clear what I mean by "libertarianism," because here too there is a plurality of understandings, and some of them will make this justificatory relationship more plausible than others.

Virtue Ethics

What is typically thought to differentiate a virtue ethic from other forms of ethics is that it focuses moral concern on the character of the agent, rather than on his or her actions. Even less is it concerned with the states of the world that those actions produce, as on most consequentialist accounts. Virtues are thought to be relatively stable traits of character: the ways we are and others come to know us to be. Vices too are stable traits of character. What differentiates them from virtues is that virtuous traits are those we value—those we judge positively, we might say—whereas vices are those traits repugnant to us. On the virtue ethical way of understanding morality, these stable character traits are the primary focus of moral evaluation.

It would be a mistake to infer that actions, or the states of the world that follow from them, don't matter to virtue ethics. Certainly they do. But their place in a virtue ethical theory is determined by the role they play in understanding the dispositions or traits that are, potentially, virtuous or vicious. They do not have moral weight independent of the role they play in understanding the moral value of those traits. Though we certainly care about good events and catastrophes, what matters morally is what we do in the face of such states of the world, as persons with the characters we have made for ourselves.

Because we obviously care about people's characters, we'd expect most plausible moral theories to make some substantial theoretical place for them. And most such theories do. On a consequentialist theory such as John Stuart Mill's, for example, virtue is a propensity to produce good outcomes—outcomes that can be assessed as morally valuable by the basic tenets of the theory, independent of the actions or character that produced them.[1] Thus, though Mill has a theory of virtue, in it, virtue logically depends on the prior criteria he has established for evaluating states of the world and the actions that have produced them. Something similar could be said of Kant (though of course his theory is not consequentialist) in the kind of place he makes for virtue. What is distinctive of

---

[1] John Stuart Mill, *Utilitarianism*, ed. George Sher (Indianapolis, IN: Hackett Publishing Company, 2001 [1861]), chap. 2.

virtue ethics is the reversal of priorities. It is character that matters first, and we explicate the moral significance of actions and states of affairs consequentially.

So described, there are many forms of virtue ethics. And although there might be convergence on what traits go on the lists of virtues and vices, there are also lots of differences, and even deeper differences, on the reasons some traits go on the virtue list and others on the vice list. Not all offer the same degree of support for libertarianism. So I need to be specific about the form of virtue ethic I have in mind.

Eudaimonist Virtue Ethics

One venerable form of virtue ethics—a form going back to Socrates, Plato, and Aristotle—gives primary theoretical place to eudaimonia. Eudaimonia is more or less happiness, but care is required here. We use happiness to mean many things, from the mood of the moment to a quality of life. What the Greeks have in mind with eudaimonia is much less like the former and much more like the latter. You might be happy in the sense of having a good life, even if just now you are not in a very good mood at all. It is that quality of life the Greeks call eudaimonia. When we wish a newly married couple every happiness, we are deploying the idea the Greeks intend with eudaimonia.

How does eudaimonia shape a virtue ethic? It provides the criterion by which we determine which dispositions or traits count as virtues. Those traits that contribute positively and significantly to our living happy lives count as virtues; vices are just those that do not. That does not mean that virtuous action is undertaken only for the sake of those happy lives; virtuous action has its own aims (on Aristotle's view, always the "fine and noble"). Instead, the work of eudaimonia is criterial. We should not suppose such a criterion is easy to come by, or simple, or uncontested. An adequate account of virtues on such a view is a hard-won fruit of life and reflection. However, two members of any plausible such account—virtues that are invariably recognized as traits that contribute to a good human life—deserve discussion here, because they are crucial to what follows. They are practical wisdom (Greek: *phronesis*) and justice (Greek: *dikaiosune*). What needs explaining is how each contributes to a good life, and what specifically it requires.

Aristotle thinks of practical wisdom as the capacity to deliberate and act well about "what sorts of thing conduce to the good life in general."[2] His argument for the centrality of practical wisdom to the good life starts with the kind of beings we are. We are, he argues, creatures who live our lives by deploying practical rationality.[3] We can, of course, deploy practical rationality in ways that do *not* conduce to good lives; only when we succeed in living well does what we do count as *wisdom*.

Other creatures live their lives in different ways. Giraffes live by grazing foliage that other herbivores cannot reach. Gazelles live by grazing grasses and by sprinting away from predators. Lions live by catching unwary or weak gazelles. Those forms of life are distinct and recognizable, the sorts of things we learn about

---

[2] Aristotle, *Nicomachean Ethics*, bk. VI, chap. 5, in *The Complete Works of Aristotle: The Revised Oxford Translation*, vol. 2, ed. Jonathan Barnes, trans. W. D. Ross with revision by J. O. Urmson (Princeton, NJ: Princeton University Press, 1984), pp. 1729–867.

[3] Ibid., bk. I, chap. 7.

in natural history museums. In the same vein, humans live by deploying capabilities that only we seem to have. We reason to plan and set ends, as well as to forge cooperative relationships with others of our kind. Aristotle's fairly straightforward reasoning, then, is that if this is how we live, living well is a matter of deploying those capabilities well. It is excellence in practical reason, or practical wisdom. And excellence in practical wisdom, in turn, is understood as what successfully aims at living well. The two ideas must be understood in tandem.

The significance for us of practical rationality—and, when successful, practical wisdom—is reflected in the networks of ends that shape our lives. Ends are goals, and we can and do have innumerable ends. The resources necessary to realize them are scarce, so the enterprise of living a life of end seeking is one requiring continual and incessant judgment of tradeoffs. Some of the ends may be indeterminate, so that judgment is required even to know what successful pursuit of such an end would consist of. (When we marry, for example, we begin with only a hazy idea of what the end of a good marriage looks like. We find out what it means in detail only through being married—and through the course of innumerable judgments and experience.) Making those judgments well—in such a way as to live the kind of life we aspire to live—is what constitutes practical wisdom as a virtue. It is not easy, and it cannot be realized except by the application of practical rationality, with virtue of character, to our lives.

Practical wisdom has another important feature. Aristotle believes that we develop and maintain the virtues (or, sadly, the vices) by force of habit. Of course, we start with a moral education from our parents and teachers. None of us starts from ground zero, which is why it matters so much that we have a good start. We have passions and appetites, but—precisely because we have the capacity for practical rationality—as that capacity develops we can *choose* what we will do. And, importantly, there is a feedback loop here: the choices we make shape our passions and appetites. That is why habit is so important: as adults, this is how we shape who we become. So what we do makes us into what we are. What we become reflects the exercise of choice on our part; once more, the work of practical reason. We exercise choice not only in determining what to do but also in deciding what to be.

That we live by exercising practical rationality is obvious and important, but it is equally obvious and important that we live socially. Humans neither live nor thrive independently. We live with others of our kind. How we manage our relations with those others, then, is also centrally important to our living well. Many of the virtues of character bear on these relations, but none does so with greater import than justice.

The best understanding of the nature of the virtue of justice has, I believe, shifted somewhat since the early Greek theorists. Plato conceived of justice as "having and doing one's own."[4] Justice in the city (or *polis*) meant each kind of citizen performing his or her own task. Justice in the individual meant the rational, passionate, and appetitive parts of the psyche each playing its appropriate role. Aristotle saw justice as being more directly connected

---

[4] Plato, *Republic*, in *Complete Works*, ed. John Cooper, trans. G.M.A. Grube with revision by C.D.C. Reeve (Indianapolis, IN: Hackett Publishing, 1997), pp. 971–1223.

with action: he thought that the "narrow" sense of justice (that is, the sense in which justice is something more specific than just doing the right thing) could be understood in two ways. First, as a matter of proportionality: equals, he argued, deserve equal treatment, and unequals deserve unequal treatment.[5] Second, there is rectification: if I steal $100 from you, or make you $100 worse off, justice requires that my benefit be negated and that you be made whole. That is, justice requires that I give up $100, and you get it back.

It is hard to argue with those insights, but moral philosophy outside of virtue ethics has made progress in understanding what is due us in ways that, I believe, we should read into the virtue of justice. Consider slavery, a practice the ancients at least tolerated, if not (as in Aristotle's case) outright endorsed. Slavery is manifestly unjust (however long it took humankind to come to that realization), and it seems that no just person would engage in slaveholding or tolerate its institutionalization. However (as Aristotle's own case demonstrates), it is not clear how the justice of the ancient Greeks could show this. There would seem to be more to what the virtue of justice requires than Plato's or Aristotle's conceptions succeeded in capturing.

One way of putting what is missing is to say that the just person recognizes the moral standing of others in ways that rule out slavery. What exactly this moral standing might come to will be somewhat controversial, but there are core elements recognizable in our everyday practice.

---

[5] Aristotle, *Nicomachean Ethics*, bk. V.

One of those elements is rights and their recognition. Of course, people have legal rights, but those rights depend on the legal regimes they live under. We also have moral rights and entitlements. We have the standing to demand that others not do certain things to us—to enslave us, to harm us, in many cases to lie to us, to break faith with us, and so on. As Aristotle indicated, we have the standing to demand proportionality of various sorts in how we are treated (to be treated as we are due) and to complain if others treat us badly in various ways. To say that someone has rights is to say that he or she has a kind of standing that the just person ought to recognize.

A second (and not unrelated) element is accountability. Suppose you harm me; you strike me in the face. Now, the law might or might not have something to say about such an event, but we ordinarily think morality certainly does. A utilitarian might say that the problem with your doing so is that you fail to maximize the greatest utility. A divine command theorist might say that in doing so, you violate God's law. But just left at that, even if either of those statements is true, it cannot be the whole truth. You have done something to me: you have wronged me. Crucially, you are accountable to me for the wrong you have done me. Any moral theory that leaves out the kinds of relations between us in which we are accountable to one another for the way we treat each other is inadequate. This kind of accountability is also a reflection of the standing that a just person should recognize others as having.

Finally, part of our moral standing is our capacity to change our moral relations with others in ways that reflect rights, obligations, and accountability. Consider, for example, our capacity to promise or to contract. If we make a deal that I will pick you up at the airport for $50, then each of us has conveyed rights to the other that we did not earlier have. I have a right against you that you pay me $50, while you have a right against me that I be there to pick you up when you arrive. Each of us is accountable to the other for doing what he or she has agreed to do. Each of us has those rights because (and just because) the other has given it. An important part of our moral standing, part of what the just person recognizes, is this capacity to change our moral relations with others in these ways.

All those elements and more are part of what we might call the "operational" aspect of being a just person. Many of its elements have been recognized since people first began theorizing about what it meant to be virtuous. Others have been more recently acknowledged. But at the core, there is more to being a just person than just these operational components, though it is certainly tied to those components. The just person sees others in a different way than the unjust person does. Consider the attitude of a human predator (perhaps a psychopath). To that person, humans are prey. To be sure, humans are importantly different from other possible prey: they have advanced rational capacities. They are (perhaps) better at detecting the kind of threat that a predator poses to them and are certainly capable of defending themselves against and perhaps retaliating against such a predator, with more force than any other potential prey. So the predator is wary of their capacities for reason and action. Their capacities figure into the predator's reasoning only tactically or strategically as potential ways in which they might impinge on his efforts to get what he wants.

The just person whom we will call Socrates, conversely, sees others as having advanced rational capacities and more. But his regard for others is not *merely* tactical or strategic, as it is for the predator. Socrates sees others as sources of reasons and obligations, in the ways we have just surveyed and more, because of the kind of beings they are. Others matter to Socrates, we might say, for their sake, rather than for his sake. In Aristotle's terms, the reasons Socrates has for regarding them are final—they are ends—rather than being merely instrumental to his own purposes.[6]

I have claimed that practical wisdom and justice count as central and important virtues in the view we are exploring here, but also that what counts as a virtue is a matter of what contributes to our happiness. The importance of practical wisdom for happiness is evident: it consists in the capacity to use practical rationality effectively in living a good life. But what about justice? After all, many have understood the requirements of morality (and especially of justice) to amount to constraints on our pursuit of happiness. Why think that it is an important part of an account of the kind of virtue that contributes to happiness?

The heart of the response to this question lies with our essential sociality. We are not atomistic individuals; as Aristotle recognized, we thrive in the company of others of our kind. The relations we have with others not only concern how we provide for our material needs (as Marx focused upon) but also concern our relations with others as rational, planning agents, as beings who

---

[6] This is famously Kant's way of cashing out the way he believes we ought to regard others. Though that formulation is his, the framework of ends is naturally (and originally) Aristotle's.

apprehend and act on reasons. Our relations with others include and occur within the "field" of those rational capacities. We have interests in the reasons that others provide us and that we provide them (we might call them "normative interests"). All of those dimensions of our social life have to go well for us to be happy, and they are the province of the virtue of justice. For us to thrive, we need to live in a network of recognition of others as having the kind of standing that constrains us from enslaving them, harming or lying to them, and so on. In other words, we need to see others in the way I have argued the just person sees others.

Consider an example (from philosopher T. M. Scanlon). Suppose you have a friend, someone you have until now considered a very good friend. But now (let us assume) you have some grave liver disorder, incurable, and you are in need of a transplant. And your friend tells you: "You and your friendship are so important to me that I will do anything to get you the liver you need. If I can't find a donor, I will kill someone to get you that liver." Something is clearly wrong with such a friend; indeed, you are likely not to consider him or her a friend, let alone a close friend, much longer.

The toxicity of that sort of injustice is incompatible with friendship. The wrongness of the way your erstwhile friend is willing to act will kill off the vital connections that we enjoy with others, connections that sustain our friendships and make our lives worth living. A bit of reflection will reveal that these sorts of sensibilities and forms of responsiveness underwrite every relation we have with other human beings. Unless we are living the kind of deformed human life that hermits live, justice is essential to happiness.

In summary, then, the kind of virtue ethic I have sketched—a eudaimonist virtue theory—maintains that we should aspire to be virtuous people. We should do so in order to live good lives, but the point is that the virtues are the keys to such lives. And although the list of virtues may itself be a matter of some contention, there is no plausible contention that among the most important elements of that list are practical wisdom and justice. So now, the question is, if that is all true, what is the connection to libertarian political theory? Why think that our political lives should be ordered as libertarians believe, if in fact such a virtue ethic is the right account of morality?

Libertarianism

That story depends, obviously, on what libertarians believe, so we must start there. And, indeed, my conception of what is at the heart of libertarianism differs a bit from the standard story. If we start with what is distinctive about that conception, the connections with virtue will be more apparent.

Frequently (perhaps generally), libertarianism is understood as a view based on the nonaggression principle: the use of force or violence against people or their property is never to be initiated and is permitted only in response to the aggression of others. That principle is, so far as I know, true; its limitations do not stem from its falsehood. The problem is that it cannot be foundational: it can be informative only against the backdrop of a further theory identifying for us what counts as aggression and what does not. Examples of this point are simple and obvious.

May I wrest from you the book that you are carrying? Likely not; that would appear to be aggression. But that is not so if you have just wrested the book from me, in which case I am not initiating force but responding to it. That is, of course, unless I had previously stolen the book from you, in which case you were responding to aggression, and I am now aggravating my initial aggression against you. Whether or not I am aggressing against you depends entirely on the background conditions of our encounter. In particular, it depends on our entitlements: whether I am aggressing against you in a way the nonaggression principle forbids really depends on whether I am entitled to use force against you. The nonaggression principle can't answer the question of whether or not I am so entitled, so it cannot be foundational. Although this feature of the nonaggression principle is often acknowledged in passing by authors deploying it, I believe it indicates that we should look elsewhere for what normative principles actually can be foundational for libertarian theory.

I find that foundation in the idea of equality of authority to obligate (or equality of authority for short). If I can obligate you in some way, you must likewise be able to obligate me in that way. That none of us has any authority to lay obligations on others in a way that they cannot reciprocate has been a core principle in liberal thought since John Locke, and it provides the right sort of underwriting to the nonaggression principle. Of course, this principle applies (as liberals since Locke have observed) only to those who *have* the capacity to live and act rationally. We do not accord this authority to those in the grips of insanity, nor to children until they are of age to join the community of full moral agents.

Those reservations aside, if we begin with the capacity to obligate each other equally, either we both have the liberty of aggressing against each other in the way the nonaggression principle focuses upon, or neither of us does. I will not pause here to make the case for the latter of those interpretations. Cases of the initiation of force are wrong or unjust in all and only those cases in which the forcing person has an obligation not to use force, and the person being forced has a claim or right not to be so forced. We want the network of obligations within which we move, act, and relate to others to be predicated on an equality of those obligations.

Libertarian complaints about the unjust imposition of force or coercion by the state are always grounded on violations of the equality of authority. Consider for example drug prohibition. One way we could frame the libertarian complaint against drug prohibition is to say that in its enforcement, it allows for aggression: it permits coercive force to be applied to those who would choose to use drugs that others disapprove of. And that is a valid complaint. However, as I have indicated, it cannot be the root of the matter. The root of the complaint lies in a violation of the equality of authority. Those who write and execute laws prohibiting the use of drugs claim the authority to obligate us to abide by those laws. Law carries the supposition of moral force: that is, it is not just the threat of penalties that bids us comply with them, but the idea that we are morally obligated to do so. So legislation imposes obligations on us that we would not otherwise have (or so the story goes) not to buy drugs, sell them, use them, and so on.

But those who claim this authority would not agree that it is equal and reciprocal. That is, they would not accept the authority of *others* to impose obligations on them as to what they can put in their bodies. Nobody wants to be subject to the arbitrary authority of others (that is, authority grounded in reasons that are accepted only by the authority, not by those on whom the authority is to be imposed) to impose obligations on them as to how they are to treat their own bodies. So those prohibiting the use of drugs claim an unequal authority. The exercise of that putative authority reflects an inequality in the capacity to obligate others, and libertarians reject it.

Or consider libertarian moral complaints about minimum wage laws. (There are, of course, economic complaints that I leave aside here.) Those who would impose such laws claim the authority to impose obligations on others not to engage in agreements (labor contracts, specifically) that in their judgment ought not to be engaged in. But they cannot possibly grant reciprocal authority to others to constrain the agreements they themselves may engage in just by an exercise of judgment. Such a moral framework would be one in which none of us would be treated as—or be capable of acting as—mature moral agents.

In fact, once the general structure of the problem is appreciated, it is easy to see that the basic source of the moral complaint libertarians make lies in the nature of the state itself, insofar as we understand the state to be an institution that claims for itself a monopoly on the rightful use of force in a given territory. Such a monopoly is incompatible with equality of authority to obligate: it is premised on the assumption that some among us have an authority to obligate (that is, to obligate to abide by its laws or to submit to its use of force) that is not reciprocated. So construed, the libertarian moral challenge is to the authority of the state itself. That is a radical challenge. Any justification for state authority must show either how it is compatible with equality of authority or how it carries sufficient moral force to subordinate a commitment to equality of authority. Both are quite demanding requirements, which is as it should be for those who seek to use force on others and who claim that those others have an obligation to submit.

From Virtue to Liberty

So construed, libertarianism readily finds support from virtue ethics. That support comes from two directions. First, the kind of freedom that libertarianism insists on for each individual is a necessary and appropriate social framework for the development and exercise of the virtues, including but not limited to practical wisdom and justice. Second, and perhaps more urgently, the virtue of justice requires that we treat others as having the sort of standing that is institutionalized in a society mediated by libertarian principles. Let's take these points in order.

First, the development of virtue and its realization in a good life require freedom from the imposition of constraints of others, including the exercise of unequal authority. We must be free to set and pursue our own ends, rather than having them imposed on us or having the tradeoffs among them dictated to us. We are, of course, bound to give others scope of action as we require it ourselves, so this isn't a matter of needing a world without limits. Such a world is quite irrelevant, not to say impossible, for creatures who live socially, such as ourselves. But the lives we lead need, within those parameters, to be free of others unilaterally imposing their judgment on how we should live, the ends we should value and pursue, and so on.

It is through choice and action that we become virtuous, and it is in virtuous agency that we are happy. Having our practical agency and authority over our own lives usurped by the (putative) authority of others is incompatible with that scope of action. So there is, at most, very little room for state interference in the ways individuals choose to live their lives.

It is perhaps worth echoing here as well a eudaimonist version of the observation that others usually don't know as well as we how we can best live our lives. This observation yields two kinds of objections to the intervention in the exercise of practical agency that virtue requires. One is epistemic: nobody else can know what you do about your life or the way its elements fit together to make it your life. F. A. Hayek made much of the economic costs of usurping the knowledge individuals have of the "particulars of time and place" in which they act.[7] Nothing I say here undermines Hayek's point, but it is only part of the problem. Apart from the concern about the knowledge lost to the production of social good of concern to Hayek, there is the loss to your good when your authority to exercise your own judgment is usurped.

The other objection is moral. The kind of interference with exercise of practical judgment that coercive command involves represents an exercise of just the sort of unequal, nonreciprocal authority that the just person will not engage in or abide. As we

---

[7] F. A. Hayek, "The Use of Knowledge in Society," *American Economic Review* 35 (1945): 519–30.

have seen, our lives are lived by finding, choosing, acting on, and making tradeoffs between ends. The choices we make about such tradeoffs make us, literally, the individuals we are, and because those lives are our own, the choices about those tradeoffs must be our own as well. That is what respect for ourselves and others requires, and it is what a just person will be unwilling to abridge.

But concern for the development of virtue by itself doesn't necessarily yield a commitment to a libertarian political structure. What does so, I believe, are the requirements of the virtue of justice. Those take a bit more unpacking. We can start with what Plato thought it required, which is (to a rough approximation) taking care of one's own business and giving others their due. It's hard to argue with that as being central to being a just person. Of course, it is somewhat vague on crucial details, which is part of what makes it uncontroversial as far as it goes.

That is a point that Aristotle noticed, and he attempted to both augment and sharpen it, in useful ways. His version of "giving others their due" is what he frames as a matter of justice in distribution, and it consists (he says) in treating equals equally and unequals unequally.[8] That requirement amounts to a kind of "proportionate" thinking: the idea is that when people deserve more of something (or when there is some basis for thinking they are entitled to more), they get more, and similarly when they deserve less or are entitled to less. Aristotle himself notes the contentions he papers over with this idea, because we can agree with the recipe while disagreeing on the kinds of things that make us deserve

---

[8] Aristotle, *Nicomachean Ethics*, bk. V, chap. 3.

more or be entitled to more. Still, this too seems a plausible part of what the just and virtuous person does.

But as I have argued, our conception of how the just person will see others has been enriched to include a kind of respect for others, for their agency, for their standing as moral equals. The just person sees that kind of respect as due to others in virtue of the kind of beings they are. Respect and equality of authority are their share. Those points together would seem to bar the virtuous person from doing a significant amount of what modern governments require their agents to do.

Consider what is required to conduct a war on drugs. Agents of the government invade the property and lives (and sometimes bodies) of others who have done neither them nor anyone else harm. They intervene in consensual transactions between other people. Prohibition in the case of minors can be even more draconian. And, of course, in the course of enforcing the various laws enjoining the use of drugs, they undertake the standard coercive measures of imprisoning others, taking their property (in fining them), and so on. None of those actions would seem to fall within the purview of the just person in the absence of the apparatus of the state lending putative legitimacy to them.

Can the fact that the state is licensing such conduct make it somehow consistent with the judgments a just person would make? If we take seriously the constraints of equality of authority to obligate (which, I am suggesting, is part of a modern augmentation to the ancient conception of what it meant to be just), it is hard to see how the judgments of some (though vested with the trappings of the state) could have the authority to obligate (or release from obligation) those responding to the demands of virtue in their treatment of others.[9]

To take another example (in some ways more mundane), consider that to be legally employed, each American must secure the permission of the U.S. government. This permission typically comes with the submission of a Form I-9 to the Department of Homeland Security. Thus, the U.S. government deems itself to have the authority to tell two people who intend to reach an employment agreement that they may not do so without its permission. In other words, their right to do what they will with their bodies and labor—without in any way harming others—is limited to what the U.S. government determines it may be.

That limitation, I submit, is something no virtuous person could endorse, accept, or practice. Consider the two dimensions of support I have indicated that connect virtue and libertarianism. One arises from the exercise of practical rationality and agency, which is the backbone of virtue itself. We cannot be virtuous nor can we live virtuous lives—the lives that are best for us to lead— without the exercise of practical reason and judgment. That exercise essentially involves determining how to promote our ends, and in the social world, that determination very often or generally means in combination with others. And to do so with others in ways that are effective and just requires that we reach mutually acceptable agreements on how to do so. The inhibition or

[9] Michael Huemer makes this case quite vividly in his argument for anarchism in *The Problem of Political Authority* (New York: Palgrave Macmillan, 2013).

constraint of those activities is itself inimical to the development of wisdom and virtue in those so constrained.

The other part of the story is the demands of justice and the recognition of an equality of authority. Put otherwise, the just person refuses to accept unequal or nonreciprocal relationships of authority. But that authority is precisely the form of authority being exerted in subordinating the judgment of another as to what contracts one may enter into to one's own. The authority of those who would limit such contracts (to say nothing of other terms of contract that do not infringe on the moral standing of others) cannot possibly be reciprocated. The point of the authority being exerted is that it is supreme and thus unequal. No just person could engage in such a practice.

Now, there are, of course, occasions on which just persons will do things that would otherwise not be just, occasioned by other instances of unjust conduct. Rectificatory justice involves just this sort of action. If Betty has stolen $100 from Wilma, justice in rectification requires that $100 be taken from Betty and returned to Wilma, and this justice plausibly would license the just person to do so. So the virtuous person could justly take money from Betty to set things right, whereas normally such taking would be unjust. Some kinds of enforcement actions such as this not only are permitted by the requirements of justice but also are required by it. Can such an argument be given to license the undertakings by the state that libertarians object to? Two points are worth making here.

The first is that typically it cannot. There is nothing, for example, in the war on drugs that has any connection with rectification of injustice. For that matter, most of what is done in the name of the war on terror also lacks such justification, though arguably it could hold in some cases, as well perhaps in many exercises of police powers in defense of the peace and safety of other people.

However, second, notice that there is nothing special in such cases about the state's role in performing these tasks. What makes such special actions permissible in such cases is not that the state is licensing them, but that the actions are warranted by the demands of justice. There are practical questions to be sure about whether private methods of answering to those demands can be as or more effective than state methods, but the crucial thing once again is that there is nothing special morally about the state undertaking such functions, and that is the best case, from the standpoint of justice, for the virtue of carrying out the state's tasks.

Those considerations, however, are not in the end the deepest problems for state agency from the perspective of being just agents. The state, by nature, claims a monopoly on the legitimate use of force. To preserve this monopoly, the state reserves for itself the final determination as to what counts as legitimate. It reserves to itself the exclusive right to final judgment as to what the legal requirements on itself and its subject will be—and thus on the nature and extent of the moral framework in which citizens live with it and with each other. And that means the state, by nature, is committed to a nonreciprocal relation of authority with respect to its citizens. Its agents act under the color of this authority, so they too claim to stand in a relation of nonreciprocal, unequal, authority to obligate others. And this is a relation between moral agents that a just agent can neither accept nor tolerate.

A clear example may be seen in the structure of authority in the United States of America (the case with which I am most familiar, but only the details, not the substance, of the issue differ in other polities). Although nominally the authority of the state rests in "the people," disputes as to how that authority is to be understood—its nature and extent—are determined in practice by the courts, including (for federal matters) the Supreme Court. It is those courts that decide grievances citizens have against the persons and undertaking of the state, and that authority is not reciprocal. For example, those courts decide whether or not citizens are entitled to challenge the operations of government in court by suing it. Their interpretation of the laws is final and dispositive, at least until they choose to revisit matters. Those in position to exercise legal authority are therefore committed to an unequal and nonreciprocal relation of authority with the subjects of the laws.

This kind of asymmetry or failure of reciprocity is not accidental or contingent, a feature that different institutional structures could correct. It is built into the claim of monopoly authority to use force legitimately. That claim can never be implemented reciprocally among moral agents; the very idea of monopoly is anti-reciprocal. So there is a fundamental problem with the authority structure that is essential to the state, to which the just agent must object. Perhaps, as an empirical matter, we cannot live without state provision of the coercive framework to secure the possibility of virtuous action and interaction. (More on this is in the next section. I doubt that this is the case, but the empirical evidence that it is not so is thin.) That, in sum, is the virtue ethical case for the minimal (in the limit, the nonexistent) state. That is the connection between virtue ethics and libertarianism.

Objections

Two general kinds of objections might be mounted to this strategy of grounding libertarian political theory in virtue ethics. One kind would be an "external" critique, rejecting the virtue ethics foundation I have outlined here. Because the topic of this chapter is how virtue ethics might provide a moral foundation for libertarianism, we can for present purposes set such objections aside.

More relevant are "internal" critiques, maintaining that, even if one accepts virtue ethics, it doesn't follow that libertarianism merits support. How might such critiques be framed? I see four major possibilities. One has an obvious historical base: Plato and Aristotle (among others) were the earliest and are still among the best proponents of a virtue ethic, but neither advocates anything like a libertarian state. If they didn't see the inference, why should we? The remaining three possibilities draw on more contemporary concerns. First, one might worry that the requirements of virtue ethics (and the virtue of justice in particular) as I have understood them are incompatible with a stable or peaceful society. Second, one might claim that other elements of virtue (other virtues) mitigate the libertarian force of those requirements. Finally, one might claim that the virtue of justice does not, despite my argument, carry with it the requirements I have cited as necessitating libertarian political arrangements. Let's take these up in order.

Plato and Aristotle had their own differences when it comes to political philosophy, but those differences are swamped by the distance from either of them to contemporary political philosophy. Neither, for example, was liberal, in the way that modern Western societies are and in the way that we have compelling moral reason to endorse. (To take an obvious example, Aristotle's politics not only tolerated but also justified slavery and the subordination of women.) Still, we can draw a challenge from their vision. For them, a good political constitution was one that played a material role in making citizens virtuous. We, like Aristotle, readily acknowledge the role of parents and teachers in this undertaking. If virtue is our priority, why not think we should endorse a state that overall has making us virtuous as its prime concern?

The answers to that question are both moral and practical. The basic moral concerns we have already surveyed. To undertake the role of forming virtuous citizens, the state and its agents must become people who, as a matter of institutional practice, must practice vice. They must, for example, see themselves as entitled to impose their conceptions of virtue and an appropriate pursuit of worthwhile ends on their political subordinates. They must establish institutions (in particular, educational institutions) that regiment the thought (especially what they take to be the nonvirtuous or vicious thought) of their subjects. (Of course, our existing system of public education does this regimentation already, but that fact does not make it congruent with the demands of justice.) Crucially, they must make a practice of substituting their own exercises of practical rationality for the judgments of others.

Notice the difference here between the case of parents and teachers and that of the state. Parents and teachers do impose their own judgment on that of their charges, but those charges are not adult humans with full moral capacities. But adults with those capacities are precisely those the state would need to claim authority over in order to accomplish this "tutorial" goal. And as we have seen, those authority relations are not something a virtuous person can do or endorse.[10]

Practically, the concerns are myriad. Socrates observed that few great Athenian statesmen were capable of improving the virtue of their fellow citizens,[11] and nobody since has demonstrated that they can do any better. Institutions of state are, simply put, bad forms of human sociality. They substitute coercion for cooperation, force for intelligence, and in so doing are corrosive to moral virtue.[12] They are among the last instrumentalities we should look to for making people virtuous. So we should not follow Plato and Aristotle in tracing through the political implications of virtue ethics.

What about the more contemporary concerns? The first is motivated by the thought that there are bad actors in the world—people who prey on others through theft or violence, in quite unvirtuous

---

[10] An interesting complication to this story is Aristotle's thought that justice requires that citizens rule and are ruled in turn (*Politics*, bk. III, chap. 16, in *The Complete Works of Aristotle: The Revised Oxford Translation*, vol. 2, ed. Jonathan Barnes, trans. B. Jowett, pp. 1986–2130.). This recipe can be, I believe, an expression of equality of authority. However, for it to be so, "rulership" must occur in adjudicating particular cases, not in other legislative or executive action, for it is in adjudication that the final obligations of individuals to the norms governing them are determined.

[11] Plato, *Gorgias*, in *Complete Works*, pp. 791–869.

[12] One of the clearest indictments of this tendency is one of the earliest. In Plato's *Gorgias*, Plato has Socrates bring out the systematic bias against truth seeking among those who most valorize the capacity to persuade others, as politicians (among others) must do.

(even vicious) ways. We ought not pretend that all people are virtuous or just. Equally, however, we ought not to think that the just or virtuous person must simply "roll over" against injustice and vice. The organizing thought of the virtue of justice—that it is rendering to others what is due them—is compatible with forceful (and forcible) responses to wrongdoing. It may justify punishment, though it is uncertain what sorts of penal arrangements might be compatible with the full scope of the virtue of justice, including not subordinating the judgment of others to one's own, but treating them as of reciprocal authority. Even if punishment cannot be justified for the just, however, justice allows (or requires) forcible resistance to injustice and restitution to its victims. "Rectificatory" justice, as Aristotle understood it, takes up exactly this idea.[13] More generally: just people engage others in reciprocity and support that reciprocity in the institutions and social arrangements that govern their lives. Nothing in that picture requires that they tolerate victimization of themselves or others.

One motivation for the next objection would be that somehow the virtues can conflict, so that justice might come into conflict with some other virtue (say, generosity or compassion), in such a way that the demands of justice would be curtailed by the demands of the other virtue. Now, on the conception of virtue ethics I am considering, the virtues are thought to be not only incapable of conflict but also mutually entailing—as requiring one another in order to be fully realized.[14] But one might hold that

[13] Aristotle, *Nicomachean Ethics*, bk. V, chap. 4.
[14] Aristotle, *Nicomachean Ethics*, bk. VI, chap. 13.

justice properly understood included within its scope restraint on the sorts of limitations of authority that (I have argued) support libertarianism.

At this point, this concern merges with the last of the critiques enumerated above. We ought not think, so it goes, that justice requires what I have said it does. It might not be hedged by other virtues, but might instead require other things of us. Perhaps being a just individual requires supporting a social system that provides a social safety net for the indigent. Or perhaps, more generally, a state is needed to provide laws, adjudication, and defense for all; and part of what the just person sees is that he must support that state financially and in other ways it demands of him, and that he must subordinate his own judgment to it.

I do not have a knockdown response to such concerns. What I have provided here is only a sketch of a conception of what justice requires of us as individuals, and there are assuredly other conceptions. However, three general points may be made to address such a possibility.

First, just because the virtues are mutually entailing, just people will not be immune to the claims upon them from those in exigent need. They themselves will be responsive to the claims and will support and engage in institutions that combat such a need. What they will not do is suppose that they are entitled to impose their judgment about what needs merit what attention—or what measures might best be taken to meet such needs—on others who do not agree with their judgment. Just people will not suppose that they have an authority to obligate others in light of such convictions, in a way that they cannot reciprocate. They will likely not suppose, that is, that the state is the right channel for exercising proper concern for the needs of others nor that it is appropriate to impose a legal obligation on others to be subject to the measures the just person thinks appropriate.

Second, most theories that would impose such an obligation on citizens (that is, some duty that just people might recognize as incumbent on them as part of what it is to be virtuous) begin with assumptions or claims about what the just state (or just society) might look like. Then, the claims about the obligations of citizens to support such institutions follow. If we take virtue ethics of the sort I have sketched here seriously, that is a tendentious way to proceed.

The requirements of the justice of virtue are predicated on what is necessary for us to live with others of our kind in relationships that allow us to be virtuous and to live well. A conception of citizenship or obligation to the state that conflicts with such requirements (that is, by beginning with the assumption that a state must be realized and satisfy certain demands of fairness or justice) lacks the theoretical authority to undermine what we know about living with one another in families, friendships, partnerships, community. Only if we do not take the claims of virtue seriously can we set aside such concerns.

Finally, the issue of authority of judgment remains. It is a staple—in fact, arguably the foundation—of liberal conceptions of political legitimacy that we are moral equals, that none of us has the authority to direct or subordinate others in ways that cannot be reciprocal, even on the basis of what seems to us to be right, to be commanded by God, and so on. To think otherwise, we know, is a recipe for conflict and warfare, and ultimately we get neither virtuous nor happy people in consequence. The demands of justice are grounded in part on that recognition. But that authority of command is what is required for the state to do its distinctive work. If some of us are to have the moral standing to have nonreciprocal authority over others, that story will require telling—and it will have to be some story. A eudaimonist virtue ethics makes space for us to understand how we can see ourselves and those around us as mutually engaged in living good lives, and in regulating our interactions accordingly through just conduct. If we take it seriously, we will see that libertarian limits on state authority are more than justified.

7

Objectivism

Neera K. Badhwar

Ayn Rand was born in 1905 in precommunist Russia, and lived through both the Kerensky and the Bolshevik revolutions. Communists expropriated her father's pharmacy, leaving the family to endure many hard times and the young Rand to learn firsthand the evils of totalitarianism. Rand decided to be a fiction writer when she was nine years old. Her greatest literary influences were Victor Hugo, for what she later called his "romantic realism," and Fyodor Dostoevsky, for his psychological acuity.

Rand fell in love with the West she saw in American and European movies, and America became her model of a free country when she studied its history in high school. She immigrated to the United States in 1926, where she honed her English language abilities by writing screen plays, short stories, and plays. She eventually published four best-selling novels and innumerable essays, comments, and columns.

To understand Rand's ethical and political philosophy, one must read not only her nonfiction but also her fiction. *We the*

Living shows how totalitarianism exalts the worst and destroys the best. *The Fountainhead* depicts the ideal man as one of vision and integrity—a man who lives firsthand and succeeds in over-coming the forces of ignorance and mediocrity. *Atlas Shrugged* provides both a glimpse of an ideal world, Atlantis, and a slow-motion look at the gradual disintegration of a society governed by the "aristocracy of pull": bureaucrats and mediocre businessmen and intellectuals in a perpetual game of favors, counterfavors, and threats, out to destroy those who engage in "unfair" competition by excelling at their work without any political favors.

It is partly due to her novels that Rand has the influence she does outside the academy. It is also partly due to her novels that she lacks such influence inside the academy. Whereas many peo-ple find her depiction of heroic characters inspiring, many others find it wooden and unconvincing. Her nonfiction, too, divides readers. Some are persuaded by her genuine insights and polemi-cal style; others are put off by her style and the lack of awareness of possible objections to her arguments. They are also put off by her misinterpretations and snap judgments of most philosophers.

Rand calls her philosophy "Objectivism" to emphasize the importance of recognizing (a) that reality is "an objective abso-lute," existing independently of our wishes or fears, and (b) that reason, rather than feelings or revelation, is our only means of knowledge and survival.[1] The name Objectivism also emphasizes the importance of recognizing that values are objective rather than subjective or intrinsic. Subjectivism holds that values are

---

[1] Ayn Rand, "Introducing Objectivism," *Objectivist Newsletter*, August 1962, p. 35.

determined wholly by our wishes and desires independent of the nature of the external world, whereas intrinsicism holds that they are inherent in the external world, independent of our nature.[2] By contrast, Objectivism holds that values depend both on our nature as rational beings and on the external world in which we live.

In ethics, Rand advocates ethical egoism—the view that we need morality for our own good, rather than for the general good or for others' good. She also argues that ethical egoism is the indispensable foundation of liberty, because liberty is needed for our own survival and happiness as rational beings who think and act by choice. The only alternative to ethical egoism, she claims, is altruism, whose essence is self-sacrifice, and we don't need liberty in order to sacrifice our lives and happiness. This is not, of course, the standard understanding of altruism in the academic literature, where altruism is usually defined as doing something for another for that person's sake but not necessarily at the expense of one's own rational desires or goals. Rand's conception of ethical egoism also differs from contemporary conceptions. I will begin by explaining this conception and then will proceed to discuss her defense of liberty, capitalism, and the minimal state.

According to ethical egoism, moral principles and virtues tell us what sort of person to be and how to act in order to advance our own good. But what if advancing our own good requires us to trample over other people? One form of ethical egoism says, "Well, then, you ought to trample over other people." But a world of such egoists would soon end up killing each other. And an

---

[2] Ayn Rand, "What Is Capitalism?" *Capitalism: The Unknown Ideal* (New York: New American Library, 1967), pp. 21ff.

ethical theory that leaves those who practice it dead is neither very egoistic nor very ethical. It is no wonder then that this is not what Rand means by ethical egoism.[3] What, then, does she mean? Elsewhere I have argued that Rand's essays and novels support more than one interpretation, but here I will limit myself to the most plausible one.[4]

Rand argues that ethics "is a code of values to guide man's choices and actions—the choices and actions that determine the purpose and the course of his life" and that it is "an *objective, metaphysical necessity of man's survival*."[5] By this statement, Rand means not merely physical survival but "survival *qua* man," that is, "the terms, methods, conditions and goals required for the survival of a rational being through the whole of his lifespan—in all those aspects of existence which are open to his choice."[6] The ultimate goal for every individual is his or her own survival and happiness. But since every individual rightfully has this goal, every individual's pursuit of it has to be compatible, in principle, with other individuals' pursuits of their ultimate goals. The "*human* good," she declares, "does not require human sacrifices and cannot be achieved by the sacrifice of anyone to anyone."[7]

---

[3] Michael Huemer, however, attributes just this kind of egoism to Rand in "Critique of the 'Objectivist Ethics'" (http://www.owl232.net/rand5.htm).

[4] Neera K. Badhwar and Roderick T. Long, "Ayn Rand," *Stanford Encyclopedia of Philosophy*, rev. ed., (Stanford, CA: Stanford University, 2016).

[5] Ayn Rand, "The Objectivist Ethics," *The Virtue of Selfishness: A New Concept of Egoism* (New York: New American Library, 1964), pp. 13, 23 [emphasis in original].

[6] Ibid., pp. 25, 27.

[7] Rand, "Objectivist Ethics," p. 31 [emphasis in original].

In what sense, however, is survival or happiness through immoral means not a "*human* good"? Since only human beings act immorally, it seems that the good achieved through immoral means is very much a human good. Further, why can't one person's good be achieved by sacrificing another person's? Countless people have gained their wealth and eminence through fraud or violence. The answer to these questions is that Rand is thinking of "human good," "survival *qua* man," and "happiness" in partly moralized terms even though she never acknowledges this point.

Happiness, according to Rand, is the existentially and psychologically "successful state of life." It is "a state of non-contradictory joy—a joy without penalty or guilt," achievable only by "the man who desires nothing but rational goals, seeks nothing but rational values and finds his joy in nothing but rational actions." [8] Happiness here is not a feeling we have episodically but an objectively worthwhile and emotionally positive state of life—what Aristotle calls *eudaimonia*. Rand holds that the pursuit of happiness is inseparable from the activity of maintaining one's life through the rational pursuit of rational goals. [9]

Because rationality is a virtue—indeed, the chief virtue that entails all the other virtues—the rational pursuit of rational goals makes virtue partly constitutive of the ultimate goal of survival *qua* man and happiness. (Note that, unlike virtuous acts, virtue as such is a character trait, an evaluative disposition to characteristically think, feel, and act in certain ways. Rand never makes this

---

[8] Ibid., pp. 27, 32.
[9] Ibid., pp. 29, 32.

explicit, but she depicts it clearly enough in her portraits of her fictional heroes.) But doesn't the view that virtue is partly constitutive of the ultimate goal of survival and happiness contradict her oft-repeated claim that virtue is not an end in itself but a means or instrument to survival and happiness? For reasons I give now, the answer is "not necessarily."

Sometimes when a philosopher says that virtue or morality is an end in itself, he means that it has no necessary connection to anything else that we care about: happiness, survival, or the things that produce or enable them. Kant is the foremost defender of this position. Morality is one thing, and the goods of this world another. Rand is surely right that in this sense virtue is not an end in itself—or that, if it were, practically no one would care about it. Sometimes, however, when a philosopher says that virtue is an end in itself, he means that it is partly constitutive of the ultimate end of a good human life, without denying that virtue also has instrumental value. This position is defended by Aristotle and neo-Aristotelians. I've argued in other work that this is also the position supported by many of Rand's statements and by her depiction of her heroes.[10]

Virtue is clearly partly constitutive of the happiness of her heroes, who often risk death and suffering for the sake of their moral principles, because the alternative—betraying their principles—would

---

[10] Neera K. Badhwar, *Is Virtue Only a Means to Happiness? An Analysis of Virtue and Happiness in Ayn Rand's Writings* (Poughkeepsie, NY: Objectivist Center, 2001). Long takes a similar position. See Roderick T. Long, *Reason and Value: Aristotle vs. Rand* (Poughkeepsie, NY: Objectivist Center, 2000).

be even worse for them. Human happiness does require success in one's worthwhile projects, but even more important, it requires a sense of justified pride in oneself, and justified pride requires virtue. This is why *The Fountainhead*'s Howard Roark can be seen as acting in his self-interest when he turns down commissions that would have made him the wealthiest and most sought-after architect in the country—at the price of his architectural vision. Roark chooses integrity over this kind of success.

The heroes of *Atlas Shrugged* renounce even more when they withdraw from the world. In both novels, Rand's heroes ultimately succeed in work and love, because it is an important part of Rand's project to show that, in a decent society, virtue is efficacious, that it helps us to succeed in our worthwhile goals.

This interpretation of Rand's view of virtue as both instrumental to, and partly constitutive of, happiness is, as we'll see, also the only interpretation that is compatible with Rand's defense of liberty and individual rights.

Liberty

Rand's argument for liberty is rights-based rather than consequentialist or contractarian. In other words, her argument is based on the premise that we all have rights by our very nature as beings who must choose to think and act, rather than on the premise that liberty brings about the best consequences or that people have agreed, or would agree, to a system of liberty.

At the same time, Rand holds that, in fact, a system of liberty would bring about the best consequences and that, partly for this reason, people would agree to it. Individuals are ends in themselves, not means to others' ends. As such, they are entitled to lead their life and pursue their happiness as they see fit, so long as they don't forcibly interfere with others' like pursuit.[11]

Rand argues that a right is "a moral principle defining and sanctioning a man's freedom of action in a social context."[12] "A right is that which can be exercised without anyone's permission."[13] All that is needed for freedom of action is the absence of physical coercion or fraud by others—including the government. All rights, thus, are negative, requiring of others nothing other than noninitiation of force or fraud—more pithily, nothing more than that they mind their own business.

Like other conceptions of rights, Rand's is also hierarchical. She states,

> There is only one fundamental right (all the others are its consequences or corollaries): a man's right to his own life. Life is a process of self-sustaining and self-generated action; the right to life means the right to engage in self-sustaining and self-generated action—which means: the freedom to take all the actions required by the nature of a rational being for the support, the furtherance, the fulfillment and the enjoyment of his own life. (Such is the meaning of the right to life, liberty and the pursuit of happiness.)[14]

[11] Rand, "Introducing Objectivism," p. 35.

[12] Rand, "Man's Rights," *Virtue of Selfishness*, p. 93.

[13] Ayn Rand, "Textbook of Americanism," *The Ayn Rand Column*, rev. ed. (New Millford, CT: Second Renaissance Books, 1998), p. 83.

[14] Rand, "Man's Rights," p. 93.

And again,

> Rights are conditions of existence required by man's
> nature for his proper survival. . . . If life on earth is his
> purpose, he has a right to live as a rational being: nature
> forbids him the irrational. Any group, any gang, any
> nation that attempts to negate man's rights, is wrong,
> which means: is evil, which means: is anti-life.[15]

Rand is making three highly significant points here, two absolutely necessary to liberty, the third possibly fatal. The first point
is that rights are claims to take certain actions without interference rather than to be given anything. They are claims to liberty
of action, not to whatever I might need or think I need—even if I
need it for acting. This is entailed by the very concept of negative
rights. For example, to earn a living I might need a car, and I have
a right to acquire a car in a peaceful exchange with someone who
wants to sell me a car. If I can't find anyone who wants to sell me
one I can afford, I can try to borrow money or beg for a free car. If
I'm lucky, I'll succeed in one of these attempts. But if I don't, it's
too bad. I have no "positive" right to a car just because I need one.

An individual's right is an enforceable claim against others—a
claim that the government is obligated to enforce. The view that
I have a positive right to a car implies that the government ought
to coerce others into providing me with a car. But such coercion,
even if it is indirect, through taxation, violates others' negative

---

[15] Galt's speech, in Ayn Rand, *For the New Intellectual: The Philosophy of Ayn Rand*
(New York: Random House, 1963), p. 182.

rights to be left alone so long as they are not aggressing or committing fraud against me. Positive rights are incompatible with negative rights. Hence, I don't have a right to a car, only to take the (rights-respecting) actions necessary for acquiring one.

The second point Rand is making about rights is that rights are held by individuals, because their function is the protection of the individual's freedom from interference by other individuals, groups, or government. So-called collective or group rights are a negation of individual rights, because they are nothing more than some individuals' power to force other individuals to obey their edicts. Individual rights are held against the collective—"the expression 'collective rights' is a contradiction in terms."[16] Indeed, the "principle of individual rights is the only moral base of all groups or associations."[17]

The third point Rand is making is that all rights are rights to actions that we need to take, as rational beings, for our own life and happiness. This is the problematic claim, for it entails that we have no right to take actions that are inimical to our life and happiness.[18] And if we have no such rights, then we may be forcibly prevented from doing things that are bad for us. Suppose, for example, that I have inherited a tidy sum of money, and now just want to enjoy the easy pleasures of lying around drinking beer, watching sitcoms, and snorting coke. My behavior is clearly self-destructive and irrational. So if all rights are rights to actions that we need to take, as rational beings, for our own life and happiness, Rand's

[16] Rand, "Textbook of Americanism," p. 83.

[17] Rand, "Collectivized 'Rights,'" *Virtue of Selfishness*, p. 102.

[18] Several philosophers have made this criticism. For references, see Neera K. Badhwar and Roderick Long, "Ayn Rand," http://plato.stanford.edu/entries/ayn-rand/.

view implies that it's permissible for the government to force me to do something more worthwhile, such as studying or working, under threat of punishment. But this is not a very rights-respecting view, and a society in which such coercion is practiced is not a very rights-respecting society. And Rand's conception of a proper government as a limited government entails that she would concur with this. She argues that a proper government must be confined to only two tasks: (a) protecting us from domestic and foreign violence and fraud and (b) settling disputes according to objective laws. There is no room in her night-watchman conception of the state for paternalistic or moral legislation allowing the government to coercively prevent people from self-destructive or immoral behavior.

How, then, can we reconcile this view of the proper role of government with Rand's claim that "[r]ights are conditions of existence required by man's nature for his proper survival," where "are" is the "are" of identity? One possibility is that in saying this, she is thinking of what gives rise to rights and what makes them valuable to most of us.[19] It seems undeniable that if human beings had been incapable of valuing their own—or anyone else's—proper survival or happiness, we would have been incapable of valuing rights—or, for that matter, anything at all. Again, if human beings had been incapable of thinking and acting long range, if it had been in our nature to always act impulsively, we would have been incapable of living by principles, or even of conceiving of them. Hence, since rights are principles sanctioning an individual's freedom of action,

[19] Such a "genetic" query is an important aspect of Rand's methodology. For example, she asks what gives rise to values, to the need for an ethical code, to the concept of justice, and so on.

we would have had no rights or even a concept of rights. But the fact that the capacity for thinking and acting long range, valuing our own or others' proper survival and happiness, is essential for having rights doesn't entail that rights must be limited to the freedom to take the actions that are rationally necessary for our life and happiness, period. Take, for example, the proverbial couch potato. A couch potato has the capacity to think and act long range, to value his long-term survival and happiness, even if his actions are irrational and self-destructive. This capacity is enough to make him a rights bearer. Respecting his rights may or may not do him any good, but it does respect him as an autonomous being responsible for his own life. A society that respects people's rights respects even the couch potato's rights.

Other statements by Rand show her recognition that what matters is liberty, whether it's exercised rationally or irrationally, so long as the exercise does not violate anyone else's rights. As she declares, "[A] right is the moral sanction of . . . [the individual's] freedom to act on his own judgment, for his own goals, by his own voluntary, uncoerced choice."[20] Again, freedom is said to be "the fundamental requirement of man's mind" because "the choice to exercise his rational faculty *or not* depends on the individual."[21] She does not say that freedom is needed only for making rational judgments, or only for exercising one's rational faculty.[22] But Rand is, at best, inconsistent on this point.

[20] Rand, "Collectivized 'Rights,'" *Virtue of Selfishness*, p. 102.

[21] Rand, "Capitalism," p. 17 [emphasis added].

[22] Sometimes Rand thinks of irrationality as the failure to exercise one's rational faculty rather than as a misuse of it.

Turning now to the other specific rights that human beings have, two of the most important are freedom of speech and property. As with other rights, the right to free speech "means freedom from interference, suppression or punitive action by the government—and nothing else."[23] It does not mean the right to be given a podium or newspaper in order to express one's views or, for that matter, the right to be given an appreciative audience. The right to property is "the right to gain, to keep, to use and to dispose of material values"[24]—not a right to *have* property, but simply a right to act to gain it, and once gained, to use it or sell it or give it away. And all these actions must themselves be respectful of other people's rights. A diamond ring gained by theft does not become the thief's property, no matter how hard he had to work for it or how ingenious his plan. Nor does the right to use one's property mean that one may use it to violate the rights of others. For example, if I live in an apartment, I have no right to play my radio as loudly as possible at 1:00 a.m., thus disturbing my neighbors' sleep.[25]

The next question is: Why should we respect each other's rights? It's good for me that other people respect my rights to my life, liberty, and happiness, but how is it good for me to respect their rights? On an egoist ethics, it has to be good for me to be justified. One answer is the instrumental answer given by the 17th-century English philosopher Thomas Hobbes: we should respect others'

[23] Rand, "The Fascist New Frontier," *Ayn Rand Column*, p. 106.

[24] Rand, "Man's Rights," p. 93.

[25] See Ayn Rand, "The Left: Old and New," *Return of the Primitive: The Anti-Industrial Revolution* (New York: Meridian, 1999), p. 167.

rights because we can't hope to get away with violating them. But this answer is not enough because there *are* times when we can get away with it.

Rand adds another reason: immorality requires self-deception, which, in turn, leads to psychological conflict and, if pursued as a policy, a sense of emptiness. But for many people, an occasional deception or worse causes no psychological conflict, and for too many people even the *policy* of deceiving, defrauding, or robbing others for the sake of their own goals causes no conflict or sense of emptiness. Given the variability of human nature, this conclusion should not be surprising. Moreover, surely we ought to respect others' rights *because they have rights* and not because it might be psychologically bad for us.

Here again, Rand's neo-Aristotelian conception of survival *qua* man and happiness comes to the rescue, albeit inconsistently. To live a life proper to a human being—to achieve a happiness worth having—requires living virtuously, and each virtue is defined partly in terms of a recognition and acceptance of some fact or facts, an acceptance understood by the agent to be indispensable for gaining, maintaining, or expressing his or her ultimate value: a happiness worth having. For example, integrity is "the recognition of the fact that you cannot fake your consciousness,"[26] a recognition that is expressed in loyalty to one's rational values and convictions,[27] and honesty is "the recognition of the fact that you cannot fake existence," a recognition that is expressed in truthfulness in

---

[26] Ayn Rand, *Atlas Shrugged* (New York: Random House, 1957), p. 936.

[27] Rand, "The Ethics of Emergencies," *The Virtue of Selfishness*, p. 46.

thought and speech.[28] Justice is the recognition of the fact that we ought to give others their due and part of what is due them is respect for their rights.[29]

An important question about rights is whether they can conflict. Rand denies this possibility if they are properly defined as protections of freedom of action against physical force or fraud. So-called "positive rights" conflict with negative rights because they are claims to benefits for certain people at the expense of other people's freedom of action. For example, my "positive right" to have you bake me a cake for my gay wedding conflicts with your (negative) right to refuse to participate in an act that you regard as being against your religion. It has been argued, however, that even negative rights can conflict. To use an earlier example, my right to use my property as I see fit seems to entail that I have a right to play loud music whenever I like, even though you also have a right not to be disturbed at 1:00 a.m. However, Rand would say that I don't have such a right because the sound of the music is not confined to my property. To paraphrase the old saying, my right to play loud music at 1:00 a.m. ends where your ears begin.

Rand also argues that not only rights, but even rational interests, don't conflict, at least in a free society.[30] In her words,

---

[28] Rand, *Atlas Shrugged*, pp. 936–37.

[29] Rand herself defines justice more narrowly as "the recognition of the fact that you cannot fake the character of men as you cannot fake the character of nature . . . that every man must be judged for what he is and treated accordingly" (Galt's speech, *For the New Intellectual*, p. 129). But the point she is making here is a special case of giving people what is due them, and human beings are due respect for their rights because they are rights bearers.

[30] Rand, "The 'Conflicts' of Men's Interests," *Virtue of Selfishness*, pp. 50–56.

"[T]here is no conflict of interests among men who do not desire the unearned, who do not make sacrifices nor accept them, who deal with one another as *traders*, giving value for value."[31] This harmony of different people's rational interests has been taken by some commentators to be essential for the existence of rights and a peaceful society.

But what is Rand's argument for the proposition that rational interests don't conflict? It seems that conflicts of rational interests abound. To take the case she herself considers: two people apply for a job, but only one gets it.[32] Assuming that both are qualified, hasn't the loser's rational interest been frustrated because the other person got the job? True, the loser hasn't been treated unfairly and hasn't sacrificed his interests, as Rand points out, but this point is irrelevant to the question of a conflict of rational interests.

Rand argues that, assuming that the employer was rational, the better person got the job. But what if the employer wasn't rational—or not on this occasion? Or he was rational but made an innocent mistake of judgment about the better candidate? Quite apart from questions of rationality or vision, in a buyer's market, employers often practically toss a coin to decide whom to hire, or do so on the basis of quite irrelevant factors, such as liking one applicant's sense of humor better than the other's. There is nothing irrational about this when two (or more) applicants turn out to be equally qualified. To take an even simpler case: I want that little doggie in the window, but so do you, and you get there

---

[31] Rand, "Objectivist Ethics," p. 31 [emphasis in original].
[32] Rand, "Conflicts," p. 50.

first and buy him. Commonsensically, our interests conflict even though they are rational. The only way to remove the appearance of conflict is to declare retrospectively that I never had an interest in the little doggie. But this is just a "sour grapes" rationalization. Why would I have tried to get to the store to buy the little doggie, or felt disappointment when I failed to buy him, if I didn't have an interest in him?

These criticisms, however, are compatible with Rand's general point that *acting dishonestly or unjustly* in order to get the job—or the doggie—is not in our overall, ultimate interest. Better to break rock in a quarry, like Howard Roark, than to sell out. They are also compatible with the fact that rational interests do not necessarily—that is, *by their very nature*—conflict. The conflicts are contingent on extraneous factors, such as that there is only one job or one doggie for two rationally interested people. If rational interests necessarily conflicted, there would be no rights—indeed, there would be a war of all against all. But there is no good argument for Rand's claim that rational interests *cannot* conflict. Nor does acknowledging this endanger the existence of rights.

Capitalism

Capitalism is a social system based on the recognition of individual rights, including property rights, in which all property is privately owned.

—Ayn Rand, *Capitalism: The Unknown Ideal*

By "capitalism," Rand means "a full, pure, uncontrolled, unregulated laissez faire capitalism—with a separation of state and economics, in the same way and for the same reasons as the separation of state and church."[33] Just as the state's interference in religious matters and religion's interference in state matters led to a corruption of both state and religion, so the state's interference in economic matters and business lobbying for special favors has led to a corruption of both politics and business.

Capitalism is the "politico-economic expression of the principle that a man's life, freedom, and happiness are his by moral right"—that is, of the principle of ethical egoism.[34] The doctrine of individual rights recognizes this principle by protecting people's freedom to pursue their own interests, so long as they respect the rights of others to do the same. It recognizes that no individuals may be forced to sacrifice themselves for the sake of the nation or society, or for another individual.

By Rand's definitions, no so-called capitalist society is genuinely capitalist. At best, contemporary societies are mixed, with elements of capitalism and socialism or fascism in the brew.[35] In a pure capitalist society, force may be used only in retaliation against the one who initiates force; and, except when the threat is immediate, this retaliatory function is given to the government. Indeed, Rand describes the government as "the means of placing the retaliatory use of force under *objective control*."[36]

[33] Rand, "Objectivist Ethics," p. 33.

[34] Rand, "Alienation," *Capitalism: The Unknown Ideal*, p. 284.

[35] Under fascism, individuals own private property but the government controls their use of it through regulations; under socialism, the government controls property without having a title to it. See "Fascist New Frontier," p. 98. Rand thought that America was more fascist than socialist ("The New Fascism: Rule by Consensus," *Capitalism*).

[36] Rand, "Capitalism," p. 19 [emphasis in original].

The government may not, however, prevent people from making peaceful transactions or, for that matter, coerce them into making any particular transaction. But this is exactly what it does when it prevents, say, Uber and its would-be customers from making the contracts they want to make, or when it requires businesses to raise their minimum wage.

Capitalism is morally justified because it respects our rational nature by leaving us free to discover or create values, as well as to trade them to mutual benefit.[37] Capitalism thus exemplifies the principle of justice. It also advances the common good by creating prosperity, but this, according to Rand, is not its justification. Ever focused on the creative mind, Rand holds that the ultimate driver of the economy is not the consumer (demand) but the innovator (supply). Contrary to imitators—those "who attempt to cater to what they think is the public's known taste"—innovators continually raise "the public's knowledge and taste to ever higher levels,"[38] even if it takes time for the public to realize the value of the product.

An important example of such a revolutionary product from our own time is Steve Jobs's computer, the Lisa. The Lisa failed to gain much market share, but Jobs's Apple computers soon gained in popularity, beating out cheaper personal computers. However, Rand does not recognize that innovators can also use clever new methods to spread urban myths and debase taste in order to make money. Thus, although the Internet provides innovators with a platform to spread knowledge and advertise products that improve people's lives, it also provides them with a platform to spread misinformation and

[37] Ibid., p. 24.
[38] Ibid., p. 25.

advertise products that are overall harmful or encourage a debasement of taste. Of course, Rand might claim that anyone who does this is an imitator, not an innovator; but using clever new methods to make people more ignorant than they already are, or to debase their taste, is hard to see as imitative. It would therefore be more accurate to say that a capitalist economy offers innovators the opportunity to increase our knowledge and improve our taste—but it also offers them the opportunity to do the opposite.

Rand challenges the widespread view that capitalism leads to wars, on the grounds that capitalism "bans force from social relationships," including relationships with the residents of other nations, by advocating free trade, "[that is], the abolition of trade barriers, of protective tariffs, of special privileges."[39] It is thus "the only system fundamentally opposed to war." No wonder, then, that "*capitalism gave mankind the longest period of peace in history*—a period during which there were no wars involving the entire civilized world—from the end of the Napoleonic wars in 1815 to the outbreak of World War I in 1914."[40] Although pure laissez faire capitalism has never existed, Rand believes that this period came closer to it than any before or since.

Rand is right that genuine capitalism creates conditions for peace by substituting free trade for war, but her statement that there were no wars from 1815 to 1914 is exaggerated. There were the Mexican-American War; the U.S. Civil War; and many European conquests of countries in Asia, Africa, and Latin America. The opponents or victims were not capitalist in any of these

---

[39] Rand, "The Roots of War," *Capitalism: The Unknown Ideal*, pp. 38–39.

[40] Ibid. [emphasis in original].

cases, but all the same, the more capitalist side waged war against the noncapitalist side. In particular, several European countries departed from the peaceful principles of free trade to conquer, colonize, and exploit the peoples of poorer countries.

Rand also holds that all freedoms—economic, personal, and political—stand or fall together, because coercing people in one sphere requires coercing them in others. Striking examples could be found in the slaveholding South. Slavery was, of course, the most egregious violation of the rights of enslaved individuals, but slavery also spawned violations of the rights of slaveholders and other whites. Most Southern states passed laws against manumission out of fear that freed blacks would subvert the slaveholding order and drafted young men to catch runaway slaves. They also censored speech, outlawing any talk of abolition. The North was freer not only economically but also politically and personally.

Still, economic and personal freedoms don't always go hand in hand. The freer economy of the North did not prevent most Northern states from imposing legal segregation in public places like schools, water fountains, lunch counters, and buses or from outlawing interracial marriage.[41] All these laws have been struck down now in our far less capitalist system.

Capitalism gradually extended the right of women to own property and participate as independent agents in the economy; but thanks to cultural changes, women have far more economic freedom now in our mixed economy than they did in the 19th century.

---

[41] See Douglas Harper, *Slavery in the North*, 2003, http://slavenorth.com/exclusion.htm and https://en.wikipedia.org/wiki/Racial_segregation_in_the_United_States.

In matters of sexual preference and reproduction as well, people are far freer now than then. For example, before 1962, sodomy was a felony in every U.S. state, and anti-sodomy laws were struck down by the Supreme Court only in 2003. The federal Comstock Act of 1873 outlawed not only abortion but also contraception, and even dissemination of information about contraception. Most states had similar laws. The first open attempt at disseminating birth control information and devices was made only in 1916—that is, after the end of the most economically free period. And abortion continued to be illegal until 1973.

To take another contemporary example, the Index of Economic Freedom often rates Singapore as one of the freest economies, but on measures of personal and political freedom, Singapore fares rather badly. Why "personal" freedoms and economic freedom so often fail to go hand in hand remains an open question.

Rand herself is a consistent defender of all freedoms. Writing about laws against birth control and abortion, she argues that they deny women as well as men the right "*to their own life and happiness*—the right not to be regarded as the means to any end"—in this case, procreation, like "stud-farm" animals.[42] On racism, she writes that it is "the lowest, most crudely primitive form of collectivism. It is the notion of ascribing moral, social or political significance to a man's genetic lineage . . . . [It claims] that a man's convictions, values and character are determined before he is born, by physical factors beyond his control."[43]

[42] Rand, "Of Living Death," *The Voice of Reason: Essays in Objectivist Thought* (New York: New American Library, 1990), pp. 55, 58–59 [emphasis in original].

[43] Rand, "Racism," *Virtue of Selfishness*, p. 126.

The Minimal State vs. Anarchism

In a rights-respecting libertarian society, human relationships are *voluntary*. People are free to cooperate or go their own peaceful way, leaving others free to do likewise. In such a society, only retaliatory force against rights violators—those who initiate force or fraud—is permissible. But the right to retaliatory force cannot be left to every individual without risking chaos and a general breakdown of society. Except when the danger is imminent, we need to cede this right to the government, which Rand defines as *"the means of placing the retaliatory use of physical force under objective control—*[that is], under objectively defined laws."[44]

Since Rand believes that the only function of a government is to protect us from domestic or foreign aggression or fraud, she holds that all legislation must be limited to protection of our rights. The government has no right to prohibit people from peaceful activities on moral grounds (even if the activities are actually immoral), or to force them to support social programs for "the greater good." To do so is to violate their rights to live their lives as they see fit. But a government can be prevented from overstepping its proper function only if it is tightly controlled by law—only if it is "a government of laws and not of men."[45] In a society with such a government, "a private individual may do anything except that which is legally *forbidden*; a government official may do nothing except that which is legally *permitted*."[46] This is the way to subordinate "might" to "right."

[44] Rand, "The Nature of Government," *Virtue of Selfishness*, p. 108 [emphasis in original].
[45] Ibid., p. 109.
[46] Ibid., p. 109. [emphasis in original].

Rand rejects the view that a free society must be anarchist on the grounds that without a government individuals would have to go around armed out of fear of attacks, or join gangs, and society would dissolve into gang warfare.[47] Even if every person in a given society were "fully rational and faultlessly moral," the society could not function as an anarchy, because there is always the possibility of honest disagreements, and their resolution requires "*objective laws*" and an arbiter that all sides can accept.[48] In *Atlas Shrugged*, however, Rand depicts her utopia, Galt's Gulch, as a society without a government: a "voluntary association of men held together by nothing but every man's [rational] self-interest," without any formal organization.[49] There is only a judge to arbitrate disagreements, although he has never been called on to arbitrate. Galt's Gulch is, thus, an anarchist society, although Rand never calls it that. Perhaps Rand would say that a small community of like-minded people who know each other well and rely on each other for all their needs can conduct their own affairs peacefully and justly, but that this is too much to expect of people in a big society, even if they are all rational and committed to justice.

Anarchists charge, however, that a government holding a monopoly on retaliatory force is itself guilty of initiating force against the citizens who have to accept its rule, whether they consent to it or not. A monopoly government also initiates force against its would-be competitors. Because protecting rights by

---

[47] Ibid., p. 108.

[48] Ibid., p. 112 [emphasis in original].

[49] Rand, *Atlas Shrugged*, p. 690.

banning the initiation of force is the linchpin of Rand's social morality, she is inconsistent to reject anarchism.[50] Moreover, a territorial monopoly on law and force (government) is not necessary, because people can establish a just and effective legal system in a competitive market of security providers.[51] The Law Merchant, a body of law established and enforced in private courts by the merchants of various countries in the late Middle Ages and early Renaissance, illustrates the possibility of an effective voluntary legal system.[52]

Rand rejects the idea of "competing governments" (more precisely, competing security agencies) because, she says, they are incompatible with a single, objective system of law and, thus, with rights and peaceful cooperation.[53] Competing agencies will, or might, have competing systems of law, with no way of reconciling differences. This criticism is rejected by anarchists, who point out that most of Western law grew out of competitively evolved systems of law, such as Roman law, Anglo-Saxon law, and the Law Merchant. But even if Rand and other minimal statists are right that anarchism is impractical, they have no

---

[50] Roy Childs, "Objectivism and the State: An Open Letter to Ayn Rand," reprinted in *Liberty Against Power: Essays by Roy A. Childs, Jr.*, ed. J. Taylor (San Francisco: Fox & Wilkes, 1969, 1994) and Murray Rothbard, *For a New Liberty: The Libertarian Manifesto*, revised edition (New York: Macmillan, 1978) [Rothbard 1978 available online (pdf)]

[51] Roderick T. Long, "Market Anarchism as Constitutionalism," in *Anarchism/Minarchism: Is a Government Part of a Free Country?* ed. Roderick T. Long and Tibor R. Machan (Burlington, VT: Ashgate, 2008), pp. 133–54.

[52] Roderick T. Long, "Why Objective Law Requires Anarchy," *Formulations* 6 (Autumn 1998), http://freenation.org/a/f61l1.html.

[53] Rand, "Nature of Government," p. 112.

defense against the objection that a monopoly state is guilty of initiating force.

Conclusion

Crude ethical egoism is inconsistent with the unconditional obligation to respect others' rights. But an egoism that sees virtue as partly constitutive of the individual's good does not have this problem, and it is this sort of egoism that Rand defends in much of her writing. Like other defenders of negative rights, Rand sees rights as claims to freedom of action and not to desired or even desirable outcomes. Her defense of capitalism as an "unknown ideal" is distinctive by virtue of her insistence (a) that capitalism is the political-economic system in which there is a complete separation of the state and the economy and (b) that this separation is necessary for freeing the individual to pursue his own happiness by creating values and trading with others.

Rand argues that justice and peace require a state, but the state must be minimal, restricted to a protection of our rights. When it goes beyond this basic function, the state itself becomes a violator of rights.

Ethical Intuitionism

Michael Huemer

I am an advocate of two controversial philosophical views: *ethical intuitionism* and *libertarianism*. Ethical intuitionism is a general theory about the nature of values and our knowledge thereof. The theory is *logically consistent* with almost any moral or political views. Nevertheless, certain ethical views are especially natural ones for an intuitionist to hold. Furthermore, those ethical views fit naturally with libertarian political philosophy. So, although I don't claim that libertarianism can be derived from ethical intuitionism, I do think that libertarian intuitionism is a very natural and coherent position. In what follows, I aim to explain why.

Major Tenets of Ethical Intuitionism

I have written about intuitionism at length elsewhere.[1] Here, I will just offer a sketch of the view. Two main ideas are central to any ethical intuitionist position.

---

[1] Michael Huemer, *Ethical Intuitionism* (New York: Palgrave Macmillan, 2005).

Moral Realism

The first tenet of intuitionism is *moral realism*. This is the view that there are objective values (or objective evaluative properties, objective evaluative facts, objectively true value statements). That is, there are at least some true statements of the form "*x* is good," "*x* is bad," or "*x* should (or shouldn't) do *y*," such that those statements do not depend for their truth on observers' attitudes toward *x* or *y*.

Who would disagree with moral realism? A number of people do. Some believe that what is right or wrong is determined entirely by what society approves or disapproves of. Thus, the truth of any "should" statement always depends on one's culture. Others believe that what is good, bad, right, or wrong depends on the attitudes of the individual. Others believe that evaluative statements, in general, are neither true nor false. Finally, some believe that all (positive) evaluative statements are false, because in reality, nothing has any evaluative properties.[2] Those views are known, respectively, as relativism, subjectivism, noncognitivism, and nihilism. The intuitionist rejects all four of those views.

What would be an example of an objective evaluative truth? During the 1970s, Ted Bundy, one of history's most notorious psychopaths, murdered a series of more than 30 women, apparently for entertainment purposes. (He was finally executed in Florida in 1989.) Bundy's behavior was, to say the least, extremely bad and wrong. That is not an indeterminate statement

---

[2] A *positive* statement says that something has some property, whereas a negative statement denies that something has some property.

(neither true nor false), and it certainly isn't a *false* statement; it's true. And it's not true because society says so. Rather, if our society somehow accepted Bundy's behavior, our society would just be horribly misguided. Nor is it true because *I* said so. If I somehow approved of Bundy, *I* would just be horribly misguided. In general, "Bundy's actions were bad" is true independent of observers' attitudes. There are many similar examples.

Intuition and Moral Knowledge

The second main tenet of intuitionism is that *ethical intuition* enables us to gain knowledge of at least some of the objective evaluative truths. There is more than one understanding of "ethical intuition"; here, I will just sketch my own understanding. In my view, an ethical intuition is a type of *appearance.* An appearance is a type of mental state, in which something *seems* to one to be the case. This appearance differs from belief, because it is possible to either believe or disbelieve what seems to one to be the case. Appearances typically *cause* beliefs.

There are several species of appearances, including sensory, mnemonic, and intellectual. For example, when I see a squirrel outside my window, I have a *sensory* appearance in which it seems that a squirrel is outside the window. When I think back to this morning, I have a *mnemonic* appearance in which I seem to remember having a delicious tofu scramble for breakfast. When I think about geometry, I have an *intellectual* appearance in which it seems to me that the shortest path between any two points must be a straight line.

That last is an example of an "intuition" (in the philosophers' technical sense). An intuition is an initial, intellectual appearance.

That is, it is a mental state in which something seems to one to be the case upon intellectual reflection, where this appearance does not depend on entertaining an inference to that conclusion. When I think about what is the shortest path between two points, I do not entertain an argument that it must be a straight line; rather, it just seems immediately obvious that it must be a straight line.

An "ethical intuition" is simply an intuition of some evaluative proposition. It is an initial, intellectual appearance that something is good, bad, right, or wrong. For example, when I reflect, it just seems obvious that pleasure is intrinsically good (good for its own sake).

All rational beliefs are based on appearances. With few exceptions, when you believe that P, you believe it because it seems to you that P, or perhaps because it seems to you that Q, *and* it seems to you that Q supports P (or it seems to you that R, and it seems to you that R supports Q, and it seems to you that Q supports P, etc.). Your belief is thus caused by and based on one or more appearances.

The exceptions are cases in which you form beliefs based on emotions, desires, leaps of faith, or some such obviously non-rational source. No other alternatives exist. (There is not, for example, the alternative of a belief based on an infinite series of other beliefs or a belief based on a fact that is never presented in any appearances.)

A belief is justified, in my view, provided that the belief is based on an appearance that one has no reason to doubt. If P seems true to you, and there are no reasons to doubt P or to doubt the reliability of the appearance, then it makes sense to believe P.[3] Ethical beliefs are sometimes justified, because sometimes one has the intuition that x is good (or bad, or right, or wrong), and one has no reason to doubt it.

There is more to say about *knowledge*, but the preceding is the most important part. When we ask, "How do we know x?" the main thing we want to know is how we are justified in believing x (this being a crucial necessary condition on knowing). The preceding explains how we are sometimes justified in believing evaluative truths.

Against Theory

In addition to the above two essential points, there is a third important aspect of the approach taken by many intuitionists (myself included): intuitionists tend to be anti-theoretical. That is, we tend to think that relatively specific, concrete judgments take precedence over general, theoretical judgments.[4] What does this "taking precedence" amount to? Four closely related things can be said to explain it.

First, the way human cognition normally works is that we come to know concrete, specific things first, and general, abstract things later—if at all. In fact, the justification for a general theory usually

---

[3] See Michael Huemer, *Skepticism and the Veil of Perception* (Lanham, MD: Rowman and Littlefield, 2001), pp. 98–115; and Michael Huemer, "Compassionate Phenomenal Conservatism," *Philosophy and Phenomenological Research* 74 (2007): 30–55.

[4] H. A. Prichard's *Moral Obligation* (Oxford, UK: Clarendon, 1957) is an extreme case; cf. Jonathan Dancy, "Moral Particularism," in *Stanford Encyclopedia of Philosophy*, ed. Edward N. Zalta, 2013, http://plato.stanford.edu/archives/fall2013/entries/moral-particularism/. Not all intuitionists share this view, but the view is much more common among intuitionists than among other philosophers.

depends on our first having justified beliefs about specific cases. For instance, to be justified in accepting some general account of what justice is, one must first know in many individual cases what is a just or unjust action.

Second, specific judgments are usually more reliable and better justified than general, theoretical judgments. Consider beliefs about the physical world to start with. Almost every *theory* about the physical world that was ever accepted was wrong (Aristotle's physics, Ptolemaic astronomy, the theory of the four elements, etc.). Conversely, of the beliefs about *specific* physical objects ("that cat is furry," "the apples are on the counter," "a river is at the base of the hill," etc.), probably almost all have been correct. I think much the same is true in almost every field: most abstract theories are false, whereas most concrete judgments are true. The record for *philosophical* theories, by the way, is especially bad.

Third, as a corollary to the preceding two points, if you have a general theory that turns out to conflict with the judgment you would be inclined to accept about some particular case, then, almost always, the theory is wrong. For instance, let's say you initially accept the theory that no person should ever violate another person's rights (including property rights). Then you consider a case in which a person trespasses on another person's land because that trespass is necessary to take someone to the hospital during a medical emergency. On its face, the trespass seems OK, though a violation of the landowner's property right. You could revise your theory so as to accept that violating someone's rights is sometimes permissible, or you could stick to your guns and insist that the trespass was wrong. The former choice is the correct one.

Fourth, suppose you are interested in the answer to some relatively specific question (say, what is the right immigration policy?). You should usually try to answer the question using the most concrete premises that will provide an answer (and that are also highly plausible). You typically should *not* take a detour through some very general theory (say, a general theory of when coercion is justified). As a rule, such detours will make you *much* less likely to arrive at the truth.[5] Another way of putting the methodological point is, *don't answer more than you have to.* When asked whether immigration restrictions are justified, you don't have to answer when in general a coercive act is justified, what in general is the good, or what is the nature of justice. So don't.

Why, then, have I been addressing abstract, theoretical questions throughout this section? Do we really need to address such questions to figure out what is the best political ideology?

No, we don't. You could follow my argument for libertarianism without knowing about intuitionism. My book on political philosophy never mentions intuitionism. But for this chapter, I was specifically asked to address the relationship between intuitionism and libertarianism. And it is true that my views on those two subjects cohere. But I think you should be a libertarian whether or not ethical intuitionism is true, and I think you should be an intuitionist whether or not libertarianism is true.

---

[5] Note: none of those things is a universal, necessary truth. There are undoubtedly *some* cases in which a theoretical judgment takes precedence over concrete judgments, in each of the four senses mentioned here.

Why Libertarianism? The Argument from Skepticism about Authority

I have discussed the case for libertarianism at length elsewhere.[6] Here, I will briefly sketch my reasons for endorsing a libertarian political philosophy, with special attention to how these reasons cohere with an intuitionist account of ethics.

The Role of Commonsense Morality in Political Philosophy

I believe that political philosophy ought to start from ethics: to figure out how the government should behave in some situation, we should first reflect on how we think people should behave in analogous situations, because the government is just a certain group of people. Furthermore, ethics, as I've suggested earlier, ought to start from our ethical intuitions, that is, the ethical propositions that seem obvious on reflection.

Sometimes, an individual's ethical intuitions conflict with the intuitions of other people. That conflict is particularly common when it comes to intuitions that bear on controversial political issues. Of particular import, those of differing political ideologies will often have conflicting ethical intuitions. For instance, those on the left and those on the right of the political spectrum tend to have different intuitions about the value of equality: left-wing thinkers find wealth inequalities intuitively, intrinsically problematic, whereas right-wing thinkers are much less likely to see any intuitive problem with it.

---

[6] Michael Huemer, *The Problem of Political Authority* (New York: Palgrave Macmillan, 2013).

Given moral realism, someone's intuitions must be mistaken. However, we have no good reason to assume that other people are much more likely to have mistaken intuitions than we ourselves are. Therefore, pending further argument, we should withhold judgment on controversial issues where people's intuitions diverge radically, especially when intuitions diverge along ideological lines.

On what, then, should we base our ethical beliefs? A natural methodological approach is this: one should look for the least controversial ethical intuitions and try to build other normative beliefs upon those. In the realm of politics, it is especially important to seek evaluative premises that would seem correct to reasonable people of different ideological inclinations, whether they be left-wing, right-wing, libertarian, or something else. No premises are accepted by everyone, but if some ethical premise seems obvious to the great majority of people regardless of their political orientation, then that premise should be assumed correct unless and until we have good reasons for thinking otherwise. In addition, the ideas presented earlier suggest that these should mainly be intuitive ethical judgments about specific cases. If we have a widespread, specific intuition, that is a reasonable starting point; no further *theory* or *argument* is needed.[7]

---

[7] At this point, you might wonder about these questions: Why not say the same thing about *political* premises? Why not start our political theorizing from the consensus political views? We'll discuss this later in the section titled "What about Political Intuitions?"

Some Commonsense Ethical Intuitions

Here is an example. Imagine that I live in a village that has some poor people who are not being adequately cared for. Suppose I go around the village demanding contributions for a charity that I run to aid the poor. If anyone refuses to contribute, I kidnap them at gunpoint and lock them in a cage for an extended period. What is the moral status of my behavior?

Most people intuit that this behavior would be wrong. It is of course laudable to run a charity to aid the poor; what is not permissible is to collect contributions by force and to imprison noncontributors. One need not give a *theory* of why this is wrong nor *argue* that it is wrong, because it just seems wrong to nearly everyone, regardless of whether one is left-wing, right-wing, libertarian, or other, and this appearance suffices for justified belief, in the absence of specific grounds for doubt.

On its face, my behavior in that scenario seems analogous to that of a government collecting funds for social welfare programs through taxation, where those who refuse to pay the taxes will be arrested and jailed. From here, it becomes the burden of those who support such government actions to explain why those actions are morally permissible, either by showing how the government's actions are really different from the actions in my example (in a way that makes the government's behavior much better) or by showing how the actions in my example are really justified (though that would be very difficult). If the defenders of government social welfare programs cannot discharge this burden, then we should conclude that government social welfare programs are impermissible.

Note how this argument differs from the sort of arguments traditionally advanced by libertarian absolute rights theorists, such as Murray Rothbard, Ayn Rand, and (perhaps) Robert Nozick.[8] They argue, roughly, that because it is always wrong to initiate coercion and because taxation requires the initiation of coercion, taxation must be wrong. By contrast, I argue that because taxation for the purpose of supporting social welfare programs is on its face analogous to behavior that would seem wrong if it were done by anyone other than the government, there is a presumption that such taxation is wrong. It is the burden of those who support social welfare programs to rebut this presumption.

My argument, I think, has a more reliable ethical starting point. Of course, this also makes the rest of the argument more difficult, because we must listen to what the defenders of social welfare programs have to say in their defense and because we can never be sure that they will not devise some new argument for why government social welfare programs are really disanalogous to the seemingly wrongful behavior in my example.

This kind of argument can be made on behalf of any of the standard libertarian political positions. The policies that libertarians advocate for the government are just the policies that almost anyone would advocate for any private agent; it is thus easy to

---

[8] See Murray Rothbard, *For a New Liberty* (Lanham, MD: University Press of America, 1978); Ayn Rand, *Atlas Shrugged* (New York: Signet, 1957); and Robert Nozick, *Anarchy, State, and Utopia* (New York: Basic Books, 1974).

argue that there should be a presumption in favor of libertarian policies. Consider three more examples:[9]

1. Imagine that I declare to everyone in my village that no one may consume certain substances that I have determined to be unhealthful. I then go around kidnapping people who consume those substances and locking them in cages for years at a time. This behavior on my part would seem unacceptable. But on its face, the behavior is analogous to the government's policy of drug prohibition. So this establishes a presumption that drug prohibition is also impermissible.

   Notice that my kidnappings would not be rendered permissible by my showing that the unhealthful substances are *really bad* for my neighbors' health. Nor would they be rendered permissible by my showing that some of my neighbors have lost their jobs and become losers in life because they loved those unhealthful substances so much. Because those sorts of reasons would not be enough to give me the right to kidnap my neighbors and hold them prisoner, prima facie, they don't give the government the right to do so either.

---

[9] I have discussed each of those issues at much greater length elsewhere. For a fuller statement of the arguments concerning drug prohibition, see Michael Huemer, "America's Unjust Drug War," in *The New Prohibition*, ed. Bill Masters (St. Louis, MO: Accurate Press, 2004), pp. 133–44. On gun control, see Michael Huemer, "Is There a Right to Own a Gun?" *Social Theory and Practice* 29 (2003): 297–324. On immigration, see Michael Huemer, "Is There a Right to Immigrate?" *Social Theory and Practice* 36 (2010): 429–61.

2. Imagine that I declare that I am forbidding any of my neighbors to own certain kinds of guns (though I myself own some of these weapons). I then learn that my next-door neighbor has one of the proscribed weapons. So I kidnap him at gunpoint and, again, lock him in a cage. This action seems wrong on my part. It also seems analogous to the government's behavior in enacting and enforcing its gun control laws.

Plausibly, my kidnapping would be permissible if I had strong evidence that my next-door neighbor in particular was planning to shoot an innocent person, and taking him captive was my only way to prevent the shooting. But I can't kidnap and imprison him merely because some other people in the country (a tiny proportion of all those who own such weapons) have used the kinds of weapons in question to commit crimes. So, prima facie, the government also is not justified in imprisoning people merely because they own weapons that some other people have used to commit crimes.

3. Imagine that I learn that a hungry person, Marvin, is planning to travel to a local marketplace to buy some food. I know that some merchants in the marketplace are willing to trade with Marvin, enabling him to satisfy his needs. I, however, accost Marvin on the road, forcibly barring him from the marketplace. As a result, Marvin goes hungry. This behavior on my part would be seriously wrong; I would then be responsible for Marvin's starvation. This example

is analogous to the government's immigration restrictions. Potential immigrants would like to come into the country, where there are people who are willing to trade with them and thereby help them satisfy their needs. The U.S. government hires armed guards to forcibly prevent these individuals from entering the country to work.

Notice that my treatment of Marvin would not be rendered permissible by any of the following considerations: (a) I wanted to prevent some of the people already at the marketplace from having to compete with Marvin economically, (b) I was afraid that Marvin might influence the culture of the marketplace in ways that I wouldn't like, and (c) I was worried that if Marvin got to the marketplace, I myself would give him some free food because of a charity program I run to aid the poor. All of those considerations would be absurd justifications for my coercively interfering with Marvin. But they are analogous to the most common justifications offered for immigration restrictions (immigrants compete with low-skill American workers, immigrants might change our culture, immigrants consume government benefits). So prima facie, those reasons do not justify the government's coercive intervention either.

Political Authority

It appears, then, that the essential difference between libertarians and nonlibertarians is that libertarians apply the same ethical standards to the government's behavior that they apply to the behavior of nongovernmental agents, whereas nonlibertarians believe the government is special in a way that exempts it from some of the moral constraints that apply to other agents.

This special moral status that the government is thought to have has a name: "authority"—more specifically, "political authority." The government can take your money, and you're obligated to hand it over, because the government has authority. I can't take your money, and you have no obligation to hand it over to me, because I *don't* have any authority. Note that those who believe in authority think that we are obligated to obey the law, and the government is entitled to enforce the law, even when the law is misguided (within limits).[10] It's not just that you should follow the laws that are actually beneficial, wise, or just; you're supposed to be obligated to follow the law just because it is the law.

So another way of describing the core motivation of libertarianism is this: libertarians are skeptical of authority. My defense of libertarianism starts from the presumption that this skepticism is justified, unless and until someone can articulate a satisfactory account of the basis for the government's authority. As a matter of fact, I claim, no one can: all attempts to explain why the government is special, such that it may do things that no other agent may do, have failed.

Obviously, I cannot discuss every possible such attempt, though I have discussed the most important attempts elsewhere.[11] Here, I'll briefly sketch three such attempts and how they fail.

---

[10] Perhaps if the error in the law becomes too extreme—for example, if you are ordered to participate in genocide—you won't have to follow the law any longer. But the doctrine of authority means that the government has substantial leeway, some wide range within which it can make errors and we still have to obey it.

[11] Huemer, *Problem of Political Authority*, chaps. 2–5.

The implicit social contract theory. Some argue that the government may coerce us in a wide variety of ways, because we have all agreed to grant the government this right, in exchange for the government's protecting us. This is the social contract theory. Usually, it is said that we accepted this contract "implicitly," perhaps by using government services or by living in the geographical area that the government controls, or merely by refraining from explicitly protesting.

In standard contract doctrine as it applies in any other context, there are at least three important principles about valid contracts:

- Both parties must have a reasonable way of opting out, where this does not include one party being compelled to undertake enormous costs that the other party has no independent right to impose on him. For example, I cannot make you an employment offer and then declare that if you don't agree to work for me, you must signal this nonagreement by cutting off your left arm; that is not a reasonable way of opting out.

- If one party explicitly states that he does not agree, then one cannot claim that he implicitly agreed anyway.

- Both parties must undertake obligations to each other, and if one party explicitly repudiates his obligations under the contract, then the other party is no longer bound to do his own part.

The putative social contract violates all three principles. First, because governments have taken control of every habitable land mass on the planet, there is no way of opting out. Second, even if you explicitly state that you don't agree, the government will still impose its conditions on you. Third, the government recognizes no obligation to do anything for you. This position has been established in a number of court cases in which plaintiffs have sued the government for negligently failing to protect them; in each case, the court summarily dismissed the lawsuit on the grounds that the government isn't obligated to protect any specific individual.[12]

The hypothetical contract theory. This theory is perhaps the most popular view among contemporary political philosophers, mainly because of the work of John Rawls. In this theory, the government has authority because we *would* have agreed to the social contract, in a hypothetical scenario in which we were all perfectly reasonable and deciding on the fundamental principles of our society. This matters because the fact that we would agree to some arrangement shows that the arrangement is fair and reasonable.

Imagine that I make you an employment offer. My offer is so *fair* and *reasonable* that any reasonable person would accept it. Nevertheless, you decline. Is it now permissible for me to force you to accept my offer (that is, enslave you), in virtue of the fact that it was a fair and reasonable offer, which you would have agreed to in a certain hypothetical scenario? If not, then of what moral relevance is a hypothetical contract?

---

[12] I invite the reader to read these amazing court decisions: *Warren v. District of Columbia*, 444 A. 2d 1, D.C. Ct. of Ap. (1981); *Hartzler v. City of San Jose*, 46 Cal. App. 3d 6 (1975); *DeShaney v. Winnebago County*, 489 U.S. 189 (1989); and *Riss v. New York*, 22 N.Y. 2d 579, 293 (1968).

The authority of democracy. Some claim that we are obligated to obey the laws because they were made democratically and therefore reflect the will of the majority of people. Now, that last claim is naive; many laws actually fail to reflect the will of the majority for a variety of reasons.[13] But suppose we set that aside and assume that some particular law reflects the will of the majority. So what?

Imagine that I am out with a group of nine friends at a bar. We've racked up a good-sized bill, and the question arises as to how the bill shall be divided: Should it be divided equally, or should each person pay for what that individual ordered? One of my friends proposes that *I* should pay 70 percent of the bill, with the rest being divided among the others. I decline. (I didn't order anything close to 70 percent of the drinks.) They take a vote. It turns out that everyone at the table except me wants me to pay most of the bill. Am I now obligated to pay the 70 percent? Are the others entitled to *force* me to do so? If not, then of what relevance is the will of the majority?[14]

Of course, there is more to say about each of these theories, and there are more theories to consider. But things go much the same with all the arguments in defense of authority: they rely on claims that would not for a moment be deemed plausible in any other context.

---

[13] For some of those reasons, see Huemer, *Problem of Political Authority*, pp. 72–73, 209–21.

[14] The 70 percent figure was not picked randomly. In America, the top 10 percent of taxpayers pay 70 percent of the income taxes. Steve Hargreaves, "The Rich Pay Majority of U.S. Income Taxes," CNN Money, March 12, 2013, http://money.cnn .com/2013/03/12/news/economy/rich-taxes.

The upshot of the failure of all accounts of authority is that the libertarian presumption stands. That is, because no one can satisfactorily explain why the government should be exempt from the moral rules that apply to everyone else, we should, in fact, judge the government according to the same rules we apply to others. Because libertarian policies would seem obviously correct for any nongovernmental agent, the government, too, should adopt libertarian policies.

Minimal State or Anarchy?

Some libertarians are minimal statists: they believe that we should have a government limited to enforcing people's negative rights to be free from force and fraud. Other libertarians, myself included, are anarchists: we believe that the ideal society is one in which the functions of the minimal state have been privatized.

Presenting the arguments on either side of that debate is beyond the scope of this chapter. Here I will just comment on the central locus of dispute and what it has to do with ethical intuitionism. The answer to that question is "very little"—the dispute between anarchists and minimal statists turns mainly on empirical questions of social science, not on any differing beliefs (intuitive or otherwise) about ethics.

Most minimal statists believe that government is needed to prevent a complete breakdown of social order. Most anarchists believe that a peaceful and orderly society is possible without government, because the functions of providing security and resolving disputes can be privatized. Reasonable anarchists agree that *if* government were necessary to provide order and security, then society ought to have government. And reasonable minimal statists agree that if government were *not* needed to provide order and security, then society ought *not* to have government.

Commonsense morality suffices to justify libertarianism—that is, to show that *at most* a minimal state is justified—or so I claim. Commonsense morality does not, however, suffice to justify anarchism. To justify anarchism, one must, in addition, support the empirical belief that private provision of order and security is feasible. The latter is a complicated task, in which ethical intuitions have essentially no role to play. On this, then, I shall say no more.

The Argument from Moral Progress

One important argument for moral realism is based on the observed phenomenon of moral progress.

The Phenomenon of Moral Progress

Over the span of human history—whether we look on the scale of decades, centuries, or millennia—we see significant changes in values and practices. Those changes are not random; they appear to be moving us consistently in a specific direction, and they are consistent across societies all over the world.[15]

The direction of moral change can be described broadly as a *liberalization* of values and practices. "Liberalism," as I use the term herein, refers to a certain broad ethical orientation (not to be

---

[15] See Steven Pinker, *The Better Angels of Our Nature: Why Violence Has Declined* (New York: Viking, 2011); and Huemer, *Problem of Political Authority*, pp. 321–24. For a more detailed version of the argument sketched in this section, see Michael Huemer, "A Liberal Realist Answer to Debunking Skeptics: The Empirical Case for Realism," *Philosophical Studies* 173 (2016): 1983–2010.

confused with "liberalism" in contemporary American politics), characterized by three main values: (a) a commitment to the moral equality of persons, (b) a respect for the dignity and rights of individuals, and (c) a reluctance to resort to force or violence.

The liberalization of values is consistent across many different issues. For example, slavery was widespread throughout human history, yet in the past two centuries, it was abolished in every nation in the world. Wars of conquest were common throughout history and often regarded (at least when successful) as glorious and manly; yet war has become steadily rarer over the past century and especially the past few decades, and virtually no one any longer regards a war of conquest as honorable.

Some of the world's greatest empires (notably the British Empire and the French Empire) were relinquished in the past century. Prejudice on the basis of race, sex, religion, and other traits has dramatically declined in the past few decades, especially following the civil rights movement.

Gladiatorial combat was a common and accepted form of entertainment in ancient Rome, and it didn't seem to occur to anyone at the time that forcing men to fight to the death was wrong. Two hundred years ago, men fought duels to settle points of honor, and a great many things were seen as sufficient reasons for initiating such mortal combat. Today, only a crazy person would endorse gladiatorial combat or dueling. Throughout history, almost all governments were dictatorships; today, democracy has taken over about half the world and continues to expand.

Some of those changes have occurred in recent decades, some in recent centuries, and some over millennia. But virtually every major shift in values is in the direction of liberalism, and this trend is worldwide. It may be the most important and interesting trend in all of human history.

The Explanation of Moral Progress

What explains the trend? I cannot address every explanation that someone might offer. Instead, I will just state what I think is the best explanation: human values and practices have become progressively more liberal, because liberalism is the objectively correct moral stance. Over the span of history, human beings have made dramatic progress in almost all areas of intellectual endeavor. In all of the sciences, mathematics, the study of history, and philosophy, human thought has become dramatically more sophisticated. In most areas, we now know that the theories that were once accepted were almost completely wrong. So if there are ethical facts, we might reasonably expect that in ethics, too, human beings would gradually progress from theories that were almost completely wrong to theories that are more sophisticated and accurate.

Here is a more detailed account of how moral progress occurs. Human values are influenced by a variety of factors in addition to purely rational intuitions. Those other factors include instincts, emotions, cultural traditions, and self-interest. The other factors act as biases, which led primitive humans to have ethical views that were badly misguided. However, because human beings also possess a capacity for rational ethical intuitions based on intellectual reflection, and because some individuals are more rational than others, there will periodically be individuals who see something wrong with the values of their society. Those individuals do not see the whole moral truth; they are still influenced by various biases, and they will find it psychologically difficult to adopt a position too far from the prevailing norms in their society. They merely get *closer* to the moral truth than the rest of their society, because they are, by definition, *less* biased than the average member of their society. Those individuals then initiate movements to reform their society. That is what occurred in the case of the abolitionist movement, the women's suffrage movement, and the civil rights movement, for example. The moral reformers will have a tendency to move their society at least some distance in the direction of justice.

Once this movement has taken place, a new cultural norm is established, one closer to the moral truth than the old one. At that point, a new generation of moral reformers may arise, again seeing some of what is wrong with their society, and again adopting a position slightly closer to the moral truth than what the rest of their society has embraced.

By this sort of process, society moves progressively closer to the correct moral stance over time. Add to this the supposition that liberalism is, in fact, the moral truth, and we have an explanation for why societies around the world have been liberalizing over the decades and centuries.

This explanation depends on the assumption that there is such a thing as objective (or at least universal) moral truth, which we can access through ethical intuition. If, as I claim, no better explanations are available for the historical trend, then we have reason to embrace that assumption. In general, it is reasonable to postulate those things that are necessary for explaining (well) the observed facts.

Libertarianism as a Coherent Liberalism

So one of my main arguments for moral realism is also an argument for liberalism as the correct moral stance. Now, what is the relationship between *liberalism* and *libertarianism*? The answer is that, as I use the terms, libertarianism is a species of liberalism. Furthermore, it is the most coherent form of liberalism, or so I shall maintain. Therefore, if liberalism is correct, then probably libertarianism is correct.

Recall that I ascribed to the "liberal" three major, interconnected attitudes:

1. Commitment to the moral equality of persons

2. Respect for the dignity of the individual

3. Aversion to coercion

All of those values stand in tension with the concept of political authority. I do not mean that a liberal *cannot* believe in authority, but that the rejection of authority fits better with liberalism. Given that the core motivation of libertarianism, as I understand it, is skepticism about authority, libertarianism is to that extent a more coherent form of liberalism than any form that embraces authority.

Now, why is the notion of authority in tension with liberalism? The doctrine of political authority is fundamentally inegalitarian. To ascribe political authority to some agent is explicitly to place that agent *above* others, in such a way that the agent is entitled to order everyone else around, and other people have to do what that agent says *just because that agent says so*. This doctrine seems on its face to impugn the dignity of everyone who is "under" the authority, insofar as they are supposed to follow the authority figure's directions regardless of their own judgment and regardless of whether the authority figure's directions are actually correct.

Is this true of *all* kinds of "authority"? I don't think so; I think the criticism applies only to forms of authority that, like political authority, are forcibly imposed on one. By contrast, for instance, a manager's authority over an employee is normally not objectionably inegalitarian, because the employee's autonomy is respected in the form of his choice as to whether to undertake the employee-employer relationship, as well as his freedom to terminate the relationship at will.

The doctrine of *political* authority supports widespread coercion, because the use or threat of violence is essential to the enforcement of government commands. To ascribe authority to the state is, among other things, to grant the state an entitlement to *force* obedience. For those individuals who do not obey, the state will send armed guards to take them captive. All of this, it seems to me, is blatantly and extremely illiberal.

One might say that there are nonetheless good arguments for the existence of political authority, or that there are good reasons for acting *as if* there were such a thing even if in fact authority is an illusion. This argument doesn't change the fact that there is a tension inherent in any position that claims to value equality, to respect individual dignity, and to oppose unnecessary coercion, while simultaneously positing a special organization that is entitled to force everyone else to obey its commands, regardless of whether those commands are actually wise or beneficial, even though no other agent would be entitled to use force in similar circumstances. And this is no small tension; the idea of political authority is, it seems to me, a *very large* illiberal aspect of any political philosophy that includes it. We therefore have reason to suspect that, as values and practices liberalize further, the libertarian's skepticism of authority will become ever more widespread.

Libertarianism vs. Egalitarianism

Critics might contend that, although skepticism of authority may be a liberal attitude, other important aspects of libertarianism are illiberal. Most notably, libertarians typically reject government social welfare programs as going beyond the legitimate functions of the state.

Relatedly, although libertarians certainly embrace equality in *one* sense—that every person has equal rights and equal moral status—they tend to reject any ideal in the vicinity of equality of wealth or welfare. Thus, a libertarian society would most likely be one in which there was a large gap between the rich and the poor. By contrast, (left-wing) egalitarians believe not only that individuals have equal rights and equal moral status, but also that inequalities in wealth are bad and should be reduced or eliminated by government programs. On this front, society has been moving away from libertarianism and toward egalitarianism over the past century, as governments have dramatically expanded social welfare programs and wealth redistribution. If, therefore, one takes to heart the argument for moral realism based on moral progress, one might conclude that the objectively correct values are liberal egalitarian values, rather than libertarian values.

This argument is important. On the question of the extent to which the argument from moral progress supports egalitarianism, I have three observations. First, left-wing egalitarianism has hardly enjoyed unmitigated successes in the past century. The most extreme form of egalitarianism has suffered decisive defeats, as communist regimes around the world have collapsed in the past 30 years, and very few people advocate communism any longer.[16] Obviously, this does not show that some more moderate form of egalitarianism won't ultimately triumph. But it does show that one cannot read the triumph of egalitarianism from the events of the past century in any simple and straightforward way.

Second, the kind of equality that libertarianism supports is more fundamental and important than the kind that left-wing egalitarianism supports. Libertarianism allows some to possess much more property than others, so in that sense, it supports (or at least tolerates) inequality. The doctrine of political authority, however, allows some to literally rule over others, to force others to obey their commands, whether or not those commands are wise and beneficial. It exempts the agents of the state from the moral

---

[16] Some people deny that the experience of the 20th century refutes communism, because regimes like those of the Soviet Union and Eastern Europe before the 1990s were not *true* communism. I think this is a deep mistake. Be that as it may, the point here is not to argue directly about the merits of communism. The point here is that ideologically, egalitarianism suffered major setbacks in the 20th century, connected with the events that most people call "the collapse of communism."

constraints that apply to everyone else. This seems to me a much starker and more offensive kind of inequality than an inequality in the quantity of wealth different individuals possess. And it is just this offensive sort of inequality that is demanded by left-wing egalitarianism. If egalitarians were content to advocate for private charity efforts, no libertarian would object.

The dispute between libertarians and egalitarians centers on the egalitarians' advocacy of government coercion to support social welfare programs.[17] Most egalitarians would *not* support similar coercion if carried out by a private individual or organization. Egalitarians are therefore committed to an inequality of moral status between the state and private agents.

Third, I want to explain how the trend of expanding social welfare programs may constitute moral progress, even if libertarianism is correct. The key point is that most people have taken the authority of the state for granted. That has been true for about as long as states have existed, and it remains true today (even if today the support for authority is at its nadir). Now, *given* the assumption that the state has authority and thus has a legitimate claim on whatever amount of money it chooses to take from its citizens (in accordance with its

[17] Some people dispute whether taxation is really a violation of taxpayers' property rights, because they question whether we really own our pretax incomes. See Liam Murphy and Thomas Nagel, *The Myth of Ownership: Taxes and Justice* (Oxford, UK: Oxford University Press, 2002); Stephen Holmes and Cass Sunstein, *The Cost of Rights: Why Liberty Depends on Taxes* (New York: W.W. Norton, 1999). I address this sort of view briefly in *Problem of Political Authority*, pp. 145–48, and at greater length in "Is Wealth Redistribution a Rights Violation?" in *The Routledge Handbook of Libertarianism*, ed. Jason Brennan, David Schmidtz, and Bas van der Vossen (New York: Routledge, forthcoming).

laws), the state ought to use some of its money to help the least fortunate members of society. This would be the compassionate thing to do and perhaps the only course of action consistent with an appropriate level of concern for the interests of everyone. The reason the state should not in fact do this, in my view, is that the state has no legitimate authority. But *that* view (i.e., skepticism about authority) has nothing to do with why the state did not run large social welfare programs before the 20th century. Rather, in earlier centuries the state did not run large social welfare programs because the government *did not care* about the poor. The shift to a government that cares (or at least pretends to care) about the poor constitutes moral progress.

In other words, we need to consider two distinct dimensions along which moral attitudes may vary: (A) deference to authority and (B) concern for the poor. For most of human history, the dominant combination of attitudes has been A + ~B (deference to authority combined with indifference to the poor). The correct combination of attitudes is the diametrical opposite: ~A + B (skepticism of authority combined with concern for the poor). Over the past century, our society has moved, roughly, from A + ~B to A + B. This is progress, albeit on only one dimension. It just so happens that in this case, making progress on just one of two dimensions leads one away from the policies that would be adopted if one made progress on both dimensions.

Questions and Objections

In this section, I address commonly raised questions and objections concerning intuitionism and/or my appeal to common sense morality.

Mistaken Intuitions

Most objections to ethical intuitionism appear to rest on mis-understandings. Perhaps the most common type of objection is this: "I can think of a few examples of false intuitions," or even, "I can think of a few examples of false beliefs that were once widely held." How is that supposed to be an objection to ethical intuitionism?

On one way of reading it, the former version of the objection rests on the mistaken assumption that ethical intuitionism is or entails the claim "all intuitions are true." The latter version of the objection appears to rest on the same assumption, in addition to another mistaken assumption, that "intuition" means "widely shared belief."

To the best of my knowledge, no serious thinker in the history of philosophy has ever held the view that all intuitions are true. (Also, no intuitionist has defined "intuition" as "widely shared belief.") This is analogous to the fact that no thinker has held that all sensory appearances are veridical, or that all apparent memories are correct, or that all inferences are sound.

Ethical intuitionism *does* involve the claim that it is rational to assume that intuitions are correct unless and until there are grounds for doubting those intuitions. This is analogous to the fact that it is rational to assume that one's sensory experiences are veridical or that one's memories are accurate—unless and until there are specific grounds for doubting them. Those theses are not refuted or even called into question by the observation that sometimes there *are* grounds for doubt.

Another way of reading the objection is that it seeks to provide inductive evidence that intuitions in general are unreliable, thus giving us grounds for doubting all intuitions, and thereby perhaps calling all moral knowledge into question. Philosophical skeptics, similarly, cite examples of a variety of sensory illusions to which human beings are subject, in the attempt to show that the senses are unreliable.

But if that is the idea, then one would have to take a large, random sample of intuitions in order to assess how reliable they are in general. One cannot simply selectively search through one's memory for a handful of cases of false intuitions. If we are counting such intuitions as "pain is bad," "murder is wrong," and "theft is wrong," it is easy to think of many examples of intuitions that we have no reason for doubting.

Disagreement

Another very common objection is along the lines of "sometimes, people have conflicting intuitions." This may simply be a variant of the preceding objection and may be based on the assumption that intuitionism holds that all intuitions are true. If all intuitions were true, then indeed there could be no conflicting intuitions. But once we understand that intuitionism does not in fact include that absurd thesis, it is unclear how the existence of disagreement poses an objection.

Sometimes, it appears that the objection is that intuitionists have failed to provide a method for resolving all disagreements. Although this objection might be a real practical problem, it is unclear how it is supposed to provide evidence that intuitionism is not in fact true. The inference would seemingly have to be something like this:

1. Intuitionism fails to provide a way of resolving all ethical disagreements.

2. If a metaethical theory fails to provide a way of resolving all ethical disagreements, then the theory is false.

3. So intuitionism is false.

But it is mysterious why one would believe the second premise. Indeed, *no* metaethical theory has ever provided a way of resolving all ethical disagreements (that is why there are still ethical disagreements), but presumably it is not the case that all metaethical theories are false.

Biases

Sometimes, people who take themselves to be objecting to ethical intuitionism point to biases that can affect people's ethical intuitions or judgments. What is a bias? A bias is simply an influence that tends to be unreliable or to lead one away from the truth. For instance, people might be influenced by religious teachings (which the objector takes to be unreliable) or by the teachings of their parents, or they might want to adopt the beliefs that serve their own interests.

This, however, really is not an objection to intuitionism. Again, intuitionism is not the view that all intuitions are true (still less is it the view that all ethical *beliefs* are true). If one takes certain intuitions to be biased, then all that follows is that one should withhold assent from those intuitions.

However, the ethical intuitions on which I rely to defend libertarianism are not plausibly regarded as biases. For instance, the idea that I should not kidnap people who eat certain unhealthful substances and imprison them for several years does not appear to be a bias caused by religion or upbringing or self-interest. If someone thinks that is a product of bias, they would have to explain how they think that is so. It is not enough to say that ethical biases exist in general, or that some *other* ethical beliefs are biased.

Nor is it our burden to show in general that it *isn't* the product of a bias (when given no specific account of how it would be). In general, we do not come to know things by first having an appearance, then proving that there *aren't* any factors influencing that appearance that would make it unreliable, and then finally accepting the content of the appearance. (Among other things, notice that that would involve an infinite regress, since establishing the absence of biases would require us to have some *other* knowledge, which would start the process over again.) Rather, we start by believing what seems to be the case, and we stand ready to revise that belief if (but only if!) we acquire reasons for doubting that the appearance is reliable. That is how perceptual knowledge, memory knowledge, scientific knowledge, moral knowledge, and all other forms of knowledge work.

Hypocritical Objections

Many philosophical objectors are hypocritical, self-refuting, or both, in the sense that the objectors are doing the very thing that they say one should not do, or are relying on the very sort of belief they say one should not rely on. This is particularly common when the topic is ethical intuitionism. Here, I want to call attention to this category of objection and to recommend against its use. Here are some examples:

1. "Any objection to the idea that we should rely on what seems true to us unless we have grounds for doubt." Essentially all such objections are hypocritical and self-refuting in the sense that the objections themselves rest on how things seem to the person making the objection; thus, if the objection is correct, then the objector is not justified in making it. A special (extremely common) case is the intuition-based objection to relying on intuitions.

2. "Intuitionists fail to provide a method for resolving all ethical disagreements." This objection would be hypocritical in the sense that the objector himself is invariably someone who has not provided a method for resolving all ethical disagreements. (*No one* has provided such a method, that is, not one that actually works. If they had, philosophers would have used that method, and all ethical disagreements would now be resolved.)

3. "We aren't justified in holding to our ethical beliefs, because some people disagree with them." But then, some people also disagree with the idea that we aren't justified in holding to our ethical beliefs, so *that* idea must also be unjustified.

4. "We shouldn't trust intuition, because sometimes intuitions have led us astray." If that's true, then we presumably shouldn't trust any means of belief formation that sometimes goes wrong. If so, then we should not rely on philosophical arguments, including the very argument just quoted, because sometimes (almost always, actually) philosophical arguments lead us astray.

5. "Your method of arriving at political conclusions is not sufficiently reliable, because our ethical beliefs could be prejudices." If the objector is actually a skeptic with no moral or political views, then that person's position may be coherent. Otherwise, it is hypocritical, because no method of forming ethical or political beliefs eliminates all possibility of being influenced by the prejudices of the day. My method is, in fact, the least prone to bias, because I start from ethical premises that are very widely shared regardless of ideology. The alternatives would be (a) to accept no starting premises (and thus to be a skeptic) or (b) to start from premises that are controversial or ideologically biased (how could that be better?).

My general recommendation: don't object to my approach to supporting libertarianism, unless (a) you have somehow discovered some evaluative premises that are more plausible and less controversial than, for example, the premise "I shouldn't kidnap people at gunpoint and imprison them just for consuming substances I deem unhealthful," and (b) your premises somehow show that mine are untrue, for example, that it actually *is* permissible for me to kidnap and imprison people for consuming unhealthful substances.

Virtually all nonintuitionists are hypocritical: they adopt and retain ethical beliefs in precisely the way that intuitionists do— namely, they believe what seems right to them, until they have grounds for doubting it—with the sole difference being that they are less self-aware, that is, they don't *say* that this is what they are doing. Then they hold forth about how bad it is to do that.

What about Political Intuitions?

The preceding objections are all confused. This one is not: most people intuit that the government (or at least *some* governments) has authority; that is, the government just seems somehow morally special. When the government kills people, it seems less bad than when private parties commit murder; when the government conscripts people, it seems less bad than private slavery; when the government taxes people, it seems less bad than private extortion. Why wouldn't this be good enough, given my own views about intuition, to defend unlibertarian policies? Why shouldn't a nonlibertarian say, "There is no need to give a theory of why the government has authority, nor an argument that the government has authority, because it just *seems* that it does"?

That would be an unsatisfactory stance to take for several reasons. First, the notion of political authority is really not nearly as uncontroversial as the intuitive ethical judgments referred to in the earlier section titled "Some Commonsense Ethical

Intuitions." Attitudes toward authority vary greatly with political ideology, with all or most libertarians intuitively rejecting the notion of political authority (indeed, to some of us, the idea seems bizarre and obviously false).

Even among nonlibertarians, it is not so much that most people *have the intuition* that the government has authority or that most people *believe* that the government has authority, as that they are habitually disposed to presuppose the government's authority. Most people, I suspect, have never actually thought about whether or why the government has legitimate authority. When explicitly confronted with the fact that the government performs many actions that would be considered wrongful for any other agent, very few people say: "Yeah, so what? It's the government, so obviously it's OK." Rather, most people can very easily be brought to feel that there is a philosophical problem here.

When I present the issue to students, for example, it is very easy to motivate the problem, and no one ever suggests that no reason is needed for why the government is special. By contrast, for instance, when you point out that although it is wrong to destroy a human being, it is not considered similarly wrong to destroy a clod of dirt, no one gets puzzled.

Second, most people—even if they think it intuitive that the state has some sort of authority—will also have the intuition that this cannot be a brute fact—that there must be a *grounding* for this authority or an answer to *what gives* the state its authority. And hardly anyone thinks the explanation could just be "Well, it's the government." (By contrast, for instance, plenty of people think it's a brute fact that pain is bad, or that the answer to what's bad about pain is just

"Well, it hurts.") This being so, the failure of every explanation we can think of for what gives the state its authority ought to make one suspect that the state in fact has no such authority.

Third and most interesting, not all intuitions are equally trustworthy. Some intuitions and beliefs are the product of psychological biases. When we have specific reasons for believing that an intuition is the product of bias, we should distrust that intuition. In particular, a good deal of evidence, both from experimental psychology and from history, shows that most people have strong pro-authority biases.[18]

For example, the famous Milgram experiment shows that most people are willing to electrocute another (innocent) person, if ordered to do so by an authority figure.[19] Milgram explicitly draws the parallel to the willingness of ordinary Germans to participate in the persecution of Jews during World War II.

American soldiers, too, have participated in atrocities, such as the infamous My Lai massacre, in response to orders from an authority figure. Now, the point here is not merely that institutions of authority are dangerous. The point is that those who are subject to an authority figure will very often *feel* a sense of that person's authority, even if that alleged authority is completely illegitimate, or the person is clearly overstepping whatever legitimate authority he might have.

---

[18] I discuss this at length in *Problem of Political Authority*, chap. 6 (which I'm told is the most interesting chapter of the book), where I also cite a variety of potential sources for this pro-authority bias.

[19] Stanley Milgram, *Obedience to Authority: An Experimental View* (New York: Harper, 2009).

Notice that there is no need here to argue about what constitutes legitimate authority or how we determine its bounds, because *those cases* are uncontroversial. No one thinks the scientist in Milgram's experiment had the right to order the electrocution of the subjects, or that the officers at My Lai had the right to order the massacre. But the people in those situations *felt* a need to obey. Because of this, it is likely that we would all feel a sense of our government's authority, even if that alleged authority were illegitimate, or the government were grossly overstepping its bounds.

Notice that in this third point, I am not merely saying that political intuitions in general can be biased. I am citing evidence of a bias *in a specific direction, on a specific issue*. Much more evidence of this pro-authority bias is discussed in Chapter 6 of *The Problem of Political Authority*.

The distinction here is like the distinction between saying in general that sensory illusions are possible, and saying that you have evidence of a specific sensory illusion in the circumstances that you are, in fact, presently in. The general knowledge that sensory illusions exist does not cast doubt, for example, on my present perception of the table in front of me. However, my knowledge that light rays are bent when going from air into water *does* cast doubt on my perception in the specific case where I am looking at a stick half submerged in water. Similarly, the general knowledge that intuitions can be mistaken does not cast doubt on my intuition that I shouldn't extort money from other people. But the existence of widespread pro-authority biases (together with some mechanisms that would tend to generate them) *does* cast doubt on the specific belief that government has a special sort of authority, particularly when no one can give a plausible account of why it has that authority.

Concluding Thoughts

I doubt that many readers would be converted to either intuitionism or libertarianism by the preceding discussion. At minimum, a persuasive case for intuitionism would have to address the main alternative theories about the nature of ethics, in addition to responding in greater detail to a greater variety of the objections to intuitionism. A persuasive case for libertarianism would have to address more accounts of authority, and to do so in greater detail. Either of those cases would be a book-length project (which is why I have in fact devoted books to each).

My aims in this chapter have been more modest. I hope to have shown how an intuitionist theory of ethics fits together in a natural way with a libertarian political philosophy. I hope to have said enough to show that this combination of views forms an interesting position, and perhaps to stimulate the reader to do further reading on the subject.

A final comment: How does my defense of libertarianism relate to other popular approaches, such as those based on natural rights or utilitarianism? I think that my arguments are compatible with natural rights and utilitarian premises, but they do not *require* either. Both the utilitarian and the natural rights libertarian reject political authority. Utilitarians reject authority because they hold that everyone is subject to exactly the same moral principle, namely, that one should always maximize utility; there is thus no special moral status for the state. Natural rights libertarians must also reject authority, if their argument for libertarianism is to succeed, for unless the idea of authority is rejected, the possibility would remain that the state is entitled to do what would be a rights violation if it were done by a private party. Natural rights theorists and utilitarians are also generally liberals (though they will have different reasons for endorsing liberalism); thus, virtually all the examples of moral progress over the past several centuries could have been defended either on natural rights grounds or on utilitarian grounds.

So I think either a utilitarian or a natural rights theorist should accept my main premises. From there, it is not necessary to further attempt to specify the correct moral theory, because as long as we have this much (the truth of liberalism, the illusoriness of authority), we should arrive at libertarian political conclusions.[20]

[20] My thanks to Aaron Powell and Grant Babcock for numerous helpful comments on an earlier version of this chapter.

Moral Pluralism

Jason Brennan

That's All, Folks!

Most people have moral beliefs, but few have anything as robust as a *moral theory*. A moral theory is meant to systematize and explain what makes actions right or wrong, states of affairs and motives good or bad, and traits virtuous or vicious. Moral theories are meant to explain rather than to guide: a moral theory explains how morality fits together.[1]

It's not clear that people need a moral theory so defined. Many people are good moral agents despite not knowing moral theory, or even despite accepting a bad moral theory.[2] The skill of *doing* is different from the skill of *explaining*. One might be good at doing

---

[1] For a thorough account of the theoretical goals of moral theory, see Jason Brennan, "Beyond the Bottom Line: The Theoretical Aims of Moral Theory," *Oxford Journal of Legal Studies* 28 (2008): 277–96.

[2] I had a neighbor who accepted divine command theory, a theory refuted more than 2,000 years ago, but he was still just as good a person as anyone else I've met.

even if one lacks the ability to explain what one is doing, or even if one has a bad explanation of what one is doing.

Jimi Hendrix was an excellent blues-rock guitarist despite not knowing music theory. He couldn't explain his own music as well as some music analysts, but he sure could play. Or consider that Tom Brady is an excellent football player, whereas Bill Belichick is an excellent coach. Brady can play better than Belichick, but Belichick has a better *theory* of football than Brady. In the same way, a moral theorist might have a better account of what morality is and how it all fits together than an average person, but that doesn't necessarily make the moral theorist a better person.[3]

In our daily lives, most of us get by just fine without invoking a moral theory. Suppose I'm in some difficult moral situation. I don't need to appeal to a broad moral principle by asking, "Is acting on this maxim in this situation something I could rationally will the whole world to do?" Nor would I ask, "Does this action produce the maximal expected utility?" Instead, I've got a handful of commonsense moral principles, such as these:

1. Give people what they deserve.

2. Don't harm others or aggress against them.

3. Respect people's property.

4. Provide an appropriate amount of charity to help those in need.

---

[3] For experimental evidence to that effect, see Eric Schwitzgebel and Joshua Rust, "The Moral Behavior of Ethicists," *Companion to Experimental Philosophy*, ed. Justin Sytsma and Wesley Buckwalter (New York: Oxford University Press, forthcoming).

5. Keep your word, and be honest to those who deserve it.

6. Reciprocate with those who have helped you.

7. Don't take advantage of others' misfortune.

8. Provide for those whom you owe a duty of care.

9. Don't violate others' rights.

I might quickly go down the list, and as long as I'm not violating these rules, I conclude whatever I'm doing is fine.

In commonsense morality, those norms strike us as useful rules of thumb. Sometimes, there are exceptions to the rules: for example, although I can't kill you for fun, I can kill you to stop you from killing other innocent people. Sometimes, there are conflicts: for example, Jean Valjean might have to steal bread to feed his starving sister's children. Sometimes, there are complexities: for example, it's unclear what some job candidate deserves, or which applicant is more deserving, or just what counts as a basis for desert for any particular job. Still, in commonsense morality, wise people weigh competing principles, use their best judgment, make a decision, and move on. They don't appear to make use of, or need, a deeper moral theory.

Most moral theorists, including deontologist Immanuel Kant and utilitarian John Stuart Mill, agree that this is what it's like to be a moral agent. They agree that in our daily experience, it feels as if we are bound by and have to weigh a plurality of (often competing) mid- or low-level moral principles.[4] But Kant

---

[4] Immanuel Kant, *Practical Philosophy*, ed. Mary J. Gregor (New York: Cambridge University Press, 1999 [1788]), pp. 546–90; John Stuart Mill, *Utilitarianism* (Indianapolis, IN: Hackett, 2002 [1861]), pp. 42–60.

and Mill think the mid- and low-level principles are at most instances or approximations of one big, abstract, high-level principle. Kant thinks that we have each of the duties on the list above, but he sees that list of duties as special applications of the categorical imperative—an abstract moral law that binds all rational agents of any species.[5] For Kant, in the end, there is just *one* fundamental moral principle. Mill agrees with Kant that in the end, there is just *one* fundamental moral principle, but he disagrees about what that principle is.

Kant and Mill both agree that commonsense moral thinking works the way I've described, but they see themselves as having discovered an underlying skeleton that holds morality together and gives morality its shape.

But what if no underlying skeleton exists? Moral pluralism, sometimes called Rossian pluralism after early 20th-century philosopher W. D. Ross, claims just that.[6] Pluralism is in effect the thesis that the structure of commonsense moral thinking *is all there is to morality.* There is no unifying principle that explains all of morality.

Pluralistic theories hold that a multiplicity of basic moral duties and values exists, and these duties and values cannot be subsumed beneath one principle. For the pluralist, morality is not all one thing. Those principles can come into conflict with each other. Acting on them, applying them, and resolving conflicts requires

---

[5] Mark Timmons, *Moral Theory: An Introduction* (Lanham, MD: Rowman and Littlefield, 2002), p. 161.

[6] W. D. Ross, *The Right and the Good* (Indianapolis, IN: Hackett, 1988 [1930]).

good judgment, but no further theory gives precise principles about how to resolve the conflict or can substitute for good judgment. In any given situation, there's a truth of the matter about how to resolve conflicts, but there's no algorithm for determining that truth.

Against One-Sentence Moral Theories

All moral theories are either *monist* or *pluralist*.[7] A monist theory of right action holds that exactly one fundamental feature of actions determines whether they are right and wrong. A pluralist theory holds that more than one fundamental feature determines whether actions are right and wrong.[8] A monist might agree that in commonsense morality, many features seem to count for and against the rightness of actions, but then holds that these features *can* be reduced to one deeper or more fundamental feature. The pluralist holds that many features count for or against the rightness of actions, but these features *cannot* be reduced to one deeper or more fundamental feature.

The best argument for pluralist moral theories is to see how inadequate all the monist theories are. Monist theories fail because they try to do too much with too little; that is, they try to explain all of morality with just one basic principle or basic idea.

---

[7] I'm treating moral particularism as an extreme instance of pluralism.

[8] Technically, a moral theory has a theory of the good and a theory of the right. It could be monist about one and pluralist about the other, or monist about both, or pluralist about both. Utilitarians are monists about the good and the right, whereas Kant is a monist about the right but a pluralist about the good.

Many of the moral theories discussed elsewhere in this book hold that morality can be summarized, systematized, and explained with just one sentence. So, for instance, Kantianism holds that an action is wrong if—and only if—it violates the categorical imperative. Ethical egoism holds that an action is right if—and only if—it is expected to contribute maximally to the agent's welfare. Act utilitarianism holds that an action is right just in case it produces the greatest net aggregate utility.

But one-sentence moral theories seem problematic. Most of them seem to have absurd counterexamples. Consider, for example, hedonistic act utilitarianism. This theory begins with the plausible thought that pleasure is good and pain is bad. It seems plausible that morality is about maximizing aggregate utility, here defined as pleasure minus pain. But this principle—"an act is right just in case it maximizes net aggregate utility"—has bizarre implications. For instance, it implies that I ought to break a promise whenever doing so produces an infinitesimal gain in utility. Worse, it implies that so long as the sadist enjoys watching others suffer more than he or she hates suffering, we're obligated to submit to his torture. However plausible utilitarianism might be, it's not plausible enough to justify biting these bullets.

Kant held that we had general duties to pursue our own perfection and to adopt others' happiness as an end. He thought we have more specific duties (a) to avoid envy, ingratitude, malice, arrogance, defamation, ridicule, suicide, lying, servility, avarice, and intemperance; (b) to develop our natural and moral powers; and (c) to act upon dispositions of beneficence, gratitude, sympathy, and respect for others.[9] He thought that applying those principles in context was complicated and that philosophers could not provide any real algorithm for doing so.[10] Still, he believed that all of these lower-level principles are just instances of and derivations from the categorical imperative.

But as anyone who has slogged through a class on Kant knows, Kant's categorical imperative is notoriously difficult to apply. The universal law formulation—"An act is wrong just in case one cannot universalize the maxim of commission associated with that act"[11]—seems like a convoluted test. When Kantians try to unpack the formula, they often appear to jerry-rig the theory to get whatever results they want. A Kantian who believes abortion is wrong always manages to "prove" the categorical imperative forbids abortion, whereas a Kantian who thinks abortion is permissible "proves" it does not. Both of their arguments seem equally good (or bad). It may be that on further philosophical investigation, we'll find that the categorical imperative really does favor one over the other. But it may also just be a sign that the categorical imperative is too abstract to resolve this question.

The humanity formulation—an act is wrong just in case it fails to respect the humanity of each person as an end in itself—at first seems more promising than the universal law formulation. But upon further inspection, it looks vacuous and empty. Libertarian

---

[9] Timmons, *Moral Theory*, pp. 158–62; Kant, *Practical Philosophy*, pp. 546–90.

[10] Kant continuously warns readers that applying his principles requires knowledge that goes beyond a priori philosophical reasoning, and that knowledge cannot be codified. Kant, *Practical Philosophy*, pp. 546–90.

[11] Timmons, *Moral Theory*, p. 166.

Robert Nozick, liberal John Rawls, conservative John Finnis, and socialist G. A. Cohen each agree we should treat the humanity in each of us always as an end and never as a mere means, but they dispute just what it takes to express such respect. When they debate each other, what does the work in the debate isn't the generic idea of respecting others as ends, but instead it is reflections on mid-level principles and intuitions about specific cases.[12]

"Respect the humanity in others" seems almost as vacuous as "always consider and properly respond to the legitimate interests of anyone affected by your actions." Well, yeah, *every moral theory says that*. It's true, but it's platitudinous. Again, perhaps a decisive Kantian resolution of this debate is forthcoming, but given how well Kantianism seems to fit with so many disparate views, perhaps we shouldn't hold our breath.

David Schmidtz, a pluralist, suggests that what attracts us to one-sentence theories is a misguided search for simplicity:

> Would a monist theory be more useful? Would it even be simpler? The periodic table would in one sense be simpler if we posited only four elements—or one, for that matter— but would that make for better science? No. Astronomers once said planets *must* face circular orbits. When they finally accepted the reality of elliptical orbits, which favor two focal points, their theories became simpler, more

---

[12] For example, I have almost a line-by-line response to G. A. Cohen, *Why Not Socialism?* (Princeton, NJ: Princeton University Press, 2009) in Jason Brennan, *Why Not Capitalism?* (New York: Routledge Press, 2014), but neither Cohen nor I have to articulate a fundamental moral theory to have this debate.

elegant, and more powerful. . . . [W]hen a phenomenon looks complex . . . the simplest explanation may be that it looks complex because it is. We may find a way of doing everything with a single element, but it would be mere dogma—the opposite of science—to assume we must.[13]

Moral philosophy faces a problem such as the one astronomers faced. When astronomers tried to cling to the view that all orbits are circles—and thus have just one focal point—they had two bad options. The first option was just to deny the phenomena—their observations—altogether. In moral theory, the equivalent would be a utilitarian insisting, "No, my theory is right, and most of the purported counterexamples to utilitarianism are actually just what morality requires." The second option was to introduce arbitrarily complex epicycles into their theory to make the equations work. Soon, the theories became so vacuous they fit the phenomena, because they can fit all phenomena. In moral philosophy, the all-too-common equivalent is how it seems that every Kantian philosopher believes Kantianism tends to justify whatever political views he held before he discovered Kantianism.

For methodological reasons, it was good that philosophers repeatedly *tried* to systematize morality into one monist principle. After all, theoretical parsimony is a virtue. But it seems that we've continuously failed to produce a workable, plausible form of monism after repeated efforts. Perhaps it's time to throw in the towel and go for a pluralist theory instead.

[13] David Schmidtz, *Elements of Justice* (New York: Cambridge University Press, 2006), p. 4 [emphasis in original].

Presumptive Duties

Kant's categorical imperative is an *absolute* moral principle. To say a duty or a moral principle is absolute is to say that it can never be outweighed or trumped by a competing consideration. (Note, however, that although the categorical imperative is absolute, what the principle requires in any given context heavily depends on context.[14] So the principle is absolute, but contextual.)

In contrast, Ross doubted that any absolute moral principles existed. Instead, he thought all basic moral principles or duties were presumptive. There is a strong default presumption in favor of abiding by any of our basic duties, but other considerations could in principle outweigh or trump them.

Each presumptive duty is a consideration in favor of performing or avoiding some action. So, for instance, that doing x would keep a promise is a strong consideration in favor of x. That doing x would involve failing to rescue my children is a strong consideration against x. If those duties conflict in any way, then we would have to judge which duty trumped the other. Ross thought that in general, this involved *weighing* the duties against each other, and then acting on whatever principle was most weighty.

Ross defines our *duty proper* as what we should do, all things considered. If I have only one presumptive duty active in a given context, then that presumptive duty becomes my duty proper. If I have multiple conflicting duties, then my duty proper is whatever presumptive duty is the weightiest.[15]

---

[14] Kant makes this clear in *Practical Philosophy*, p. 584.

[15] Ross, *Right and Good*, pp. 19–20.

With that, consider a precise definition of presumptive duties, quoting Mark Timmons:

Definition: An action is a [*presumptive*] *duty* if and only if

1. It possesses some morally relevant feature that counts in favor of my doing (or not doing) the act, and

2. This feature is such that were it the only morally relevant feature of my situation, then the act (or not doing the act) would be my duty proper.[16]

Pluralist moral theories provide an appealing account of what it's like to be a moral agent making decisions on the ground. Commonsensically, it seems that there are multiple basic moral rules, that such rules can conflict, and that there's no obvious "super-rule" for resolving those conflicts. Instead, we have to use our best judgment.

Some people's best judgment is better than others. Some people are better able to reason via analogy, to think through matters in a consistent and cool way, to note similarities among cases, or to be aware of what moral factors are at stake in a given situation.[17] Some are more prone to suffer from self-serving or confirmation bias than are others. Indeed, much of contemporary moral psychology finds that people often act wrongly not because they have

---

[16] Timmons, *Moral Theory*, p. 249. Because Timmons is discussing Ross, he says "prima facie" rather than "presumptive." Philosophers today tend to prefer *pro tanto* rather than *prima facie*. I just skip the Latin terms here.

[17] See Michael Huemer, *Moral Intuitionism* (New York: Palgrave MacMillan, 2005).

mistaken moral beliefs but because they simply fail to notice that they are in morally charged situations.[18]

Which Presumptive Duties?

The ancient Greek philosopher Thales hypothesized that everything was water. We now know that water isn't an element, but a compound, and that there is more than one element. Pluralists similarly hold that there are multiple moral elements. But one big question for moral pluralists, as for chemists, is just how many elements there are. Another big question is how those elements work or interact.

Earlier, I listed nine candidates for basic presumptive duties. Ross himself divided our duties into seven basic kinds. Following the periodic table metaphor, we might consider each of them as being similar to *periods*. Each period contains a number of duties within it, which play the role of moral elements. Thus, consider this Ross's periodic table of moral elements:

1. Duties of fidelity

   • For example, duties to keep promises, to avoid deception

2. Duties of reparation

   • For example, duties to apologize for error, to accept punishment, to pay compensation for harms

---

[18] For one useful popularization of such research, see Max H. Bazerman and Ann E. Tenbrunsel, *Blind Spots: Why We Fail to Do What's Right and What to Do about It* (Princeton, NJ: Princeton University Press, 2012).

3. Duties of gratitude

- For example, duties to express thanks, to reciprocate favors

4. Duties of justice

- For example, duties to give people what they deserve

5. Duties of beneficence

- For example, duties to provide charity, to rescue those in great distress; certain duties of special obligation to loved ones (such as the duty to feed one's children)

6. Duties of self-improvement

- For example, duties to improve one's skills, to improve one's character

7. Duties of nonmaleficence

- For example, duties to respect rights, to avoid causing harm

There are disputes in physics about how best to characterize all the fundamental particles. Some chemists defend alternatives to the standard periodic table. It's not that they dispute the basic elements, but just the best way to arrange them. In the same vein, different moral pluralists might disagree about what's the best "periodic table" for moral elements.[19] They agree on a common list of duties but perhaps disagree on the details of the hierarchy. It won't be important for us to debate that here.

---

[19] For examples, compare Ross's *Right and Good* to Bernard Gert's *Morality: Its Nature and Justification* (New York: Oxford University Press, 1999) or to Schmidtz's *Elements of Justice*.

One might think that if pluralists do not all agree on the best theory of pluralism, then pluralism is no better off than monism. But that approach might be similar to saying that because physicists dispute some of the fundamental particles, we're no better off than Thales. To be a better theory than monism, pluralism just has to be better than monism. That is, it has to have more explanatory power, with less vacuity—and with fewer counterexamples or absurd implications—than the extant monist theories have.

Moral Dilemmas Are Real

One thing pluralists agree on is the fundamental structure of morality: morality is not all one thing, and different moral reasons can pull us in different directions.

On January 7, 2015, two armed terrorists threatened to kill *Charlie Hebdo* cartoonist Corrine Rey's daughter unless she unlocked the office doors. She opened the door. They let her go but stormed the office and murdered 12 people, including 9 of her coworkers. Rey faced a difficult choice: Should she save her child or her coworkers?

Thus we have a classic moral dilemma. We see it frequently in fiction. In *The Dark Knight*, the Joker makes Batman choose between saving ace district attorney Harvey Dent and saving his childhood friend and love interest Rachel.

Consider another classic dilemma. Suppose I've promised to give you a ride to the airport. On the way to pick you up, I see a hurt child lying on the side of the road. On the one hand, it seems as if I have a duty to keep my promise. On the other hand, it seems as if I have a duty to help the child. But I can't discharge both duties—if I help the child, I'll be late and you'll miss your flight, but if I keep my promise, I'll abandon the child. It seems as though I have to weigh two conflicting moral duties and to determine which duty (in this case) is more important than the other.

A *genuine moral dilemma* is a situation in which we have conflicting moral obligations or duties. We have good reasons both to do something and not to do it. Batman has good reasons to save Rachel—she is his friend—but also good reasons to let her die and save Harvey Dent instead—Dent will probably help save Gotham City from further crime. In the hurt child case, I have good reasons both to keep my word and to break it.[20]

Monistic theories hold that all apparent moral dilemmas are merely apparent. Monist theories hold that it is always possible in principle to adjudicate apparent conflicts of duties, because those conflicts aren't real. Instead, such dilemmas seem real, because day to day we rely on helpful rules of thumb in making moral decisions. But, monists say, those rules of thumb are merely that. What we really ought to do in any given situation is whatever the one fundamental moral principle requires.

For instance, an act utilitarian would say that in the example above, Batman should do whatever produces the best consequences. If he were fully informed, he'd be able to determine whether saving Rachel or Harvey has better consequences, and

---

[20] A *tragic moral dilemma* is a scenario in which no matter what one does, one acts wrongly. Ross seemed to think that so long as you picked the weightier duty, you acted rightly. Some pluralists dispute that—they think morality might be unfair, and there might be times where through no fault of your own, the best thing you can do is still wrong.

he should choose accordingly. The utilitarian would recommend that I save the child, unless the consequences of your missing your flight are very severe.

Pluralist theories hold that the conflicts are real and that adjudicating them requires good judgment. What pluralists deny, though, is that to adjudicate between conflicting duties, we need to invoke a deeper, more fundamental moral duty or principle. Consider: It seems obvious that to rescue a drowning toddler, I may break my promise to meet you for dinner. In this case, the duty to rescue trumps the duty to keep promises. It also seems obvious that if I'm on the way to my best friend's wedding, I don't need to rescue a person whose car has broken down a quarter mile from the nearest service station. In this case, the duty to keep my promise to attend the wedding trumps the duty to rescue. (If the person were in severe distress, that would change.)

If someone objected, "How do you know that, without having a deeper moral principle?" I'd say the objector is overintellectualizing morality. The baseball player can catch a ball without knowing physics equations. Jimi Hendrix can play a melodious solo without knowing music theory. Any one of us can reliably distinguish cats from dogs without being able to give necessary and sufficient conditions for cathood or doghood. And so the average person can reliably choose among moral tradeoffs without having some fundamental principle in hand. For a more detailed account of how such moral knowledge is possible, see Michael Huemer's chapter in this volume.

Going back to the periodic table metaphor: chemists learn over time how different chemical elements interact. Ross thought that as a person developed moral wisdom, so he or she would learn over time how different moral elements interact. But most of that wisdom remains tacit—we can act on it, but we can't articulate it.

Some might be turned off by this metaphor. One can imagine, for example, Ayn Rand saying that Rossian pluralists are whim-worshippers who lionize their arbitrary decisions by invoking a mysterious and otherworldly "moral insight." Ross might respond that all moral theories—including Rand's—involve making use of judgment and insight. Indeed, Rand's theory relies more upon insight than does Kant's or Mill's. Mill thought he had a formula; Rand thought she had general principles that required virtuous judgment to apply.

When people try to produce a highly rigoristic theory that leaves no room for judgment, they typically hide their prior judgments inside their principles. We have a choice here. Either we can give useful general principles that require good judgment to apply, or we can try to give a principle that attempts to cover everything, but that isn't all that useful. Ross's theory is an instance of the former; Kant's is an instance of the latter.

When I tell my students what makes for a good or bad term paper, I can give them general advice (e.g., "be original," "respond to objections," or "avoid BS"). But suppose I were to develop a metric with a set number of points for each bit of advice they follow. For example, they get five points per objection they consider. They lose two points for each extraneous sentence. That metric would give my grading the false appearance of rigor, free of subjective judgment, but it wouldn't make my grading any better nor would it make it any less based on judgment. (After all, I can't really say a priori that failing to consider an objection is always worth 5 out of 100 points.) Instead, it would inevitably lead to unfair grades. Similarly, monistic theories that try to dispense with judgment and insight inevitably lead to distortions and absurd counterexamples.

One might worry that Rossian pluralism has no way to resolve disagreements. Ross was more sanguine. He might begin by noting that disagreement is boring. Even when it's indisputable that there's an objective truth of the matter, we still see persistent disagreement. People disagree about all sorts of things—whether evolution happened, whether vaccines work or cause autism, or whether planet Earth is older than 6,000 years—about which we have overwhelming evidence for one side. The mere fact that people disagree tells us little about whether there's an objective truth of the matter.

Part of the problem is that most of us don't have consistent moral beliefs (or fully consistent beliefs about anything, really). We aren't able to hold all of our beliefs in our conscious minds at once. Most of our beliefs are latent (or "nonoccurrent"). Because of that condition, we don't notice conflicts and contradictions among them. Indeed, much of what philosophers do is point out those unnoticed contradictions and then work to resolve them.

The Demarcation Question and the Unconnected Heap

Consider the following two lists of norms:

List A

1. Do not kill.
2. Do not cause harm.

3. Do not deprive of freedom.

4. Keep your promises and agreements.

5. Do not cheat.

List B

1. Righty tighty, lefty loosey.

2. Use one finger per fret.

3. Place your pinky finger between the fourth and fifth laces on the football.

4. First depress the clutch; then shift.

5. Take Route 50 to the Key Bridge exit, and stay in the left lane.

Both lists contain various rules or norms. However, it's clear to us that list A contains *moral* norms, whereas list B contains non-moral norms. It's wrong to kill and wrong to shift before pressing the clutch, but those are different kinds of wrong. Killing is *morally* wrong; trying to shift before pressing the clutch is a bad (and ultimately expensive) driving technique.

One thing a moral theory needs to do is explain what demarcates moral norms from nonmoral norms. We can see that everything on list A is a moral norm, but what *makes* those norms moral rather than nonmoral?

One might presume that this is an easier problem for monists to solve than for pluralists. After all, monists offer us one basic principle that is meant to encapsulate all of morality. For Kant, everything on list A is an instance of the categorical imperative. For Mill, everything on list A is an instance of rule utilitarianism.

But because pluralists do not have one fundamental principle, it might seem that they have a more difficult time accounting for what distinguishes list A from list B.

This kind of reasoning leads to a common complaint about moral pluralism. It seems as if the principles are an unconnected heap. The trick for the pluralist, then, is to explain how all the presumptive duties are united in being *moral* principles, without thereby reducing everything on the list to a monist principle.

Those common complaints are about pluralist theories, but they are ultimately misguided.[21] To see why, consider that Kant and Mill are monists, but they disagree about what the fundamental principle of morality is. Still, though they disagree, they agree that list A and list B are distinct. When Kant and Mill disagree about what the fundamental moral principle is, they are not *talking past each other* but are instead talking about the same thing. So presumably Kant and Mill can agree on a *theory-neutral account* of what demarcates moral norms from nonmoral norms.

Similarly, John Rawls says that although Marxists, libertarians, classical liberals, left-liberals, communitarians, and others disagree about what justice requires, there's a sense in which they all agree on what justice is. They have the same concept of justice but have different conceptions of it. Rawls says that assigning rights and duties and determining the proper distributions of benefits and burdens are built into the concept of justice.[22]

---

[21] For example, Timmons *Moral Theory*, pp. 262–63; and Russ Shafer-Landau, *The Fundamentals of Ethics* (New York: Oxford University Press, 2010), p. 235.

[22] John Rawls, *A Theory of Justice* (Cambridge, MA: Harvard University Press, 1971), pp. 5–6.

Different conceptions (theories) of justice—utilitarian, liberal, libertarian, communitarian—disagree about what the various duties, rights, and distributions are, but they are all conceptions of justice because they all concern these same issues.

We could say that all of the moral theories discussed in this book are different *conceptions* of morality, but each of the theorists should share the same *concept* of morality. Whatever answer Kant or Mill gives to explain what demarcates moral from nonmoral norms is equally available to the Rossian pluralist.

In this vein, pluralist moral theorist Bernard Gert offers the following generic account of moral norms:

> Morality is an informal public system applying to all rational persons, governing behavior that affects others, and has the lessening of evil or harm as its goal.[23]

Gert sees this definition of morality as theory-neutral, as describing what every major moral theory agrees on. Different moral theories provide different accounts of what the norms are or what explains them, but they each seem to agree on this definition.

Now, perhaps Gert's attempt to provide a generic demarcation of morality from nonmoral norms does not quite succeed. After all, most moral theorists believe that we owe duties to ourselves, not just to others. Gert seems to think there would be no morality

---

[23] Bernard Gert, "The Definition of Morality," in *The Stanford Encyclopedia of Philosophy*, ed. Edward N Zalta (Stanford, CA: Stanford University, 2005). Gert uses "evil" in a nonmoralized way, so this definition isn't question begging.

on a desert island, but Kant, Mill, and many other moral theorists would disagree.

So perhaps Gert's definition is not generic enough. Without here trying to offer a superior definition, we might note that moral norms have the following features:

1. They are categorical. Moral norms bind us independently of particular desires we happen to have. For instance, if you don't want to throw a spiral, you can just at whim opt out of rule 3 on list B. But you can't just opt out of rule 3 on list A, even if you really want to.[24]

2. They hold for all rational agents. Moral norms bind us in virtue of our being the kinds of creatures that (a) can understand right and wrong and (b) can act on this understanding.

3. They are not mere conventions. My extending my middle finger to express disrespect rather than respect is a social convention. We could have used the middle finger to mean what we mean by a salute, but we didn't. Social conventions can—in some sense—just be modified. We could just agree starting tomorrow to switch the meaning of the

---

[24] Introductory ethics students often get tripped up on, and collapse, a number of distinctions. To say a norm is categorical is to say it binds you because you are a moral agent—you can't just opt out of it at will. The contrast to categorical is hypothetical—a hypothetical norm (e.g., "Major in accounting, not art history, if you want a job") binds you because of desires you happen to have. A different distinction is absolute versus presumptive. Absolute norms cannot be outweighed or trumped; presumptive norms can. A third distinction is noncontextual versus contextual. Noncontextual norms require the same behavior in every circumstance, whereas contextual norms require different behaviors in different circumstances.

middle finger and the military salute. Basic moral norms are different—a society may not decide not to respect rights. (Plenty do, but they *shouldn't*.) They cannot modify moral norms by fiat.

4. They serve social cooperation. Moral norms make it possible for us to live together well. They help ensure that society is a positive-sum game, where everyone benefits from social cooperation. (Gert was right that moral norms tend to reduce harm, but that's not all they do.)

Pluralists and monists of all stripes can agree to this characterization of moral norms. Thus, even though pluralists (by definition) do not accept one fundamental unifying principle, they are not thereby stuck viewing moral norms as an unconnected heap.

Methodological Moral Pluralism

The prominent bioethicist and applied ethicist Peter Singer is a type of preference-satisfaction utilitarian. Singer is famous for arguing for various controversial conclusions, for example, (a) that we shouldn't eat meat, (b) that we should give most of our money to charity, or (c) that we should euthanize severely disabled newborns.[25] Those conclusions might follow from Singer's controversial moral theory. But what's interesting about Singer is that he doesn't first try to convince you of his moral theory and then deduce those conclusions from it. Instead, he appeals to widely shared, commonsense, mid-level moral principles and intuitions,

[25] Peter Singer, *Practical Ethics*, 3rd ed. (New York: Cambridge University Press, 2011).

principles and intuitions that Kantians, Objectivists, natural law theorists, and your moral theory–lacking grandma already accept.

Similarly, the Marxist philosopher G. A. Cohen has some controversial views about egalitarianism and justice. But when he wants to argue for socialism, he does not first try to convince you to adopt his version of egalitarianism and then show you that socialism follows from it. Nor does Cohen first try to convince readers to accept heterodox Marxist economics.[26] Instead, Cohen relies on widely shared moral intuitions, intuitions shared even by conservatives, free marketers, and libertarians. He tries to show readers that they themselves already accept moral principles and ideas that show they're implicitly committed to socialism.

In contrast, consider economist Murray Rothbard, who dabbled in moral theory on the side. In *The Ethics of Liberty*, Rothbard first tries to convince us that one major moral principle—the nonaggression principle—is self-evident. He then applies that principle dogmatically to every moral issue. The supposedly self-evident principle leads to bizarre conclusions: for example, if my neighbors decide to let their newborn starve to death on their lawn, I must not take a single step onto their property to rescue the infant.[27]

---

[26] G. A. Cohen, "The Structure of Proletarian Unfreedom," *Philosophy and Public Affairs* 12 (1983): 3–33; here, p. 24, he accepts that "bourgeois economics" is basically sound.

[27] Bryan Caplan makes this complaint about Rothbard in "Thoughts on Jason Brennan's *The Ethics of Voting*," *Reason Papers* 35 (2013): 12. He cites Murray Rothbard, *The Ethics of Liberty* (New York: New York University Press, 1998), p. 100.

The reason Singer and Cohen are successful as applied ethicists, while Rothbard's writings seem question begging and unconvincing to anyone who doesn't already agree, is that Singer and Cohen appeal to widely shared *mid-level* moral principles. They both have deeper moral theories that they believe justify, systematize, or explain the mid-level principles. But they also recognize that the theories are themselves *less plausible* than are the mid-level principles. To debate their interlocutors, they don't start by invoking some highly abstract moral theory but instead start from common ground. They say to their debate partners: "You already accept A, B, and C. Don't you see that A, B, and C together imply D?"

Good applied ethics seems to be committed to what we might call *methodological moral pluralism*. Methodological moral pluralism is the view that we should do applied ethics *as if* Russian pluralism were true. A methodological pluralist might accept a monist moral theory or might be agnostic between monism and pluralism. However, the idea behind methodological moral pluralism is that although we might disagree about fundamental moral theories, we probably can each agree to a shared set of mid-level moral principles. In trying to resolve debates about what to do here and now, we should try to appeal to those more obvious mid-level principles rather than some less obvious fundamental theory.

For thinking about political philosophy, we see there is yet another reason for methodological moral pluralism. Most moral theories are highly abstract. Asking what Kantianism implies about distributive justice is a bit like asking what

Einstein's field equations tell us about the path of a falling feather. Einstein's field equations describe the general ordering of space-time. They are complicated and often cannot be used for direct calculations. They are highly abstract and devoid of specific empirical information. The equations are consistent with worlds radically different from ours, such as Gödel's universe.[28] By themselves, the field equations don't tell us much about a falling feather. To understand the falling feather, we use intermediary or mid-level physical laws and models, and the laws and models we'd use are ultimately compatible with Newtonian or relativistic physics.

Kant's theory is much the same. Kant sees his theory as highly abstract. It's meant to apply to all rational beings of any species, including any possible rational aliens with highly different forms of life and biology from our own. Kant himself thinks that applying his theory to humans and human ways of life takes a huge amount of work, and depends on philosophical anthropology, the social sciences, and plain good judgment.[29] Kant ultimately grounds his political philosophy on the categorical imperative, but it takes him hundreds of pages of work to get there. If Kant's political philosophy turns out to be mistaken, that finding might not be because his moral theory is wrong but because the intermediary work is wrong.

---

[28] Kurt Gödel, "A Remark about the Relationship between the Theory of General Relativity and Idealistic Philosophy," *Collected Works: Publications 1948–1974* (Oxford, UK: Oxford University Press, 2001 [1949]), pp. 202–7.

[29] Kant, *Practical Philosophy*, p. 65; Robert B. Louden, *Kant's Impure Ethics: From Rational Beings to Human Beings* (New York: Oxford University Press, 2000).

No Straight Path from Moral Pluralism to Libertarianism—or Any Other Political Theory

How might one argue for libertarianism on pluralist grounds? Frankly, it takes a lot of work, and that's OK. That it takes a lot of work isn't a flaw of pluralist moral theories or of libertarianism for that matter. (It would also take a lot of work to go from moral pluralism to most other plausible political theories.) The basic moral principles—avoid killing, avoid stealing, keep your promises—are obvious. But no particular political philosophy is obvious, and none follows straightforwardly from our basic moral principles.

If you've read the other chapters in this book, it should be clear that no one-to-one correspondence exists between libertarianism and any particular moral theory. A classical liberal or libertarian might accept any number of background moral theories, including any of those listed in this book, as well as others that didn't make the cut.

John Rawls and I agree that we should regard people each as an end in themselves. We agree that we owe various duties of reciprocity, fidelity, beneficence, and nonmaleficence to others. But we disagree on how to apply many of our shared moral concepts. For instance, Rawls thinks that there's a presumption in favor of an egalitarian distribution of wealth and that departures from equality have to be justified. But *why* does he think that? In my view, Rawls's problem is that he finds what I consider a misleading metaphor illuminating. In his view, my problem is that I find what he considers an illuminating metaphor misleading.

Here's the metaphor: suppose we simultaneously come across some resource that none of us have any prior claim to, such as a pie.[30] The most natural way to divide the pie—the way that would elicit the fewest complaints—would be to give everyone an equal share. But suppose it turned out to be a magic pie that would grow or shrink in size depending on how we cut it. In that case, if we were rational but not envious, we'd each prefer a bigger but unequal slice to an equally small slice.

Rawls thinks it's illuminating to think of the "social product"—all the stuff we all produce while working together—as being like this unowned pie. I think it's misleading. I think the "social surplus" is not like a pie that we all came across in the woods simultaneously and thus have an equal basic claim upon. Here, my political disagreements with Rawls aren't disagreements about fundamental moral theory but about some of the intermediary intellectual tools that we use to *apply* our shared moral principles.

Or consider that G. A. Cohen and I share many of the same ideas about what a perfectly virtuous person would be like. However, Cohen and I disagree about what a perfectly just society would be like. He believes perfectly just angels would live under a kind of anarcho-socialism, whereas I hold that perfectly just angels would predominantly live under a kind of cooperative, voluntaryist, anarcho-capitalism as seen in the children's TV series *Mickey Mouse Clubhouse*.[31]

Still, our disagreement is not over fundamental values or moral theory. Rather, as I've argued elsewhere, Cohen made a simple mistake. He compared an idealized form of socialism (a socialist

---

[30] Schmidtz, *Elements of Justice*, pp. 182–83.

[31] Cohen, *Why Not Socialism?*; Brennan, *Why Not Capitalism?*

society inhabited by angels) with realistic capitalism (a capitalist society inhabited by real people, flaws and all) and concluded that the ideal form of socialism was better. But then he mistakenly concluded that this means socialism is better *tout court*, without his stopping to ask how a capitalist system inhabited by angels would work. Here, the problem isn't that Cohen and I disagree about moral theory, but rather we disagree about how to *apply* that theory. We're disagreeing not about the fundamental standards by which to judge things desirable but instead about how well different institutions would meet those standards, because we have empirical and conceptual disputes about what those institutions do.

Further, it's implausible to think that one is going to derive libertarianism from a few moral premises without needing to consider empirical questions at great length. Part of what a political philosophy tries to do is determine the standards by which to judge social institutions. Social institutions—such as private property, democracy, or the nuclear family—are "the rules of the game in a society . . . the humanly devised constraints that shape human interaction."[32] Every major moral theory, whether consequentialist or not, holds that at least part of what would justify or condemn various institutions is how well those institutions can be expected to work. For that, we'll need economics, sociology, political science, and history.

Now, consider that the philosopher Joseph Heath and I disagree about what institutions would be best in the real world, given that

---

[32] Douglas North, *Institutions, Institutional Change, and Economic Performance* (New York: Cambridge University Press, 1990), p. 3.

people are not angels. Here, our disagreement stems not so much from differences in moral values, or even principles of justice, but rather from empirical disagreements. He thinks markets are more prone to failure than I do, whereas I think governments are more prone to failure than he does. We both agree more or less on what it means for governments and markets to work, but we disagree about how well they work.

Libertarianism as a Default

With those caveats aside, the most promising strategy for moral pluralists who want to justify classical liberal conclusions is the same strategy that Huemer takes in this volume. One could begin by noting that commonsense interpersonal morality seems to be libertarian. In our day-to-day dealings with one another, we seem bound by libertarian constraints. Even in illiberal countries, most people generally think they're morally bound to leave others alone, so long as they're not hurting others.

Consider: I am not allowed to use violence or threats of violence to get you to follow my religion, eat healthier food, or stop smoking cigarettes. I may not force you to fight my enemies or to give your money to worthy causes, no matter how worthy. I can't force my neighbors to buy tomatoes from my garden rather than tomatoes from down the street or across the world. If my neighbor wants to sell or rent his house to people from outside the neighborhood, I can't stop him. If I choose to spend my money educating my neighbor's kids, I can't then demand that the neighbors repay me with one-third their income until they die. And so on. Again, in our day-to-day dealings with one another, we seem subject to libertarian constraints.

What makes libertarians unusual is that they think most or all of those constraints and prohibitions apply to government agents as well. For various reasons, people who hold ideologies believe government and its agents are exempt from some or all of those prohibitions.

They might be right! I'm not accusing the other side of having obviously absurd unnoticed inconsistencies. Rather, it might turn out that there is a philosophical justification for allowing governments to do things to us that we may not do to one another. Perhaps this justification even implies that the reason day-to-day morality is so libertarian is that the morality of state action is not. It's an open question.

Still, from a pluralist perspective, the best way to defend libertarianism is to begin with the observation that day-to-day morality is libertarian. There is a presumption of liberty. By default, we presume people should be free to live as they see best, without having to ask permission from or justify themselves to other people. By default, *all* restrictions on liberty are presumed wrong and unjust, until shown otherwise. Coercive interference with others' liberty must be justified. Political authority and all laws are assumed unjustified until shown otherwise.

One can then turn to nonlibertarians and say: "Look, I'm not an absolutist. I'm not pounding the table and saying the presumption of liberty can never be overcome. I'm just saying it has to be overcome. Can you explain to me why we should grant governments powers that we'd forbid private individuals?"

Nonlibertarians will happily oblige. They have plenty of arguments on offer. Remember, in their view, nonlibertarian conclusions are ultimately grounded in commonsense moral ideas as well.

Thus, the final step is to refute those arguments, starting from *shared moral premises* and relying on as uncontroversial or well-established *empirical premises* as possible.[33] It's unlikely you'll arrive at one decisive argument for libertarianism. Rather, you can see nonlibertarians as making a series of separate arguments such as these: It will be a disaster if we don't have government do *x*. It will be a disaster if we don't have government do *y*. You'll need to show, for each *x* and *y*, that empowering the government to do *x* and *y* doesn't work, or isn't worth the cost.

Rawls's Argument for Social Justice

I'll end by giving an example of a challenge to libertarianism from the Rawlsian camp. Libertarians are sometimes quick to say that taxes look like theft. Because everyone agrees that theft is wrong, it seems as if our basic shared moral intuitions forbid coercive taxation. Left-liberals and even Marxists agree that people shouldn't steal, so why then would they favor taxing Peter to pay Paul? In this section, I'll explain why we cannot just derive libertarian politics straightforwardly or with ease from the widely agreed-upon presumptive duty to avoid stealing. Consider this an illustration of my earlier point: going from moral pluralism to libertarianism is hard.

Libertarians often say that when the government taxes you and redistributes your income to others, this "is on par with forced

---

[33] For example, see Jason Brennan, *Libertarianism: What Everyone Needs to Know* (New York: Oxford University Press, 2012).

labor."[34] It's as if I spend 700 out of my 2,000 yearly working hours working for other people's benefit rather than my own. I don't have a choice—the government won't let me get paid for the remaining 1,300 hours unless I agree to pay it 700 hours' worth of income. So it looks at first glance as if libertarians are right—taxation is theft, or, worse, a kind of moderate slavery.

Perhaps taxation does turn out to be a kind of theft. But it's worth seeing that Rawls has a principled response to this accusation. To see why, we need to take a step back and ask, "What justifies the institution of private property in the first place?"

John Locke—though himself an ardent defender of the right to hold and use private property—notes that in the first instance, private property seems to limit other people's property. To see why, imagine a world in which no one yet owns anything. Everyone is free to go where he likes and use what he wants. When the first person encloses a plot of land and declares it his own, he thereby in the first instance reduces other people's freedom. They used to be able to go anywhere, but now there are 40 acres they can't touch. And so, Locke realizes, we need to justify "original appropriation." It won't be enough to say that you earn a right to the land by "mixing your labor" with it. After all, when you privatize unowned land, you reduce others' freedom. So you'll need to compensate them in some way.

Locke thinks that everyone does indeed get compensated. Unowned land is not productive, whereas privatized land can

[34] For example, see Robert Nozick, *Anarchy, State, and Utopia* (New York: Basic Books, 1974), p. 169.

be 10,000 times more productive. So, Locke thinks, when land is parceled and privatized, and when people are able to sell the products of their land on a market, the systematic effect is that everyone enjoys many times more wealth than they would under a system without private property. He's absolutely right. The average American living today enjoys a standard of living about 60 times (yes, 60) higher than the average European colonist of 1600 AD.[35] Americans are thus better able to realize their conceptions of the good life and have more power to achieve their ends.

In effect, Locke thinks that what justifies the institution of private property is that it tends to leave more and better for others. But he's not claiming that every individual transaction has to benefit everyone else. It's not as though you can't sell your guitar to your friend unless doing so helps literally everyone else on earth. Rather, Locke just means that the rules of private property as a whole should tend to make everyone better off.

Libertarian Nozick and left-liberal Rawls agree. *Part* of what justifies the institution of private property is that people tend to have much better lives with it than without it. But this is where Locke and Nozick start to disagree with Rawls. They disagree about just how much the institution of private property must benefit everyone to be justifiable. For Locke and Nozick, it's more or

---

[35] See Angus Maddison's data on historical gross domestic product per capita, available on his homepage, http://www.ggdc.net/maddison/Maddison.htm. See also Angus Maddison, *Contours of the World Economy, 1–2030 AD: Essays in Macroeconomic History* (New York: Oxford University Press, 2003).

less enough that people do better with it than without it. Rawls has a stricter standard—he thinks that for a particular system of private property to be justified, it must tend to ensure that the representative member of the least advantaged working class does better than he would under alternative systems of private property.[36]

Rawls thinks that meeting this standard will require having a series of strong, democratically controlled central governments, which (a) regulate the economy in various ways and (b) provide various forms of social insurance. Rawls's argument is in effect this:

1. Normative claim. Any particular regime of private property is justified only if it satisfies the following principle: it should tend to ensure that the representative member of the least advantaged working class does at least as well as would be possible under alternative regimes.

2. Empirical claim. If we are to meet the standard in 1, it is necessary to have a liberal social democratic government, which taxes citizens to provide social insurance.

3. Implication of 1 and 2. When the government taxes citizens (in whatever amount is necessary to meet the obligations described in 1), the citizens are not entitled to the money it takes. Instead, the government is entitled to the money. Were the citizens to withhold taxes, they would be stealing from the government.

---

[36] Rawls, *Theory of Justice*, p. 80.

If Rawls is right, when the government taxes me, it isn't necessarily stealing. Rather, it might just be doing what it takes to ensure that the system of private property is justified in the first place. Accordingly, if libertarians want to challenge Rawls, it's not to declare that taxes are theft. They may be right, that's a *conclusion* of their theory of property rights, not a premise. Thus, libertarians need to instead attack Rawls's normative premise (1) or his empirical premise (2). That is, either they need to show that his standards for justifying the system of private property are too stringent—perhaps by defending a superior theory of the legitimacy of private property rights—or they need to show that a libertarian system can meet those stringent standards.[37]

Summary

Rossian pluralism is a good theory to start and end with. It's a good theory to start with, because it accurately describes what it's like to be a moral agent. The other moral theories seem artificial, because they are indeed artificial. Rossian pluralism is a description of what we actually do, on the ground, as people making moral decisions.

It's reasonable to hope for more (or, in a sense, less). It's reasonable—it's good philosophical methodology—to look for a simpler theory that reduces the number of basic moral principles as much as possible. It's good methodology to try to find one unified explanation for what separates right from wrong, good

---

[37] For example, see John Tomasi, *Free Market Fairness* (Princeton, NJ: Princeton University Press, 2012).

from bad, virtuous from vicious. But this is good methodology only if we don't end up producing a vacuous or absurd theory in the process. The problem with so many of our one-sentence moral theories—be they Kantian, virtue ethics, or consequentialist—is that they do tend to be either vacuous or absurd.

Thus, after we repeatedly try but fail to make a monist theory work, we might want to end up back where we started. There are still plenty of questions moral theorists might try to answer, such as these: What kinds of truths are moral truths? What makes moral truths true? How is moral knowledge possible? And if morality is best depicted as being like the periodic table of elements, just what's the best way to draw that table? In the end, we shouldn't demand more precision from a theory than the phenomenon being studied admits.

Rossian pluralism doesn't offer a 60-second defense of libertarianism—or any other political philosophy for that matter. But that's not a bad thing. It would be rather surprising if we could derive a political philosophy directly out of a basic moral theory, without having to first study economics and political science to learn how institutions actually function. Some libertarians are attracted to moral theories that let them bypass this difficult step, in much the same way that some bald men want to buy miracle hair-growth formula. If we're taking things seriously, though, we'll have to admit that our basic moral ideas underdetermine on their own what politics should look like, and we'll need to understand robust political economy to make a final determination about what justice requires.

Recommended Readings

The editors of *Arguments for Liberty* asked the author of each chapter to recommend books or articles about his or her moral theory. In addition to the following suggestions, readers can find many helpful articles online at the Stanford Encyclopedia of Philosophy (plato.stanford.edu) and the Internet Encyclopedia of Philosophy (www.iep.utm.edu). Each of the moral theories in this book has a comprehensive introductory entry of its own in one or both of those sources.

Chapter 1: Utilitarianism

Christopher Freiman recommends:
Rachels, James, and Stuart Rachels. *The Elements of Moral Philosophy*, Chapters 7 and 8. New York: McGraw-Hill, 2015.

> "A good introduction to utilitarianism, illustrated with plenty of real-world examples."

Mill, John Stuart. *Utilitarianism*. New York: Oxford University Press, 1998.

"The classic defense of utilitarianism. Mill's writing is accessible even to those without a background in philosophy."

Rauch, Jonathan. *Government's End: Why Washington Stopped Working*. New York: PublicAffairs, 1999.

"Rauch provides an accessible introduction to public choice theory, which is at the heart of the utilitarian case for libertarianism."

Chapter 2: Natural Rights

Eric Mack recommends:

Nozick, Robert. *Anarchy, State, and Utopia*. New York: Basic Books, 1974.

"This is a scintillating natural rights defense of minimal state libertarianism that almost single-handedly revived academic interest in libertarian doctrines. Nozick argues that, if one takes seriously the separate importance of each individual, one must recognize each individual's right to live free of coercive interference. He argues that fundamental rights are justifiably enforced by a minimal state that eschews coercive redistribution, coercive enforcement of morals, and coercive paternalism."

Locke, John. *Second Treatise of Government* (many editions, but see the 1980 edition from Hackett Publishing, Indianapolis).

"This is Locke's most important political treatise, and it is the key work of early classical liberalism. Locke famously begins with arguments for why individuals possess natural rights to life, liberty, and property and maintains that individuals have rationally consented to form a political society devoted to the protection of these rights. Only a government fundamentally focused on protecting these rights is morally legitimate. Individuals and political society have rights to discard and replace any government that threatens these rights."

Mack, Eric. *John Locke*. New York: Bloomsbury, 2013.

"This is a general and accessible account of Locke's rights-oriented classical liberalism. It contrasts Locke with crucial authoritarian writers of his day and recounts and explains Locke's affirmation of natural rights to life, liberty—including religious liberty—and property. Other themes include Locke's explanation for why private property free market orders are likely to be beneficial to everyone, Locke's defense of resistance against tyrannical rule, and Locke's influence on the American Revolution."

Bader, Ralf. *Robert Nozick*. New York: Bloomsbury, 2013.

"This is a general and accessible account of the libertarian doctrine developed by Nozick in *Anarchy, State, and Utopia*. It explains Nozick's affirmation of individual rights, his complex account of why the minimal state is legitimate, his defense of the 'historical entitlement' understanding of justice in holdings, his critique of arguments on behalf of coercive redistribution, and his contention that the minimal state is inspiring because it provides a framework within which all persons can pursue their visions of utopia."

Chapter 3: Kantianism

Jason Kuznicki recommends:

Kant, Immanuel. *Kant's Critique of Practical Reason and Other Works on the Theory of Ethics*, trans. Thomas Kingsmill Abbott, BD, Fellow and Tutor of Trinity College, Dublin, 4th revised ed. London: Longmans, Green, and Co., 1889, http://oll.libertyfund.org /titles/360.

"Contrary to popular belief, Kant's own writing is not always obscure. Interested readers should begin at the source."

Kant, Immanuel. *Kant's Principles of Politics, including his essay on Perpetual Peace. A Contribution to Political Science*, trans. W. Hastie. Edinburgh: T. & T. Clark, 1891, http://oll.libertyfund.org /titles/358.

"Readers should turn here following the *Critique of Practical Reason*."

Kant, Immanuel. *The Philosophy of Law: An Exposition of the Fundamental Principles of Jurisprudence as the Science of Right*, trans.

W. Hastie. Edinburgh: T. & T. Clark, 1887, http://oll.libertyfund
.org/titles/359.

> *The Philosophy of Law* is a public-domain English-language
> volume that contains a translation of the *Metaphysics of Mor-*
> *als* and both parts of *The Science of Right*. In the latter work
> in particular, Kant showed most clearly how his politics and
> ethics were related, and developed his distinctive theory of
> private property."

Nozick, Robert. *Anarchy, State, and Utopia*, Chapter 3. New York:
Basic Books, 1974.

> "Having read the works by Kant highlighted previously,
> connections to modern libertarianism are easy to trace—
> especially in the third chapter of Nozick's masterpiece."

White, Mark D. *Kantian Ethics and Economics*. Stanford, CA:
Stanford University Press, 2011.

> "White's book fills in many of the blanks that Kant
> left in the ethics of market activity. Readers can check
> whether they agree with White by referencing Kant's
> "Idea for a Universal History from a Cosmopolitan Per-
> spective," available online at http://yalepress.yale.edu
> /yupbooks/excerpts/kant_perpetual.pdf and "What Is
> Enlightenment?" at http://www.columbia.edu/acis/ets
> /CCREAD/etscc/kant.html."

Chapter 4: Contractarianism

Jan Narveson recommends:

Narveson, Jan. *You and The State*. Lanham, MD: Rowman & Littlefield, 2009.

> "This is a general introduction to political philosophy, and the only one I know of that makes the sort of case for libertarianism that this article does, while also examining in more depth various other theories."

Gauthier, David. *Morals by Agreement*. New York: Oxford University Press, 1986.

> "This is a classic in moral philosophy, and has much influenced my own work. Gauthier claims not to be a libertarian, but I don't see why! (See Jan Narveson, "The Only Game in Town," soon to be published in the Canadian philosophical journal *Dialogue*.)"

Friedman, Mark. *Libertarian Philosophy in the Real World*. London and New York: Bloomsbury, 2015.

> "Friedman discusses many real-world issues with a view to really applying the libertarian philosophy. Interesting for showing the complexity of that project. (The subject of libertarian foundations doesn't really get discussed in it, but readers will be able to see where applying contractarian theory on top can be helpful."

Schmidtz, David. *The Elements of Justice*. Cambridge, UK: Cambridge University Press, 2006.

"This beautifully written book also combs through the main ideas about justice, and generally supports a libertarian view on something not far from my contractarian approach."

Chapter 5: Rawls

Kevin Vallier recommends:

Rawls, John. *A Theory of Justice*. Cambridge, MA: Belknap Press of Harvard University Press, 1971.

Rawls, John. *Political Liberalism*. New York: Columbia University Press, 1993.

"These two books represent Rawls's two most important works of political philosophy, which outline the projects that Tomasi and Gaus develop in their works."

Tomasi, John. *Free-Market Fairness*. Princeton, NJ: Princeton University Press, 2012.

Gaus, Gerald. *The Order of Public Reason*. Cambridge, UK: Cambridge University Press, 2010.

"Tomasi draws on *A Theory of Justice* and Gaus's work is similar to Rawls's project in *Political Liberalism*."

Chapter 6: Virtue Ethics

Mark LeBar recommends:

LeBar, Mark. "The Virtue of Justice, Revisited," in *The Handbook of Virtue Ethics*, ed. Stan van Hooft. New York: Acumen Press, 2014, pp. 265–75.

"A brief survey of ancient Greek thinking about justice and the way it can benefit from modern ethical insights, including the need for respect for others."

LeBar, Mark. "Virtue and Politics," in *Cambridge Companion to Virtue Ethics*, ed. Daniel C. Russell. Cambridge, UK: Cambridge University Press, 2013, pp. 265–89.

"Here I argue that the political implications of virtue ethical theories must be quite limited in reach to conform with the constraints of *liberal* political theories (ones in particular that see the need for justification of their coercive authority to those they govern)."

Rasmussen, Douglas, and Douglas Den Uyl. *Norms of Liberty*. University Park, PA: Penn State University Press, 2005.

"An excellent comprehensive case that virtue requires liberty, and a political order which leaves the development and exercise of virtue up to the individual."

Chapter 7: Objectivism

Neera K. Badhwar recommends:

Rand, Ayn. *We the Living*. New York: New American Library, 1936.

"*We the Living*, Rand's first novel, is her only autobiographical work. It is, however, what she called 'an autobiography of an idea,' not a detailed description of her own life. *We the Living* shows how totalitarianism exalts the worst and destroys the best."

Rand, Ayn. *The Fountainhead*. New York: Plume, 1994.

"The novel depicts the ideal man as one of vision and integrity—a man who lives firsthand and succeeds in overcoming the forces of ignorance and mediocrity. Rand wanted to show that such an individual can inspire others and succeed in a (more or less) free society, the society of 1940s America. In this respect, *The Fountainhead* is the opposite of *We the Living*."

Rand, Ayn. *Atlas Shrugged*. New York: New American Library, 1959.

"*Atlas Shrugged* is motivated by a darker vision. It is set in an America in which a few honest and visionary individuals fight the forces of collectivism till they can fight no longer, and decide to go on strike. This is not the conventional workers' strike, but a strike by inventors, actors, writers, entrepreneurs, and industrialists, who choose to stop working for a world that victimizes them. The novel is populated by villainous and mediocre businessmen, politicians, and bureaucrats—an 'aristocracy of pull'—who are ruining America, and gives a glimpse of an ideal world, Atlantis."

Rand, Ayn. *Capitalism: The Unknown Ideal*. New York: New American Library, 1967.
Rand, Ayn. *The Virtue of Selfishness: A New Concept of Egoism*. New York: New American Library, 1964.

"These books contain many articles on rights, government, society, and ethics."

Chapter 8: Ethical Intuitionism

Michael Humer recommends:

Huemer, Michael. *The Problem of Political Authority*. New York: Palgrave Macmillan, 2013.

> "This book explains why you should be skeptical about authority, and how this supports libertarianism."

Huemer, Michael. *Ethical Intuitionism*. New York: Palgrave Macmillan, 2005.

> "This book makes the case for ethical intuitionism and against alternative views."

Huemer, Michael. "Is There a Right to Immigrate?" *Social Theory and Practice* 36 (2010): pp. 429–61, http://www.owl232.net/immigration.htm.

> "This paper uses some common-sense ethical intuitions to argue against immigration restrictions."

Huemer, Michael. "America's Unjust Drug War" in *The New Prohibition*, ed. Bill Masters. St. Louis, MO: Accurate Press, 2004, pp. 133–44, http://www.owl232.net/drugs.htm.

> "This paper uses some common-sense ethical intuitions to argue against drug prohibition."

Chapter 9: Moral Pluralism

Jason Brennan recommends:

Shafer-Landau, Russ. *What Ever Happened to Good and Evil?* Oxford, UK: Oxford University Press, 2003.

"A text by a leading moral theorist defending value pluralism, intuitionism, and moral realism."

Ross, W. D., *The Right and the Good.* Indianapolis, IN: Hackett, 1988.

"Ross's classic text is perhaps the first major example of a pluralist moral theory."

Schmidtz, David. *Elements of Justice.* Cambridge, UK: Cambridge University Press, 2006.

"Schmidtz develops a pluralist theory of justice based on four major elements: desert, reciprocity, need, and equality."

Brennan, Jason. *Libertarianism: What Everyone Needs to Know.* Oxford, UK: Oxford University Press, 2012.

"An explanation of libertarianism that relies largely on pluralist moral theory."

Contributors

Neera K. Badhwar is professor emerita of philosophy at the University of Oklahoma and a senior fellow in the F. A. Hayek Program for Advanced Study in Philosophy, Politics, and Economics at the Mercatus Center at George Mason University. She is the author of articles on various topics in ethical theory and moral psychology and of *Well-Being: Happiness in a Worthwhile Life* (2014). She also edited *Friendship: A Philosophical Reader* (1993).

Jason Brennan is the Robert J. and Elizabeth Flanagan Family Chair of Strategy, Economics, Ethics, and Public Policy at the McDonough School of Business, Georgetown University. He is the author of seven books, including *Against Democracy* (2016) and *Markets without Limits* (2015).

Christopher Freiman is an associate professor of philosophy at the College of William and Mary. He is a graduate of Duke University (BA in philosophy) and the University of Arizona

(MA, PhD in philosophy). His research interests include distributive justice, immigration, and democratic theory. His work has appeared in venues such as the *Australasian Journal of Philosophy*, *Philosophical Studies*, *Philosophy and Phenomenological Research*, *Journal of Ethics and Social Philosophy*, and *The Oxford Handbook of Political Philosophy*. His website is www.cfreiman.com and he blogs at www.bleedingheartlibertarians.com.

Michael Huemer received his BA from the University of California, Berkeley, in 1992 and his PhD from Rutgers University in 1998. He is presently professor of philosophy at the University of Colorado at Boulder. He is the author of approximately 60 academic articles in ethics, epistemology, political philosophy, and metaphysics, as well as four books: *Skepticism and the Veil of Perception* (2001), *Ethical Intuitionism* (2005), *The Problem of Political Authority* (2013), and *Approaching Infinity* (2016).

Jason Kuznicki holds a PhD in intellectual history from Johns Hopkins University, focused on the Enlightenment. He is the editor of *Cato Unbound*, a monthly journal of ideas. He was an assistant editor of the *Encyclopedia of Libertarianism*. His first book, *Technology and the End of Authority*, will be published by Palgrave Macmillan in the spring of 2017.

Mark LeBar is professor of philosophy at Florida State University. He works in moral, social, and political philosophy. His book, *The Value of Living Well* (2013), is a development of contemporary eudaimonist ethical theory. He is now working on extending that account of eudaimonism to questions about the nature and origin of the virtue of justice, and he is editing a book on the development of justice as a virtue. He coedited *Equality and Public Policy* (2014), is the editor of *Social Theory and Practice*, and has published in journals including *Ethics, American Philosophical Quarterly, Philosophical Studies, Canadian Journal of Philosophy*, and *Pacific Philosophical Quarterly*.

Eric Mack is professor of philosophy at Tulane University and a faculty member of the university's Murphy Institute of Political Economy. His many scholarly essays focus on the moral foundations of rights, the nature of natural and acquired rights, property rights and economic justice, the legitimate scope of coercive institutions, and the history of classical liberal and libertarian political theory. His recent and representative essays include "John Locke's Defense of Commercial Society" in *Wealth, Commerce, and Philosophy*; "Elbow Room for Self-Defense" in *Social Philosophy and Policy*; "Elbow Room for Rights" in *Oxford Studies in Political Philosophy*; "Nozickan Arguments for the More-Than-Minimal State" in *The Cambridge Companion to Anarchy, State, and Utopia*; "Lysander Spooner: Nineteenth-Century America's Last Natural Rights Theorist" in *Social Philosophy and Policy*; and "Robert Nozick's Political Philosophy" in *Stanford Encyclopedia of Philosophy*. He is the author of *John Locke (2009)*.

Jan Narveson is distinguished professor emeritus at the University of Waterloo in Canada. He has published seven books, notably *The Libertarian Idea* (1988 and 2001), *You and the State*

(2008), and *This Is Ethical Theory* (2010). He is the author of several hundred articles and reviews in philosophical journals and collections, among them "Pacifism, a Philosophical Analysis" (1965); "A Puzzle About Economic Justice in Rawls' Theory" (1976); "Deserving Profits" (1995); "The Invisible Hand" (2003); and "Cohen's Rescue" (2010). In 2003, he was made an officer of the Order of Canada. He founded and has for decades led the Kitchener-Waterloo Chamber Music Society.

Kevin Vallier is an associate professor of philosophy at Bowling Green State University. His research focuses on political philosophy, normative ethics, political economy, and philosophy of religion. Vallier is the author of *Liberal Politics and Public Faith: Beyond Separation* (2014) and *Must Politics Be War? In Defense of Public Reason Liberalism*, forthcoming from Oxford University Press.

Index

In page references, *n* designates a numbered note.

About the Editors

Aaron Ross Powell is a Cato Institute research fellow and founder and editor of Libertarianism.org, which presents introductory material as well as new scholarship related to libertarian philosophy, theory, and history. He is also co-host of Libertarianism.org's popular podcast, *Free Thoughts*.

Grant Babcock is Assistant Editor of Libertarianism.org and a scholar of political philosophy. He is especially interested in nonviolent action, epistemology of the social sciences, social contract theories and criticisms thereof, and finding libertarian-compatible responses to cultural problems.

Cato Institute

Founded in 1977, the Cato Institute is a public policy research foundation dedicated to broadening the parameters of policy debate to allow consideration of more options that are consistent with the principles of limited government, individual liberty, and peace. To that end, the Institute strives to achieve greater involvement of the intelligent, concerned lay public in questions of policy and the proper role of government.

The Institute is named for *Cato's Letters*, libertarian pamphlets that were widely read in the American Colonies in the early 18th century and played a major role in laying the philosophical foundation for the American Revolution.

Despite the achievement of the nation's Founders, today virtually no aspect of life is free from government encroachment. A pervasive intolerance for individual rights is shown by government's arbitrary intrusions into private economic transactions and its disregard for civil liberties. And while freedom around the globe has notably increased in the past several decades, many countries have moved in the opposite direction, and most governments still do not respect or safeguard the wide range of civil and economic liberties.

To address those issues, the Cato Institute undertakes an extensive publications program on the complete spectrum of policy issues. Books, monographs, and shorter studies are commissioned to examine the federal budget, Social Security, regulation, military spending, international trade, and myriad other issues. Major policy conferences are held throughout the year, from which papers are published thrice yearly in the *Cato Journal*. The Institute also publishes the quarterly magazine *Regulation*.

In order to maintain its independence, the Cato Institute accepts no government funding. Contributions are received from foundations, corporations, and individuals, and other revenue is generated from the sale of publications. The Institute is a nonprofit, tax-exempt, educational foundation under Section 501(c)3 of the Internal Revenue Code.

CATO INSTITUTE
1000 Massachusetts Ave., N.W.
Washington, D.C. 20001
www.cato.org